THE KIDNAPPING OF MARK TWAIN

A Bombay Mystery

ANURADHA KUMAR

SPEAKING TIGER

SPEAKING TIGER BOOKS LLP
125A, Ground Floor, Shahpur Jat, near Asiad Village,
New Delhi 110049

First published by Speaking Tiger Books 2023

ISBN: 978-93-5447-680-8
eISBN: 978-93-5447-681-5

10 9 8 7 6 5 4 3 2 1

Typeset by SÜRYA, New Delhi
Printed at HT Media Ltd, Greater Noida

Anuradha Kumar was born in Odisha. She lived in various places in India, before moving to Singapore and later the US. She lived in Mumbai for over a decade, where she worked for the *Economic and Political Weekly*. She studied history at Delhi University and management (specializing in human resource management) at the XLRI School of Business, Jamshedpur. She has an MFA in Writing from the Vermont College of Fine Arts (VCFA). Anu's stories have won awards from the Commonwealth Foundation, UK, and *The Little Magazine*, India. She writes regularly for *Scroll.in*. Her stories and essays have appeared in places like Fiftytwo.in, the India Forum, *The Missouri Review*, *Catamaran Literary Reader*, *The Common*, *Maine Literary Review*, and other places. She has written for younger readers as well. As Adity Kay, she wrote three bestselling works of historical fiction published by Hachette India: *Emperor Chandragupta*, *Emperor Vikramaditya* and *Emperor Harsha*. This present work is her 11th novel, and she hopes to write more about Henry Baker and Maya Barton. Anu now lives in New Jersey with her family.

Praise for *Coming Back to the City: Mumbai Stories*

'The lucid quality of the prose and the rounded characters makes this a book to be savoured and lingered over...deft and unobtrusive touches of description bring the characters physically alive.' —Manohar Shetty, *Hindustan Times*

'As vast and diverse as Mumbai itself, *Coming Back to the City* draws us effortlessly, completely into the lives of the people who animate the Maximum City, even as they are consumed by it...this is a delightful read.' —Ganesh Saili, *New Indian Express*

Praise for *It Takes a Murder*

'Kumar marries interesting form with fluent, conversational prose that can be charming, fortuitously phrased and (darkly) atmospheric.' —Peter Gordon, Editor, *Asian Review of Books*

'Anu Kumar's strength lies in her ability to create believable characters, demanding our empathy.' —Moazzam Sheikh, *The News*, Pakistan

Praise for *The Hottest Summer in Years*

'Anuradha's evocative prose, spliced with a racy whodunit, makes this a rare treat. It's a novel for every season.' —Jane Borges

'Anuradha Kumar has the gift of building palpable, authentic worlds that draw the reader into their charged complexities.' —Neelam Saran Gour

Praise for *A Sense of Time and Other Stories*

'Kumar never loses sight of the story as a form that entertains even while it presents complex portraits of society.' —Lopa Basu, *India Currents*, California

For my mother, Uma Chakrabarty,
and as always, Krishna Raj (1937-2004)

Contents

About this Novel: A Short Note from the Author

The events in this novel are a fictitious rendering of Mark Twain's stay in Bombay during his world tour of 1895-1896. Mark Twain had run into considerable debt, owing to bad investments, and had committed to writing a series of syndicated articles about his world travels. This later became a book called, *Following the Equator*, published in 1897.

This novel imagines a time when Mark Twain vanishes for some days, without trace, in circumstances unbeknownst even to his wife, Olivia, and daughter, Clara. The events unfold in a city represented as it was then. Familiar historical places appear like the Watson's Hotel, Colaba Causeway, Crawford Market, Victoria Terminus, the Bombay Police Headquarters, and of course, the Elephanta Caves.

There is also reference to the rising political fervour in the city, the British fear and suspicion of Russian spies in the midst of the 'Great Game,' the famous trial of Oscar Wilde in London, and America's own keenness to establish a bigger presence for itself on the world stage. In the world of detection, methods like fingerprinting were beginning to be talked about, and the British persisted with its discriminatory policies as seen in how it labelled certain ethnic and wandering groups. There were also active groups involved in eradicating social evils like addiction and others more passionately engaged in reform, for instance, in areas of women's education and widow remarriage. All this and more provides context to the unfolding events in this novel.

Prologue

That morning, Maya Barton read the day's paper, and Henry's thoughts strayed toward astrology. He was not into stuff like that, but even he could tell that the stars ruling the houses of romance and murder were never aligned sympathetically. Even if they were, they never worked in one's favour. Such erratic and dark thoughts crossed Henry Baker's mind at breakfast time. He wanted to engage Maya in warm, animated conversation about various things, but the newspaper was an inky black and white wall between them, and Maya's attention was held by the story of a girl's murder in the native part of the city. A second later, the paper curtain fell, Henry heard the rustle of the newspaper as Maya passed it to him, her finger tapping over what she had just read.

Henry's eyes quickly ran down the page. The sensational news item about the Marquess of Queensberry's accusations against Oscar Wilde headlined the front page, but at the bottom, there was a short note about a murder. A first paragraph continued onto the fourth page, and lifting the paper, so he could turn the pages easily, he read the same news that had so agitated Maya.

Bombay Gazette
Bombay, January 20, 1896

Shocking Murder in Native Lodge Brings Old Fears Back

A young woman's body was found in a guest house in the native settlement of Sewree. Close to the mangrove swamps on old Parel island, Sewree is northeast of the main Fort area of Bombay. Casi was found in her bed late in the morning, and is believed to have been strangled to death. The police superintendent, Mr R.H. Vincent, is investigating and says his men are looking at every angle. He requests people not to rely on rumours.

'We have no proof it is the work of the thugs of old,' Vincent said, and assured us that the murderer would soon be caught. Murderer? Did that mean there was only one? But the superintendent refused to say more. 'Investigations are on. And we will soon have an answer,' was all Mr Vincent let on.

Casi had arrived in the city from Khed, a village in the Ghat region, south of the city. Her husband, Tuka Ram, employed in the New Empire Cotton Mills as labour supervisor, was on night duty and informed the police only when he returned to the lodge in the morning. Tuka Ram and Casi had the room on the third floor. The couple had just been married, but Tuka Ram's first wife had refused to vacate their room in the workers' chawl in Parel. The

> woman claims to have no knowledge of the murder, but said something about karma visiting people who do evil to others. According to Tuka, some jewellery, and utensils of daily use appear to be missing. The police are not saying anything about suspects, and the superintendent said he would have updates soon.

Henry sighed, and put away the newspaper, a carefully folded neat square on the cushioned cane chair to his left. Maya was looking out of the open window, a distant look on her face.

'I knew this girl,' she said, turning toward Henry, nodding once to indicate the *Bombay Gazette,* now quiet in its chair. Her voice quivered. The curtains behind her flapped with the sea breeze, and the gentle morning light turned her hair a golden brown. Her eyes looked blue and misty. The usual defiance from her face was gone.

'I am sorry,' Henry said in a low voice. 'Poor girl,' he added, holding Maya's sad gaze with his own. He imagined the girl, Casi, in the small damp room, the kind found in guesthouses like the one mentioned. He had been in one once with his artist friend, Edwin Lord Weeks, and remembered the narrow wooden staircases with their flaky handrails, the creaky rafters on low ceilings just inches away from the head (Edwin and he were both tall men), brass water vessels outside every door, and the musty sea smell everywhere. A love story, a jealous other woman, and an unexplained death. Romance and murder, he thought, could sit companionably inside a newspaper, and in all the pulp fiction he had read in his days in London. And that had been only a year ago, that sudden thought surprised him as he ran his fingers through his hair, already frizzy despite the new gel he had used.

'It should be easy,' Henry began, his mind on Bombay's damp weather that made his hair feel sticky too soon, and then he flushed for Maya had been speaking and he had missed her initial words. It did look easy, he would tell her in a bit, for the police to nab the murderer. The guest houses in the native parts of the city were right in the middle of crowded areas. Someone would have heard something.

'She was to work in the mills too, but she'd read of the girls' school in Mazagaon. That's how I met her,' Maya said in her quick, low voice. 'Then yesterday, she came to the hospital, with...'

She tapped on her armrest, and stared at Henry, her eyes ablaze. 'It's an open and shut case,' she said, the tapping following her every word, 'this man, Tuka, the husband, did it.'

Henry was startled. Maya was racing ahead in her conjecture. A breeze lifted the thin gauze curtain, and a tendril of hair danced fitfully across Maya's forehead, distracting Henry for some moments. Then a vendor's voice floated in from outside, he was selling fresh coconuts. Henry looked down at the paper, and thought of that errant strand of hair. Every time the curtain moved, the light shifted too, and her hair flashed a burnished gold, and seconds later, turned a warm honey colour. He picked up the paper and ran his finger down the story and paused at the very end. 'It says here. That Tuka was not even there at the time.'

Maya looked at him with a mix of impatience and pity. 'That is really so obvious, Henry, isn't it? Tuka set it all up so he wouldn't be suspected. I mean....' She leaned forward, over the low glass table between them that had the paraphernalia of their recent breakfast, and said, 'That is precisely what we need to get to the bottom of. Or the police if it tries hard enough,' Her lips quivered. She rose, placing her napkin on the ceramic plate, and Henry got to his feet too. 'I'll go and see Charlotte, Dr Ellaby. She...,' Maya gestured with her hands, swept the hair away from her face, and pointed to the newspaper, 'the girl, Casi, had come to her with an injury.'

She picked up her purse and looked around for her hat. Henry looked at the other occupied tables, at the happy clinking of cutlery, the soft murmur of conversation, and masked his own disappointment. 'I thought we might go...'

'I remember,' she smiled in unexpected apology. Then leaning forward, her hand on his arm, she kissed him on the cheek, 'I am sorry, Henry, about that. We will meet soon. Very soon.' She rubbed her cheek in wry amusement, and Henry knew it was his beard. He liked keeping it neat and pointed, the latest fashion, but now he wondered if that was a good idea. Maya's face was flushed as she made a show of putting on her hat and gloves, and he drew his breath. The red in her cheeks heightened the strange blue of her eyes.

They both turned at the soft tread behind them. The turbaned bearer who had come to clear away their breakfast smiled shyly, holding his tray forward like a shield, as if not wishing to intrude on them. Henry, flustered at the sudden intimate gesture on Maya's part, found himself at a loss for words. She gathered up her stole, placed it around her shoulders, pushed her hair back more firmly this time, and rose to go. Just as she turned away, Henry said, 'Mark Twain's here tomorrow.'

'That will keep you busy then, won't it?' she asked, and not waiting for a reply, went on, 'It was nice meeting this way. And if your busy schedule, and Mark Twain's too, permits, we hope you will come over for luncheon soon.' Her face was in profile as she said this, and still looked somewhat flushed to him. Then she smiled at the bearer, who moved away just in time from her path, and made for the double doors that led to the club lobby and the entrance. Henry signed on the pad the bearer held out, looking over all the details he was sure the manager had got quite right: his room number at the club, the breakfast items, and the date, and then he felt in his pockets for some coins. The bearer bowed, 'I have arranged your table, sir, in the reading room. Not many people in today.'

Henry made his way past the door, through which Maya had just left, and turned right to walk down the hallway that was lined with clay figurines, a potted money plant or two, and thought more about her. Behind him was the lobby, where the concierge waited at his desk, making his notes, keeping an eye on the doorman and the scene outside. Sunlight came in through the slatted bamboo blinds and Henry remembered it was January. He had almost forgotten how cold New York, or even Chicago, was at this time of year. He pushed open the door to the reading room, using more force than necessary. He didn't want to think of Maya. If he did, he would just get too distracted. There was so much to do, and as the American trade consul in Bombay, he had to make an impression on the right people and those who mattered. It had been only six months so far but he hadn't travelled all this way, leaving everything that was familiar, the past and the painful, behind him for nothing. Six months in this city in the East that he was getting to like, and almost six months since he had known Maya, and he already liked her a lot more. He lifted a hand to his cheek, where her lips had alighted briefly, only moments ago, and felt a sudden happiness flood him.

I
Arrivals

The Clemenses—Samuel, better known the world over as Mark Twain, his wife Olivia, and daughter, Clara—arrived around seven the next morning, with *The Rosetta* keeping to its schedule from Colombo. Henry Baker was there to meet them, and quite on time, in a new brown sack coat that he took off minutes after reaching the Bori Bunder docks. Things always got warm quickly even if it was January. He handed the coat over to Abdul, warning him not to let it crease in any way. Abdul had been his manservant for almost as long as he, Henry, had been in India, and he learnt fast. Henry found his enthusiasm hard to take at times, but he always relented: Abdul was only eighteen, and looked even younger, tall for his age, and there was always a desperate earnestness in his dark eyes.

Now Henry pulled his watch out of his vest and checked the time yet again. He paced, heading to the quay's very edge to look farther away, out to sea, before gingerly stepping back, scraping the damp off his knickerbockers, his eyes straying toward the fishermen in their small painted boats, unloading their wares on the docks.

The boats jostled against each other, and the sea, time and again, bubbled and brushed against the wood. The sunlight flashed silver against the nets, heavy and glistening, and the trapped fish in turn made tiny mirrors of light. A thousand and more mirrors rose and fell with the waves rolling up to the rocks before easing away. Henry blinked, feeling the cold damp of the morning on his face, and the fishermen flung their fish-laden nets over the rocky ledge. The womenfolk waited, wicker baskets against their hips. They vended the fish across the city, calling out their wares as they spread across different quarters of the city: Walkeswar, Colaba, and northward in the mill area of Parel and Sewree. The gulls circled and hovered overhead, dipping low, and moments later, soaring high, and the women swatted them away, in practiced and habitual irritation. *Shoo. Shoo. Jao.* Henry heard their rhythmic imprecations, almost in unison. Two policemen descended the stony quay, their wooden sticks flapping against their knee-length shorts as they gestured to the fishermen. That meant the docks had to be cleared soon for the bigger ships to anchor. In the distance, to the east, Henry saw a first faint blob, and he wondered if that was *The Rosetta* bringing in the Clemenses.

'They will soon be away, sahib,' said Abdul, waving his umbrella all about him, swatting away flies. The sky looked clear, but it had rained the previous night, and Abdul liked to be prepared.

'Who?' asked Henry crossly, wondering if Abdul meant the fisherfolk, the fishy smell from their baskets, or the flies. For a pleasant minute or two, he had been thinking of Maya. The other morning, he had planned a carriage ride on the Apollo Bunder with its sparkling view of the morning sea, the dewy breeze on their faces, but news of the murder had put paid to his plans. He should have kept the newspaper firmly out of sight. A couple of pye-dogs came trotting up, their ears perked high as they surveyed the shore. The gulls squawked as they indignantly flew away, and the women sat on their haunches, carefully arranging their baskets of fish. Henry wondered at the kind of welcome the Clemenses were going to get.

'Never mind, Abdul. Just be careful you don't let the smell get into my coat,' he said, half-jovially. Then more seriously, he explained, 'Our guest is a writer, and there's his family too. Maybe they will want to do something other than the usual stuff. Everyone does the parties, the visit to Governor's House and Elephanta Island. There must be other things to do, I am sure.' Henry's words petered off as a breeze came up, and he lifted a hasty hand to his head, but Abdul's eyes lit up and he nodded enthusiastically. Maya had suggested an excursion way out of the city, in the Ghats leading to Poona. Something like that would speak to a writer's imagination, she'd said at the time and Henry smiled at the memory.

Half an hour later the pier at the farthest end suddenly came to life. More policemen in their yellow turbans and blue uniforms came up, coolies, dockworkers thronged that end, standing amidst crates and boxes, craning their necks south-westward from where the ship chugged in. Clouds of black smoke rose, spread against the blue sky, and the black hulk of the approaching object gradually took on a more definite shape. Two tugboats led the ship in, its siren blowing with a majesty that for moments silenced the cacophony on the pier. Passengers stood along the white railings waving to the crowds, acknowledging the cheers, as the ship came in slowly, ponderously.

Abdul helped Henry with his coat, running his hand quickly over it, smoothing out the creases, one last time. Henry took his hat off, his fingers sticky from his hair pomade, and stood smiling stiffly, trying to look as efficient and welcoming as possible. As the American Consul in Bombay—as he never failed to remind himself—he had to ensure the Clemenses had a pleasant stay in Bombay, and wherever else they travelled to in India. Mark Twain's manager, Robert Smythe, who was still in Australia, unable to travel with them owing to some personal matters in Sydney, had mailed Henry their detailed itinerary. He wished now that he had it in his pocket. It would have given him something to talk about in the carriage ride to Watson's Hotel where the Clemenses were staying.

Minutes later, as the passengers descended, and walked down the gangway, Henry caught a fleeting glimpse of the Clemenses as they headed toward the Customs House, and felt a frisson of excitement. He moved his hat from one hand to the other, wondering if he should wave it to draw attention. He was seeing the famous writer for the first time and while most other passengers looked ahead, with anxious or expectant expressions, Mark Twain looked around with what Henry thought was some writerly curiosity. His head, crowned by a shaggy salt and pepper mane, was never still for long. Samuel Langhorne Clemens—Mark Twain's actual name—was just as he appeared in his photos, even the grainy ones in the newspapers. His wife and daughter flanked him as the three of them were swept along in the general wave toward the awning leading to the Customs House.

Henry swatted a fly or two away, and prepared for another long wait. Though the customs officials had been told of the Clemenses' arrival, they could be officious, insisting on following every rule when it came to clearing luggage and other formalities. And he, Henry Baker, was still learning to throw his weight around like the ruddy, at times pompous, English officials he interacted with. The obsequiousness they took for granted from their juniors had given Henry a start in his initial days. Now he knew better than to form judgements easily. It was best to slowly learn about a new place. To let every experience seep into the skin before one figured a way to decipher them.

This manner of thinking confused him, and standing there, near the benches that made up the waiting area, the crowds around him, but not near enough to bother him, the glinting blue sky and the heat already seeping in through the canvas awning, he knew it all stemmed from Maya. She was a sort of nowhere person just like him, looking to fit in, to belong in this very cosmopolitan city of the East. Their being out of place, Henry thought, was just what had made them so compatible, that very first time they had met, quite by accident, at the Asiatic Society building. A professor-like speaker—he remembered it was someone called Jivanji, a merchant philanthropist from Gujerat—had been expounding at length about the Persian origins of cricket—not British, he declaimed time and again, to a few muttered cheers—and Maya had looked just as lost as Henry was. That had been six months ago, and he wondered if it was too soon for him to be thinking ahead, about Maya and himself, or if he should just let things be for a while.

He saw the other man then, standing not very far away, using his hat to fan himself. His wrist moving mechanically, like a fan blade. Fans were Henry's specialty, and he was trying to woo over the business community and the elite to electric fans. What he had not accounted for was that the city's electricity system still wasn't up to standard. Most of the city still relied on gas lamps lit up and diffused by an army of lighters who had their earmarked spots, and travelled in their two-wheel pony carts. They were always followed by groups of excited urchins who stood behind them, mimicking the sound of the lamps as they were lit—

Phooosh—before fleeing into the small lanes and by-lanes Henry was still learning about. Fans would save so much labour, he thought, watching the other man, who held a writing pad in his other hand, a pen tucked behind his left ear. It clearly marked him out as a newspaperman and Henry felt irritation gush over him. He wished the newspapers hadn't cottoned onto Mark Twain's arrival so very early. The famous man needed some respite. Reporters from the *Times* or the *Gazette* would right away ask him things he might have little idea about. Russia's military build-up, America's opinions on the Afghan matter, and America's plans in the Pacific, especially the Philippines. Would the accession of Hawaii mean a more belligerent America? Writers weren't diplomats, Henry reasoned and allowed himself a little smugness.

The man jumped when Henry walked up to him. He ran a finger over his moustache, over his short groomed hair and Henry knew he should have recognized him earlier. This was no reporter but someone from the police commissioner's office.

'By whose permission are you here?' Henry asked. That kind of pomposity would never work, for one could always trust a government official to do it better, and Henry hastily added on a more concerned note. 'Is something the matter?'

The other man pursed his lips, nodded crisply, and looked into the far distance, as if contemplating something serious. 'Inspector Button here,' he said, quite unnecessarily, thought Henry, as he went on,

'And I do beg pardon, sir, but we have orders. To monitor everyone who enters the city. It is for security. There's a Russian prince on this ship, and we think there may be attempts on him.'

Henry's eyes widened, 'You don't say! Attempts on his life, you mean?'

His nose scrunched up as a fisherwoman raced past him, clearly in some personal distress, the basket on her head trailing brown brackish water in her wake. 'There's goes her spot at the market today,' the inspector murmured. He ran his eyes over Henry appraisingly. 'Hmm...yes, at least we think so.'

'Why is a Russian prince here though?' Henry persisted. What with that young woman, Casi's murder only a day or so ago, and now a Russian prince in fear for his life, Bombay suddenly appeared a city pulsing with secret danger. Quite like Constantinople, Baghdad, or even Vienna. Cities forever conspiring to make history. Button fixed the pen more securely behind his ear, chewed his lip and said, 'I am not at liberty to divulge that. Or anything, really. Just that I should make a note of all arriving passengers.'

Button nodded toward the far end of the platform, where the first few ship passengers had begun coming out the Customs House door. Henry saw Clara in her long blue skirt looking all around, evidently for him, for he had cabled the ship about meeting them on their arrival. Mark Twain waited for his wife, Olivia, to catch up, he stood in the way, quite unmindful, of the other passengers who impatiently sidestepped him.

Henry stepped forward, suddenly confused whether to be effusive or serious in his greeting. Maya had once told him that he was one of the lucky few who could get through life bothered only by such minor, even pleasant confusions. He did not know whether she had spoken in jest or meant it in all seriousness. With Maya, her convoluted life, and intriguing name, one could never come to an easy conclusion about such things.

'One of these days, your father could write to the governor to rein you in,' Henry had recently told her, a deliberate light tone in his voice as he referred to her father, the Reverend Charles Barton who headed the Indian Church Mission in Lahore. They had been walking along the sea, and Maya was close to the ledge overlooking the rocks where the waves splashed time and again. The spray rose high, catching them on the face, and Henry feared she might, in an absent-minded moment, slip and hurt herself. And so very firmly, he had taken Maya's elbow and nudged her away.

Maya had only smiled, but she let herself be pulled away. 'He should be happy I am following his example. Making my way in a new city, just as he did when he first came to India.' She placed a hand on his arm, a gesture quite unconventional in a city where everyone was mindful of the proprieties, and said, 'And do I really need reining in?'

Henry held his hands up in surrender, and Maya had raised her brows and walked on ahead. He smiled ruefully at the memory. For all he knew about her,

Maya was so much a mystery. The rumour was that she had been adopted by Reverend Charles Barton, that her mother was a Kashmiri woman who had once worked for the church mission and Reverend Barton. That explained Maya's eyes that changed colour just like the sea. Blue when she felt strongly about something, and a strange hazel-green in the quiet of the morning. In the gossip circles of Delhi, Lahore, and Bombay, as Henry had heard too, there were other direct insinuations and conjectures, that Maya was the product of the Reverend's own secret liaison with the woman from Kashmir. Maya intrigued Henry in other ways too. He had never met anyone quite like her. Someone who fascinated him and irked him beyond measure.

II

All the Things to Do in a New City

Henry Baker stepped under the asbestos roof of the pier, so he had a clearer view of Mark Twain. The keen eyes, the drooping, shaving-brush moustache, the unkempt hair matched everything Henry had seen of him in photos, and he held himself straighter, and willed a smile. He had never imagined meeting Mark Twain, who lived half a world or more away, in his native Chicago, or New York.

Henry frowned. It wouldn't do to call him Mark Twain. 'Mr Twain' sounded plain ridiculous. And Mark? Perhaps that indicated some undeserved familiarity. 'Samuel L. Clemens was the name on his ticket, and schedule, and even his manager Robert Smythe had addressed him that way. 'He likes the formality,' Smythe had written. 'And sometimes he might address himself as Twain, or Mark Twain, when he writes to organizers, editors, and the like. But he can be whimsical about that. My rule is: he is Mark Twain when I arrange for his lectures, but Mr Clemens for every other thing. This name offers him anonymity too. Also, remember, he gives his money away too easily, especially when flattered, and for any invention that promises a miracle. He has a weakness for those kinds of things.' So, it would be Mr Clemens then, unless he specified otherwise. *S. L. Clemens*. It did give him, Henry thought, a certain privacy.

He noticed someone else then, a figure in a shabby brown coat, and a flat black hat who emerged around the corner, right at the other end of the port building. Henry groaned. He should have expected Arthur Pease to be around the docks at this hour. At this time of the morning, one could see some of the porters lolling against the wall, lost in the haze of their addiction. Pease always made himself a preachy and holier-than-thou nuisance, forever distributing his pamphlets that berated the British for their opium policies, the people for being weak in not resisting the drug, and he was now critical of America as well. Pease had reached out to Henry as well, soon after his arrival, when the crisis with Venezuela was at its height, insisting that Henry intercede with President Grover Cleveland. The opium crisis was another subject that America had to take on, Pease had added. Henry had felt bemused and flattered. The Venezuela crisis with Britain was really none of Pease's business, for he was no diplomat, and not even part of the government. But Henry had been so new to the city then, and he had no wish to upset the British, or any Britisher for that matter, especially when he was in the empire they lorded over. Trade, he knew, could never flourish in a state of antagonism. He had since then learnt how to avoid Pease, pleading he had to be away at meetings, and now he looked on with alarm, hoping Pease wouldn't accost Mark Twain, hand him a pamphlet or two.

But Pease had other matters on his mind. He walked in through the Customs House door, with barely a glance toward the Clemenses. That was not really surprising, Henry thought, since, probably, no one in Bombay knew of Mark Twain or his work. That was what the police superintendent, R.H. Vincent, impatient and brusque as always, had told Henry when he had asked for a sepoy or two for the Clemenses. 'For their security,' he explained as Vincent raised a quizzical eyebrow.

'Mr Baker, I really don't think that will be necessary. No one really knows who they are,' Vincent had replied slowly, looking at his sola hat, running a finger through its inner lining, as if checking for dirt. He'd tapped the hat against the table, weighing his next words. 'I haven't even read him. His books, and the newspaper columns. Maybe more people will, after this visit. But no one, really no one, even your big guys like Jeejeebhoy, Sassoon, and the rest, has heard of him. The Clemenses are safe as they are. Just get them a good servant. Check with his Mrs about the kind she may prefer.'

Henry had nodded, it did no good to argue with Vincent. Henry secretly admired him, how he got things done, simply by putting on that impatient and officious manner. Simply by acting superior, the British had managed to be conquerors, and oppressors. Something Maya was always saying to him.

'It's all in the way of speaking, behaving, and appearing. Men fool themselves and the world.'

His lips twitched as he remembered Maya again, while keeping the Clemenses firmly in sight. If there was someone who could give Twain competition with words, and the right aphorisms, it was Maya Barton.

The two women on either side of Twain soon came clearly into view, as Henry advanced, waving his hat, and smiling effusively. He hoped he wasn't overdoing it. A long journey through the warm tropics was something they weren't really used to, even he wasn't. Clara, walking on Twain's right hastily fixed her hair, ran a hand down her blue, pleated skirt. Their eyes met and she looked flustered. But Henry's moment of being flattered ceased, as she looked back at the three men who tottered behind, carrying their luggage.

Henry bowed as the three of them came closer. Abdul advanced as well, circling around them, as he made for the porters. 'It's all right,' Henry said, his first words to the Twains, the Clemenses, as he corrected himself mentally, 'my man will see to your luggage. Please don't worry.'

A look of collective relief appeared on their faces, and Henry thought how British he had sounded. He cleared his throat, bounced on his heels, and then as an afterthought, he introduced himself.

~

In the carriage, Clara and her father looked out of their windows, their eyes ablaze with excitement, while Olivia tried hard to stifle her yawns, smiling apologetically at Henry every time her head lolled drowsily on the brocaded seat. When he offered her a cushion to rest her back, she laughed, embarrassed.

The morning outside was pleasant. Clara pointed to the crows, some gulls too, that circled watchfully over the running women, the baskets of fish balanced delicately on their heads.

The carriage passed a man draped in beads, matted locks of hair hanging about his face, who sat cross-legged under the umbrella-like branches of a banyan tree. His eyes were closed, his hands stretched in a yogic position over his knees. The fisherwomen giggled. They paused their run momentarily and folded their hands before him, before carefully skirting their way around, shushing each other not to bother him. One of them plucked a marigold flower out of her hair and placed it before the meditating yogi.

'Are they really so worshipful of him? Afraid of his powers?' Clara asked breathlessly, her eyes following the action outside.

'No.' Henry was matter-of-fact, as he had seen it many times before. 'It's just fun. Once I heard the women accuse him of putting a spell on the birds, making them do his bidding. There was an argument, and he threatened to shift to another spot. It just goes on.'

Twain looked around, patted his pockets, and Olivia

answered tiredly, 'You must have put away your diary, dear. I do remember seeing it in the green suitcase.'

'I don't want to forget anything,' he muttered. 'I want to remember everything. And sometimes the way others remember just isn't right.' He tapped his fingers on the window and looked pleased with all that he saw.

Henry tried to sound assuring. 'You'll find lots of things to write about here. And you'll need lots of diaries too. There's never a dull moment in this city.' After six months, he believed his own words. There was this city, its many people, its very liveliness, the events that changed from day to day, hour to hour, and the even more vast country beyond it, that he had yet to explore, and all this made things so much more exciting than Chicago. 'And the weather's better too, at this time. It's the best time to visit,' he said, as the balmy air drifted in from the sea.

He saw the fishermen's catamarans out at sea, the smaller boats headed out to Elephanta and Butcher Island, and the lone steamship standing still at the dock. The palm leaves swayed, a man sat with his pottery wares by the street, and a young Pathan boy, his turban wrapped loosely on his head, led a horse by a rope, shouting out a price, as he raised his hand in the air repeatedly.

'January and February, I'd wager, are the best months to be in Bombay,' Henry said again to Mark Twain and to the back of Clara's head as she craned her neck to take in the city. 'May gets hot, and then boy! Wait for the monsoons in June. It just pours and pours.'

He frowned, prodded by a recent memory. Those were Maya's words, when she had told him of the time she had been caught at sea, just as the rains came. 'That was a narrow escape,' he remembered her telling him. 'The waves lashed over our boat repeatedly. And the rain wasn't giving up. If the fishermen hadn't seen me, I might have drowned. And we might never have met.'

That should have been his cue to be more romantic, and he had, as always, missed his moment.

He smiled at Clara, while her mother undid the strings of her hat, flopped it on the space by her, and asked about a servant. She had obviously been schooled about her visit. Was it really necessary, she asked with some nervousness, and could they be trusted?

Henry nodded sagely. 'They see to the small, very important things. Getting water, getting the clothes ironed and arranged, and running any errand, things like that. The hotel staff can sometimes be limited.'

Olivia glanced toward her husband, but he was scribbling away in his diary. The diary had been in Twain's pocket after all and now that he had found it, he was writing at a furious pace, as if afraid of forgetting all he had seen so far. Olivia smiled, her eyes still on her husband, 'I see. I do see your point, Mr Baker.'

Only then did Twain put his diary, a black-covered one, with gold velvet lettering away in his pocket and looked up, a pleased expression on his face. 'Well, that's one worry settled for you then, Livy. Mr Baker here has all the answers.' He picked at his coat sleeve, and said with a frown. 'Since we are going to be seeing a lot of each other, I hope, you must call me...' His voice broke off, and he shrugged, 'Sam or Mark. Either will do.'

Clara laughed, before she explained, 'Father used to be fussy. Sam for friends and family, and Mark for those who knew him better as a writer. But it got complicated. Everyone calls him Mark Twain, or Mark, and he hates Mr Twain, so you must do as he says. Choose one.'

'I am Henry, of course,' Henry said. 'You must call me that.'

Clara flushed as he said that, and it made Henry self-conscious. He had no illusions about the effect he had on others. True, Clara was far from home, and she must miss seeing Americans her own age. And there were Americans like his friend, the artist, Edwin Lord Weeks, who had had a more adventurous life, and who was away at present exploring the cave temples at Ajanta with his wife. Edwin was taller, and had a robustly luxuriant moustache that he was proud of. Then there was the magician Freddie Bancroft, whom Henry had little liking for. Bancroft was handsome, tall, and lithe with extravagant manners that pleased the British ladies and Indian memsahibs alike. Henry, for his part, was still finding his feet in a strange land after wandering through England, the Continent, and a bit of Russia. Sometimes it amazed him that Maya, intelligent and strangely attractive as she was, found his company interesting. Or did she? He swept away his wild mop of hair from his forehead. It became frizzy even in gentle heat. He had a complexion that burned easily, and a pointed beard that was at times difficult to maintain. He remembered how it had troubled Maya only the other morning. Olivia saw his preoccupied look and they exchanged friendly smiles before turning away, toward their respective windows.

They took the road from the Bunder, circled the town hall, and then the wide Elphinstone circle lined by its pillared buildings with grey slatted windows, the Cathedral with its twin tall turrets, and the red tiled roof and arched windows of the Bombay Club, before moving down the wide, well-shaded Esplanade Street. The plane trees stood still and quiet, soaking in the morning. A few more carriages appeared in the streets now, some passed them occasionally, and a few soldiers trotted past on their horses. The sound of their hooves mingled with those of the carriage horses, and the first sirens sounded from the mills in the city's heart. Watson's hotel soon appeared to their right. Henry leaned out to point it out to the Clemenses. A four-storied, glass-fronted hotel with balconies on every side, and a driveway that led into an impressive domed portico. He saw that the coachman's assistant had already jumped down from the footboard and was directing the carriage toward the driveway.

'You just walk toward the registration desk, and we will see about the servant soon,' Henry said. 'And do notice the atrium. It's all glass and goes right up to the roof. It's something exceptional and very modern. I am glad you are seeing one of the finest things about the city on your first day. It's quite a feat. You stand under the glass dome, and it feels like you are bathed in sunlight.'

There I go again, sounding like an over-talkative travel guide, Henry thought as the carriage drew to a halt. But everyone's attention was diverted by the excited shouts outside, coolies were thumping the carriage on every side. Henry glanced out and put a finger to his lips. '*Chup karo*,' he said. Momentarily, the coolies fell silent. They smiled ingratiatingly, fixed their turbans and folded their hands in supplication, and just then Abdul came up, running. He was gesturing frantically with his hands as well, shouting at the gathered men, '*Jao. Jaldi jao.* Go away, all of you. I am here to manage the sahibs' luggage.'

'Really, Abdul, you did take your time,' Henry jumped off the carriage, light on his feet. He noted Olivia looking with some concern towards Clara. 'Is something the matter?' he asked, with one eye on Abdul managing the porters.

'Oh no, it's nothing,' said Olivia, laughing apologetically. 'Poor Clara was feeling somewhat under the weather on the ship, and she never sleeps well at such times. Maybe I should be with her in her room.'

Henry nodded, 'I am sure the hotel would accommodate that, or any request you have, Mrs Clemens.' The hopeful porters were looking with expectation at another carriage that had just driven up, and cried joyfully in unison as the coachman crooked a summoning finger. The crowd of men that swarmed around the coachman dispersed the moment he lifted his whip in mock-anger. 'I don't need so many, you idiots. Get lost,' the coachman snapped repeatedly as he picked two men out of the crowd, still holding his whip high.

'Carriage got stuck up for a bit, sir. There was funeral procession,' Abdul said excitedly, his eyes roving quickly over the guests before he discreetly looked away. Henry held his hand out for the ladies, and to Mark Twain, he said, 'Abdul here, will see to the luggage. I'd trust him with my life. Well, the times when it isn't in much danger.'

And Twain was laughing as they went in. 'You have a way with words. Are you sure you aren't a writer too?'

III

An Evening with the Bengalees

That evening there was a dinner at Cowasjee Bengalee's house. If Henry had had his way, the dinner wouldn't have happened right on that first evening. But Bengalee's secretary, a hot-headed Irishman called Carsten O'Hara, had cabled Mark Twain on the ship, extending the invitation. Carsten, mindful of protocol, had even sent around an invite for Henry.

'You'd think they would have some consideration,' he told Maya the morning he walked with her down the stone-tiled Apollo Bunder, as it curved towards the Yacht Club. The boats at sea were like small specks, dotting the blue waters. 'He should have realized that the Clemenses would be tired. The seas can be rough this time of year and that can be hard for some too. But I guess Bengalee wanted to show off. An American guest, and a big writer too.'

'You should have anticipated a thing like this,' she said. 'Bengalee would never lose an opportunity, especially when he was slighted by the British. Governor

Sandhurst didn't give him a meeting relating to a matter of import duties on cotton, and the Prince of Wales preferred staying at the Sassoon house during his stay here.'

Henry reminded the three Clemenses again of the dinner invite, and he noticed how their eyes lit up. 'That should be most exciting,' said Twain. 'I believe he is one of the richest men in town. His secretary promised us quite an experience. One to remember. He must be quite like the nabobs, or the maharajas of old. I must remember to have my diary with me.'

'And I must get out my gown, Father,' said Clara. 'I do hope it's in good shape. All my skirts are so rumpled and creased.'

'I am sure, miss, you will look beautiful in anything,' Henry said gallantly, lifting his hat. She looked most flustered, and Twain smiled, in the abstracted way he had.

Henry felt discomfited, however, when he caught Olivia's speculative glance on him, a moment before she looked toward her daughter. He hoped he had not sounded over-effusive.

'I think I promised to speak about something this evening...,' Twain had been talking in a low voice, tapping his forehead, as if trying to remember something. 'They wanted me to speak about gold, the prodigious amounts apparently in Australia, though I saw none,' he chuckled, as he turned to his wife and daughter. 'Maybe I should talk about that funny sage—he called himself a yogi with great powers, didn't he?—the one who predicted some exciting adventures for me ahead?'

~

As the Clemenses moved through the atrium, looking up at the glass skylight with the iron beams crossing it, Henry stayed behind. Getting a servant was an onerous thing but with the Clemenses at least it was easy. There wasn't much to tick off on the checklist. Unlike the British, the Americans were more self-reliant. The servant, Olivia had said, just had to understand a bit of English. Abdul had managed to get two porters to lug the Clemenses' luggage up the steps, and now he stood in the portico, salaaming repeatedly in Henry's direction. Next to him stood a painfully thin man, a pleading expression on his face, a hand on his turban that looked dirty and distinctly ragged. If this were the man Abdul had picked for a servant, that unwashed, raggedy turban would have to go.

Still, after he had talked to him, Henry was pleased with Manuel. He had a nervous way about him, a twitch in his right eye, but he was reasonably conversant in English. He said he had picked up English from working as a porter for many months. 'I know English, Swahili, Persian, and then Marathi, sahib. Gujerati too.' Manuel said, counting off the languages on his fingers.

'Only English will do for now, thank you,' Henry said, briskly. 'Get yourself a new turban or take it off if you haven't got one. And remember, you are on trial.

If the sahib and memsahib don't find you suitable, we get a new servant.'

'*Ji*,' Manuel said, taking his turban off in a jiffy. One end came loose, and flapped sadly against his leg. His exposed head made him look even more shrunken, and Henry noted a certain piteous expression on Manuel's face. As if, Henry would remember later, he wanted this job desperately.

Henry kept up with his instructions to the Clemenses, as they rode in the carriage to Bengalee's house. It was still early evening and he had hoped they would want to lie in, but they were waiting for him at the reception as he came in. He had had lunch at the doctors' bungalow—as the old house in Colaba was called—where Maya lived. She shared the bungalow with Dr Charlotte Ellaby. Earlier, another lady doctor, Edith Pechey, had lived there too. Since her marriage to the American businessman, George Phipson, Edith, however, had moved out, though she came over every so often with her husband, for the occasional meal and company.

Maya and Charlotte had been very keen to hear about the Clemenses. There had been the inevitable discussion as to whether they should be referred to as the Clemenses or the Twains.

'Well, he's left that open for me. Sam or Mark will do for him. And then Mrs Clemens...' Henry said, wiping his hands on a napkin, hoping the mutton curry stains wouldn't show up later. 'She preferred to be called Livy.' Maya's cook, Ali was, like Abdul, a Pathan from Afghanistan, and known to stir up with ease the most complicated and spiciest Mughlai dishes. His biryani that took several hours and whose fragrance lingered through the house—turning it, as Maya joked, into a garden of heavenly aromas—made events at the bungalow always very popular.

'Considering the family name isn't Twain, it'd make sense to stick with Mr Clemens for him, don't you think? I was thinking about what might apply to me, of course,' Maya had said, and then she had moved onto other things, as was typical of her. 'I am sure they will love it at the Watson's. It's so much more modern, and so unusually built. That iron frame—it makes the Majestic look...dated.'

Henry had lingered long over lunch, and only a hasty look at the clock, and Abdul's discreet appearance at the window, as he tried to catch his eye, made him get quickly to his feet. Maya had sounded vague about coming to Bengalee's party, and Henry remembered this as he was driving away in a carriage to his rooms at the Byculla Club, where he would change before returning to Watson's Hotel to pick the Clemenses up for the party. She'd said she wasn't sure, and Henry tried to remember what she had said next, as he blinked in the strong afternoon light. 'I might go, or I might not,' he had heard Maya saying. 'Though I am told Mrs Bengalee is hosting a play. That should be something fun. For the Clemenses too.'

Henry had inwardly groaned. He knew what this could entail. That he would have to translate things for the Clemenses, and his Hindustani was still very patchy. He would most likely miss quite a lot of what was going on.

~

The hotel was even busier in early evening than when he had left it some hours ago. There were a few carriages lined up on the road leading to the hotel's impressive doorway, and a juggler was just setting up his act in the grounds opposite. The hotel's servants and porters lingered outside, some trying to look busy, others smoked their bidis discreetly. A few salaamed Henry robustly with a smile. The doormen greeted him over-effusively, hands to their foreheads, and bowing low.

'I gave him the evening off,' said Mark Twain. 'Soon after he had pressed my suit, and got the ladies' dresses done too. A most efficient chap, this Manuel.'

'It's not that you gave him the evening off,' Olivia countered almost immediately. 'He was hovering around a bit too much, and then I had to ask him what he wanted. And what a pantomime it was...'

Clara laughed as she added, 'He had to figure out from my gestures what I wanted.' She mimed them now, using two fingers on the pleat of her shimmering yellow skirt. 'This is what I did when I asked for the dress to be ironed. After that he said he had to go somewhere.'

'Go where?' Henry asked, trying not to show his irritation. A servant, once he had been engaged, couldn't just take off like that. Henry wished he had not engaged Manuel in such a rush. That he had not relied on Abdul. He should have relied on Maya, but of late, he had begun to rely on her a bit too much.

Everyone stared at Clara as she folded her hands, lifting them to her forehead. 'Shiva, Shiva, he kept saying.'

'That's the god of destruction, isn't he?' asked Mark Twain. 'The one who opens up his third eye and burns up the world.' He laughed, waving away the surprised glances of the women. 'Don't you women remember anything? The yogi I met in Australia told me.'

'Yes,' Henry said, 'but he does that when he's really angry, or when the world is beyond saving. So, they pray to keep him appeased.'

There was light-hearted conversation on the way to Bengalee's house. Mark Twain did not seem troubled, nor preoccupied in any way. There was nothing to indicate that the very next day he would disappear, literally pull a vanishing act, leaving everyone clueless. Henry saw him scribble something in his diary, the pencil stub making a sharp, scratchy sound as he wrote quickly, and Henry remembered that taking the Clemenses to Elephanta was also on his agenda. He hoped Manuel would be back that night.

~

Clara looked sunny and even younger in her yellow floral skirt with a white frilly blouse, and her mother was in blue. The yellow might look faded once the lights came on, the flickering gas lamps would only highlight the women's jewellery, but all this was still some hours away. Mark Twain was in grey, and wore a red tie over his upturned collar. Henry knew he cut a dashing figure himself in his light brown coat, and dark blue tie. It annoyed him that he had not been able to find his yellow polka dotted tie, and had given Abdul quite a mouthful. Against the brown of his coat, the yellow tie would have presented quite a contrast.

Mark Twain's polite cough cut into the short silence that had settled in the carriage, before he said, 'The staff were talking about a most interesting murder. If a murder can be called that...,' he paused, gave a short laugh. 'From what I was told, it was quite a thing really.'

Henry nodded sombrely, 'Yes, in the native area. A young girl, and just newly married.' He thought of the shock on Maya's face, and how devastated she had sounded. The others in the carriage with him, however, sounded animated.

'Everyone seemed shocked,' burst in Clara, her eyes big and rounded in excitement. Henry smiled thinly in understanding. It wasn't so unseemly, her excitement, considering all this was so new and alien to her still, and then her father broke in, leaning forward to get Henry's attention. 'They were talking of the thugees. The thugs, they are called that too. I read about that. The way they picked their victims, usually those who wore a lot of jewellery, and their methods of poisoning and strangulation.' He rolled his eyes, and ran a mocking finger across his throat, drawing a disapproving hiss from his wife. They laughed softly, and a silence fell quickly again, as if they recognized the incongruity of their recent humour. 'I'd like to learn more about it though,' Henry heard Mark Twain muse, as he riffled the blank pages of his diary.

Their carriage took them past the Lohar Chal Street, with smithies and utensil shops on either side while the Sonapur Lane was lined with jewellery shops and goldsmith establishments. The carriage jostled over the tram lines, and then turned right on Queen's Road, just where the Marine Lines battalion was stationed, and the beach, the waters now darkening in the sunset, appeared to their left. He discreetly pointed out the high brown walls shrouded by low-hanging trees, behind which spread the Hindu cremation and Mohammedan burial grounds. 'Even in death, the two communities remain divided,' Henry said. Only some years ago, he had read, there had been riots in another part of the country, when one community had taken out a festival procession past a mosque where a congregation had just gathered for its weekly prayers. As Maya had explained, it didn't take much for people to be affected by the symbolic, external matters that defined a religion, and that was such a pity. Mark Twain leaned forward to look out with great interest just as the carriage picked up speed, trying ineffectually to outrace another horse-drawn carriage of the Bombay Tramways that soon pulled away, the sound of hooves loud in their small boxed-in compartment.

The trams, Henry explained were originally meant to run on electricity, but setting up things was still taking time. The lines had been built some years ago, and so the horse-run carriages now ran on them, on the same routes. 'Once the electricity comes in, the trams will run the same route. Minus the horses,' he finished. The women laughed, and Twain ran a hand over his moustache before he spoke with a twinkle in his eye. 'I am willing to wager that the horses will always be much faster.'

At a point where the land curved, they could see ahead the swaying palms, the thick, bushy trees, and the blinking lights of the big houses where Bombay's rich lived. These were houses that could be the envy of cities like New York and London, and designed at times, by the same architects. The road wound up Cumballa Hill, and Henry pointed out to them the Banganga temple to their right. There was a small crowd in places on the beach. The breeze carried the call of the vendors to them, and some could be seen, through the soft waving palm fronds, as they gestured to the coconuts piled up like low hills on the sand. Others passed, jingling small bells, the wooden boxes on their shoulders full of the crunchy peanut savouries that were so popular, and farther on, a group of acrobats performed rope tricks and the applause fell and rose, in rhythm to the waves and the wind.

'I wish we could stop,' said Clara.

'Some other time, miss, and I am sure Mr Bengalee has some interesting entertainment lined up for you.

They, Mr Bengalee and his wife, have a reputation as wonderful hosts. They even had a ghost hunt when the Duke of Connaught had come some years ago,' Henry detailed.

They rode up the hill, past the Tower of Silence that he faithfully pointed out to them, a place, he explained, where the dead were left, according to the Parsee religion. As the trees loomed higher, it became almost dark in places but the evening was fragrant with the laburnum flowers strewn on the road, and the jasmine bushes that lined it on either side. It was hard to see the houses, as most stood behind high towering walls, but Henry occasionally caught a glimpse of wide driveways, an impressive gate flanked by moustached guardsmen, a colonnaded portico, tall French windows, arched or domed roofs, and the trellised balconies that ran along the upper stories.

Cowasjee Bengalee's mansion was right where the road curved around a small hill, and turned back towards the sea. As the carriage slowed, they heard the drumming and the low strains of the flute. 'Quite a musical welcome,' said Mark Twain. They joined the line of other carriages that waited to go up the driveway. The lawn stretched a lush green, and across flowerbeds of orchids and hydrangeas there were low tables and chairs with bearers in their red turbans moving between them, holding their trays high. At the far end, along the walls, there were the two white marquees, identical in every way, with their neat square shapes, and conical tops dipping and sinking in the breeze. As their carriage came to a stop, and the musicians paused for the briefest of seconds to catch their breath, a decaying smell came from the Tower of Silence, and Henry heard too the flutter of vulture wings, as the birds appeared like black blobs not too far away. It sent a cold shudder down his spine, and he noted Clara's look of concern. In that moment, there came the slow mournful strains of a violin and he smiled at her, held his hand out to help her alight, and Olivia after her.

'There will be just so much to see here. I worry you might be tired.'

The strains of the violin were soon drowned by other noises rushing in like waves. Some moved in slowly, like the buzz of nearby conversation, and then the pipers and drummers sounded again, louder this time.

'Not at all,' Mark Twain said laughing gruffly, and his moustache, as Henry had noticed, once again bobbed up and down. 'I will catch up on my sleep when we get back.'

The two women with him exchanged quick smiles, before turning to Henry. 'He means when we return home finally, to America, don't you, dear?' Olivia straightened the brooch on her dress. A starfish shaped thing, it flashed as it caught the gas lamps. Twain ran a hand over his lapel and shrugged. 'All those articles I have to write, like a machine, and everyone is so eager to read them, apparently.' His words faded on a mock frustrated note, and Henry looked for a way to change the subject. He knew the Clemenses had decided to go on a world tour after Mark Twain had lost a lot of money with his poor investment decisions. Now he was committed to writing about his travels, and Henry was sure these would be popular. Not for nothing was Mark Twain considered the most entertaining and humorous writer of his time.

'I am sure, I am sure,' Henry said, gesturing to indicate the carriage now turning around, away from the driveway. 'You will soon be just as famous here as in America. And there will lots to write about.'

Another carriage came up to the portico just then, and a man with a bejewelled turban and a loud, quavering voice standing at the very top of the carpeted stone steps announced: 'The Honourable Shahji Pallonji and his son.'

There came the rush of running feet. A big red umbrella with tapering red ribbons threaded its way past the hedges and the gazebo in the garden, and made a bobbing, dipping way toward them. Henry made out the several pairs of legs under it, making the moving, shaking umbrella look like a strange creature that had emerged from the lush greenery; a pair with tight shalwars first materialized, followed by a long silver-beaded skirt, and last of all, the series of unclad feet, racing to keep the umbrella aloft over their heads.

'Mr Twain. Er...Mr Clemens,' the umbrella lifted, and Mr Cowasjee Bengalee, one of the city's richest merchants came into view, and his wife, plump and panting for her breath, smiled, her face appearing behind his shoulder. 'Good afternoon, how do you do?' And Cowasjee Bengalee bowed. Mark Twain who had extended his hand first withdrew it hastily, bowed awkwardly, before folding his hands in a namaste. The ladies smiled, and Clara curtsied, a flush appearing on her face like it always did when she was self-conscious. Mrs Bengalee, her face creased in dimples, laughed nervously, and curtsied in turn. Henry wished he had explained to the Clemenses more about such niceties, that sometimes things like curtsies were exaggerated and unnecessary. The British were snobs who looked down on Americans and respected them only grudgingly. When the British were out of the way, Henry knew, Americans and the Indians, especially these enterprising people, the Parsees, always got along famously.

'This is the Mrs Bengalee,' their host said, stressing every word, even the out-of-place article. He was still bent halfway as he turned to his wife, who had to step back hurriedly, and the bearers holding the umbrella stepped back too. 'Benaifer to you, please,' she said, in a soft voice. 'It means the cool spring breeze from our ancient land.'

'Persia,' Henry explained helpfully. Mark Twain's eyebrows rose again, and Henry knew he must keep his explaining to a minimum. Or that he should remember to do it at the right moments. He looked around, and to his consternation, realized that things had come to a standstill. The music hadn't picked up, though a few carriages were still coming in slowly up the driveway, but almost everyone was looking at them.

Everyone, but Maya Barton, for she was nowhere to be seen. Henry was somewhat distracted as he tried to remember something that Maya had said, or not said, while Cowasjee Bengalee laughed, more heartily than before, a hand rising to fix his pince-nez glasses, and it was his wife who came to the rescue. 'I am sure everyone would like a drink. It's somewhat humid, and there's nothing more cooling than fresh coconut water.'

Henry looked at her gratefully, as she took Olivia and Clara under her wing, and moved away with them toward a marquee where a lot of women were already milling around. Then there were just the three of them standing there, looking forlorn. Henry started when he realized that Cowasjee Bengalee had been trying for the last several seconds to get his attention. The bearers holding the umbrella moved this way and that, unsure of what to do and Bengalee waved them away, laughing in his high-pitched way. 'You can go, it's not sunny nor does it look like rain. Go now.' Then he turned back to the two of them, 'Come, meet everyone. They are most excited to hear you speak.'

Mark Twain still had his eyes on the two retreating bearers, who walked in step and held the red gilded umbrella aloft, a bit away from themselves, as if afraid to even stand under its shadow. Bengalee trotted off briskly ahead. He nodded to those he passed, and looked back once, as if the new guest from America he was so anxious to display would vanish otherwise. Henry followed, smiling reassuringly at Twain, and then casually glanced toward the other marquee. As did happen in all parties and soirees, the ladies sat separate from the men, and only the bearers moved freely among the guests. Even if Maya was around, there was no way he would know. He wondered if a bearer would carry a message for him into the 'women's only' marquee, but that would involve too much explaining on his part. He sighed involuntarily, and the sad violin music caught his attention just then.

The musician had the saddest expression on his face, his eyes were closed, as he drew his bow across the strings time and again, lost in his music. Something about his face, the dark hair swept back across his forehead, his fine beard, and the pale skin reminded Henry of something. Something that someone—Inspector Button—had told him before: The Russian prince who had assassins on his trail. 'He isn't Russian at all,' said a voice behind him, and he turned to see Superintendent R.H. Vincent of the Bombay Police. 'Not Russian, but Serbian,' said the officer, nodding as he caught Henry's eye, 'and that only adds to our problems.'

'As if you don't have enough on your hands already,' said Henry smiling. Vincent always looked stressed, and these days more so. Some parts of the town had reported an outbreak of a mysterious illness, and since cholera always posed a constant threat, it was often the police who had to ensure that houses were adequately sanitized, that the very sick patients were moved to hospitals before it was too late. And in the more traditional houses, there had been much opposition to this. The locals did not like the police barging into the women's quarters, and popular leaders like Tilak had written angry editorials at this 'invasion'.

'So have you arrested that gentleman, the one who didn't want you barging into their houses?' Henry asked, politely curious.

'Tilak, you mean? They call him, "Lokmanya". Leader of his people,' Vincent rolled his eyes briefly before he became all officious once again. 'Well, he's in Poona, and yes, he's quite some trouble for us. There's little we can do, for he has a big following, and is very revered and popular. Any arrest and we will find the protests hard to manage. Then we have the young woman's murder on our hands too. The one you must have read about. And now there's this man,' Vincent jerked his square chin back towards the sad-faced violinist, 'we are not sure why he's here. Orders from superiors, all the way from London. He isn't Russian, but he could be a spy.'

'I see, he looks too...,' Henry looked for the word. Just then a bearer came up with a tray and he gladly accepted a goblet. Twain took one too and sipped slowly as he watched the crowd with open curiosity. It was wine, as a discreet sniff confirmed. Bengalee stocked the finest wine and Henry was relieved to note that the tray did not contain any glasses of the special cocktail named after another of Bengalee's fellow Parsees: *Jamshetji Jeejheebhoy*. A drink made of arrack—a spirit distilled from the coconut flower—and sweetened with coconut water, orange bitters and sugar syrup. It was something that took time getting used to, but perhaps, Bengalee, had chosen to play it safe, and not offered the *Jeejheebhoy* special. The gathering, as Henry confirmed once more on looking around, was so diverse. He saw the high rolled-up Parsi turbans, the top hats, those with homburgs, fez hats, and several wearing the traditional *phetas* too, the elegantly wrapped cotton turbans with the tasselled border.

'Do you mean artistic?' said Vincent, interrupting his thoughts. 'You mustn't let that fool you,' he went on to pontificate. 'And while we are here, I should warn you about the jewel thieves as well.'

He was talking as his eyes roved around the crowd, and that gave Henry an excuse to look around himself. There was no sign of Maya. She wasn't among the women, and not even among the men for he wouldn't put it past her to break every protocol. She had done so quite often, and gotten away lightly too, with only a hint of scandal. Such as the time she had interrupted an all-men's gathering at Town Hall, ostensibly to speak for the court ruling on the 'age of consent' bill. A legal act that raised the marriageable age for a Hindu woman, from ten years to twelve, had, however, upset several of the conservatives. As one venerable speaker after another argued against the interference of foreigners, especially the British, in what tradition dictated and age-old customs sanctioned, Maya, had flung pamphlets advocating reform, especially on women's matters, from the overhead galleries. The papers had fluttered, waving and drifting in the breeze that came in from the windows, and thrown everything into confusion. The meeting had been disrupted as some in the audience dashed around for those errant pamphlets, letting Maya make a quick exit. Later, none of the men could accurately describe to the police who the intruder had been.

Maya enjoyed recounting her adventures to Harry, and he loved listening to them, every time she got in the mood. There was the time she had accompanied the Bombay Sappers regiment to Waziristan, a region near the border with Afghanistan. She had sneaked into the Afghan capital, Kabul, to meet with a British woman doctor, Lilias Hamilton, then working there. Hamilton's book, *A Vizier's Daughter: A Tale of the Hazara War*, was published soon after, and Maya's visit had come to light as well. That had set off a full-fledged diplomatic crisis—she was accused of acting in British interests, and of even being a spy—and things calmed down only because the Amir was then engaged in a conflict with another tribe.

'I don't see your lady,' said Vincent suddenly, and Henry flushed inadvertently.

'She isn't...'

Vincent was laughing as he moved away, as if he had made Henry admit to something. Henry flushed, a retort always came slow to him, and Vincent nodded genially as the garrulous Professor Wilson came across his path. Henry had missed his chance to ask about the murder in the guest house that had got Maya so agitated, and if the jewel thieves were suspects in the case, but Vincent was now threading his way toward the group of Parsi engineers who had just returned from London. Professor Wilson lumbered up close, like a heavy lolling ship and Henry took his hat off in greeting, then fanned himself pretending it was the heat. Hoping the professor wouldn't engage him in a chat, he put on an abstract expression, thinking of the electric fans he was soon going to demonstrate before the Chamber of Commerce, and he was glad to have something to think about. Maya, he was certain, hadn't turned up, maybe she was at the munshi's place at this very moment trying to learn Sanskrit. A subject, she insisted was beyond her, but Henry didn't believe her.

He circulated among the guests saying hello to those he recognized, and soon he realized how the light had dimmed around him. It became dark quite abruptly in this part of the world, a lingering late evening light giving way to sudden grey darkness. But around him, the gentle hum of conversation continued, then the occasional bark of laughter, the swish of jackets and long coats, the sound of men bowing to each other as they circulated among themselves.

He saw Mark Twain was the centre of attention in one circle and felt reassured. The writer didn't look tired, and appeared to revel in the company he was in. Was he talking about the sage he had mentioned earlier, or was he soaking in information from everyone around him, especially about the murder? He hoped Twain wouldn't put off anyone with his writerly curiosity.

Americans were a frank, curious lot and free in their ways, unlike the prim and proper British. And this city and its people were accepting too in their ways and of foreigners in particular. They just took their time about things, as Henry was learning too well.

Mark Twain would get plenty to write about, not just in Bombay but in his travels around the country too. Henry hoped he would have the time to put some of it down in his diary first. From the ladies' section, he heard peals of laughter, the clink of jewellery, and still no sign of Maya among them. As the twilight darkened farther, and the rustling of the birds sounded in the plane and mango trees about him, the bearers came forward, holding flames of light aloft. They lit the gas lamps along the driveway and in the lawns. Soon, the guests would move in, nudged indoors by the onrush of the moths, and the buzzing night insects that were never quite dispelled by the coir flames and incense sticks placed strategically. He could hear the call of the owls, the rustling in the branches, and the roll and the hiss of the waves not too far away.

At this juncture, the violinist surprisingly chose to play a more joyful tune, Johann Strauss's 'Blue Danube', and it had a calming, soothing effect. Everyone was smiling as they applauded him, and exchanged pleased, friendly nods with one another.

'Did you hear about the special *nautch* performance sahib has arranged?' Henry heard one of the guests, Sorabji Dorabji ask, 'all in honour of our new foreign friends.'

'Something that won't shock the ladies, I assure you,' added Judge Wilkinson, 'At least that's what I believe.'

'That would never be the case, Judge,' Henry said, bringing a jovial note into his voice, 'with you around.' He couldn't help feeling a bit deflated at not having spotted Maya yet. She would have livened things up, certainly for him, he thought wistfully. She had an engaging way of describing things that Henry always found beguiling. Many a time she made him laugh; she had a knack for picking out a person's foibles, but she was never really unkind. He saw Twain again, this time he was in earnest conversation with Professor Wilson. The latter was always trying to get people interested in the obscure manuscripts he dug up or those that people sold to him. One of these days, Henry remembered Maya telling him, that professor is going to get royally fooled. 'Someone will pass him a forgery and he will never know.' Henry stamped his foot, as he felt something soft run over his shoe. Not a snake surely, but a frog of some sort, and he noticed the crowd of people at the doors, eager to move inside.

Then a bearer stepped neatly into his path and handed him a note. He recognized Maya's writing right away. *There are really no thieves here.* He stared at the note, mystified, and irritated. Maya was being ambiguous, but the note meant she was around somewhere.

'Who gave you this?' But he spoke to emptiness for the man had slipped away, holding his tray aloft, bowing toward a fairly well-endowed woman whose veil was entangled in the bushes. Everyone else was heading for the white mansion, its big double doors held open and in place by two servants, the path to it lit by lanterns hanging from every tree. Cowasjee Bengalee had clearly spared no effort.

IV

Women in Disguise, Men on Stilts

The ballroom in Bengalee's mansion was rumoured to be even bigger than the Governor's house. Bengalee had many things to prove with this lavish party he had thrown. For one, it was no secret Bengalee was upset when the Prince of Wales did not grace his mansion during his recent visit to Bombay, and at the grand banquet hosted later by the Governor, the Viscount Sandhurst, Bengalee had been seated with minor native officials, and granted an audience of just five minutes with the Prince.

But the Prince's visit had been a hush hush one. The Presidency government, and Bombay was its chief city, was somewhat nervous that his visit wouldn't go down well with some sections of the populace, especially those in the native quarters. The natives had also been urged by the very popular leader, Bal Gangadhar Tilak to protest a recent Bombay court decision that allowed a young Indian woman, Rakhmabai, to divorce her husband. The Rakhmabai case was now all over the papers, and quite a hot topic of discussion. Women, the pundits said, would now begin to think too much of themselves. A woman couldn't just leave a husband she had been married to by sacred rites. The most fortunate woman, as the rites had it, was the one who remained wedded to the same husband over seven lives. Women needed to be kept in their place. All this had made Maya quite furious.

Henry clearly remembered the time he had met Rakhmabai when Maya had got her over to the doctors' bungalow in Colaba. There had been much animated discussion about finding assistance for Rakhmabai to travel to Philadelphia to study medicine, but Henry hadn't heard a thing more yet. It was possible communication was being held up, as happened every time there was a chill in relations between the two countries: Britain and America. And it was largely over Venezuela. Who would have thought a country in south America could become a spanner in the works? It troubled him. All the deals he had had in mind, with the electric fans, the new electric bicycle, and the innovations in the telegraph—for one could send pictures via the wire too—were held up on some pretext or another. The last couple of weeks he had just been soliciting one meeting after another, with businessmen and people in the government, and now he wondered if his efforts would ever lead anywhere. It would be humiliating to receive a gentle reminder from his superiors who expected a good deal all the time, but little understood the intricacies of a faraway place.

As everyone filed into the hall, the dholaks sounded, someone stepped up to the podium and read a poem composed by a fifteen-year-old girl who had evidently impressed the ruler of Hyderabad so much that he had sent her to England on a scholarship. It was quite an impromptu performance and was received by some polite clapping. Some heckling followed from the back that made the reader smile effusively in turn. He took his hat off, bowed exaggeratedly and withdrew. After a pause, the dholaks sounded again. Henry stole a glance at the roster of events placed in the main doorway, and saw what had got everyone sighing in expectation and envy. The rumours were right. There was indeed a nautch performance scheduled—a local dance performed by women complete with erotic moves that had made the form discreetly popular—followed by a play, an adaption of the story of the honest king who lost his kingdom because he never told a lie.

Everyone moved to take the seats arranged in rows on three sides of the huge ballroom. It was as big as the one in Town Hall, with chandeliers arranged in six rows, and thick maroon curtains lining the curved high French windows. Twain was writing something again in his diary, and Henry's lips turned in wry amusement, only to find himself puzzled a moment later. The diary had a red cover, and he frowned, thinking he ought to remember something, but just then everyone around him got to their feet, clapping vigorously as two young men, their small cymbals beating in rhythm, made their way to the front of the ballroom, an empty expanse left aside especially for their performance. On one side, hidden by an alcove, the musicians were clearly visible. The men on dholaks, one on the shehnai, and then someone playing a stringed instrument. Henry wondered where the sorrowful looking violinist had gone.

From two doors at the further end of the hall, the nautch girls swayed in, graceful and sinuous. The man playing the stringed instrument broke into a loud, tuneless song. The dancers, there were four of them, wore bright skirts with mirrors that caught the light from everywhere, the lamps, and the jewellery the women wore. The silver in their long dark braids glittered and flashed, and as they advanced, singing, clapping their hands, and dancing in perfect rhythm to the music, the lights slowly and gently dimmed. No one noticed though, for everyone looked on mesmerized. The dancing girls, Henry recollected reading, were part of a theatre troupe that had travelled from the Punjab. They had performed in the princely courts of Rajputana, in Gujerat, and were now in Bombay, where Cowasjee Bengalee had once again scored a coup by paying a princely sum for their performance.

The dancers clapped their hands, swayed, and whirled around, hands on their hips. Their skirts swirled, the pleats rising and falling in waves, revealing the tight salwars they wore beneath, and the thick anklets. Then they extended their arms, clasped each other's hands, and swirled around so quickly that it made Henry's head spin. The ladies in the audience raised their hands to their cheeks and gasped, in admiration and alarm. Some of the men standing all this while took the nearest empty seats, looking entranced as the women danced, coming closer together and drifting away, in repeated motions, till they moved away one final time, whirling and twisting their bodies in ways sinuous and graceful, and it was then that the male dancer in their midst was suddenly visible. His moves were quick, swift, but not as fluid as the women around him. Three of them neared the guests, clapping, leaning closer, extending their hands, hoping for tips. Some of the seated women rose and danced a few steps with them. Clara did as well, her face flushed as she linked her fingers with one of the women dancers. Her arms swung in rhythm, she followed the dancer's every movement, and laughed self-consciously when it all ended, to some loud applause. The dancers exited. The curtains at one end closed, and everyone again sat back with a hush of expectation.

The music began again, with the hesitant tapping of the dholaks, and from the other end of the ballroom, came the low gentle strains of the violin. The curtains parted, and the mythical king worshipped for his honesty, Harishchandra, appeared. He stood straight and tall, holding up a bow and arrow, seated in the hollow of a papier-mâché horse. It was, as the story went, when the king was out hunting that he disturbed a sage at his prayers. The latter, enraged, punished the king who would then lose everything he had, including his only son. The king regained them only after he had been through several tribulations, after which Shiva, the hard to please god of destruction, pleased with his perseverance, revealed himself before Harishchandra, and restored everything the king had lost. Even his recently dead son came back to life.

The actors moved in circles, swaying, and mouthing their lines, and the music rose and fell with the drama in the play. The women had their handkerchiefs out when the king picked up his dead son in his arms. The men looked agitated for the fuming sage threw his weight around a bit too much. He raised his trident often as he strode around the makeshift stage in his anger, and when at last, Shiva appeared, some of the men in the audience, who were still standing, retreated a few paces warily, while some of the veiled Hindu ladies, folded their hands reverentially. The god was dressed for the part. His face and arms were painted blue, his hair was knotted up high. He wore a deer skin robe, and a fiercely glaring, red-rimmed eye was etched on his forehead. Behind Shiva were his two trusted attendants. One with a bull's horns affixed to his head, and the other was a man so skeletal that he shivered as he walked. A stick painted to look like another leg dangled from his hip making everyone laugh.

Henry wasn't sure when he caught on, but he was certain the moment after the actors had taken their bows, folded their hands in acknowledgement of the applause. Then they moved around the audience, their heads lowered, their hands held out, for baksheesh. He saw one of the actors, someone who had played the king's devoted minion, approach him. He had a quick glimpse of blue eyes that were discreetly lowered as the actor bowed before him. Henry noticed his missing yellow tie turned into a cummerbund holding up a yellow dhoti. The hand that held out the tray was slender, distinctly feminine. Maya looked up once quickly, and then perceptibly shook her head, almost in warning. Henry reached out a hand toward her involuntarily, the tray in her hand jangled, some coins spilled over, and in the silence that followed, everyone turned to look.

Maya and he shared the briefest of glances before she bent to collect the coins. He bent too, and the people around them scattered. Around them he saw a dozen pair of feet, and knew if he looked up, he would find her blue eyes again. Yet at that moment, he found it difficult to talk to her. He was still bemused and startled, and saying anything to her would be indiscreet. He didn't want to give her away, not before a full audience, but he wished he had been in on her secret plans. The small circle in Bombay loved gossip, and rumours grew in moments, from a drop to a wave. A part of him wished it would happen so, but he was never really sure of Maya, and then, he wasn't sure of himself too. He had left home in Chicago in search of adventure, and he was still restless, still a bit hollowed out. And Maya was always two steps ahead. She had plans to travel even further than he did, to places he hadn't dreamed of going—she planned to return to Afghanistan for instance—and so far, he just hadn't been able to keep up.

The actors came on stage for a final bow, and Henry had a feeling it was already quite late in the evening. His hands strayed towards his pocket, he felt for his watch, and panicked—the thin chain of gold that was always otherwise reassuringly there, was missing. His watch was gone, as was the chain always fixed to its luminous dial. Nearby, he saw someone else fumbling in a similar way. Some of the women clutched their throats, and screams of surprise broke out seconds later. 'My necklace, it's gone.' And a man leapt to his feet yelling for his glasses, and another for his stick. 'It was just here, by my side.'

'Check your wallets,' someone said. And a lady shrieked, 'My purse is with me, but my silk scarf is gone.'

Their host appeared on stage. Cowasjee Bengalee raised his hands, pleading for calm. He folded his hands, bowed, and Henry felt sorry for him. His mind raced ahead, thinking of Maya, the way they had knelt close on the floor, picking up the scattered coins. Was Maya responsible for his watch suddenly gone missing? He heard Bengalee's voice rise pleadingly above the gasps and hisses of shock everywhere. 'Please, please, stay calm. Ladies and gentlemen, I implore you. The police are here. I am sure your things will be found.' His eyes scanned the audience anxiously for Superintendent Vincent.

'How can it be that our things are gone, with the police around?' Someone's plaintive voice rose in the crowd. Mark Twain looked around puzzled, and then he placed his hands in his pocket, and looked around with helpless alarm. Henry knew then he had lost his diary.

'There's that gang, remember,' Henry heard one of the women speak up. 'Maybe...,' she glanced around, her eyes caught Henry's and she flushed, realizing she had said something indiscreet. Among the guests, there was really no one who was a stranger, and that left only the actors, and the dancers. He felt a nudge at his elbow, and there was the bearer again, with a message, 'For you, sahib.'

Henry took a quick look, and then it was his turn to stride on to the stage. Cowasjee Bengalee twitched in some nervousness, and Henry, gesturing to the note he held, whispered something in the other man's ears. A look of gratification appeared on Cowasjee Bengalee's face. He called for silence, and Henry stepped forward.

'I am here to read out a note. I have a message. About the matter of your missing things. Well,' he cleared his throat, looked most annoyed, but still forced himself to read it through. 'The missing items, you will find them on a tray on the table outside the door. The writer of this note goes onto say that pranks may be played, jewellery items can go missing and just as quickly be returned.'

'Someone is evidently trying to teach us a lesson,' said Jamshetji laughing. 'Or maybe delivering a moral lesson for the police.' The police superintendent Vincent stood, running a hand over his moustache, gritting his teeth, and nodding as he caught Henry's eye. 'All in order, please,' he said, raising his hand. 'All in order as you go towards the door.'

Henry heard the screams of delight, the delighted guffaws, as everyone retrieved their goods. Mark Twain stood in one corner looking lost, and Henry saw Maya, now looking her normal self, walk toward the writer. She had the diary in her hand—the red, gold-embossed one Henry had seen earlier in the carriage—and smiling her slow, gentle smile, she gave it to him and introduced herself. Henry shook his head, as Maya's eyes caught his. When had she had the time to learn the masterful tricks that best suited a conjuror, Henry thought, and the answer struck him with an irrational flash of jealousy. She must have taken lessons from Freddie Bancroft, the magician, whom everyone steered clear of, and who had, in his few months in Bombay, gathered quite an unsavoury reputation.

~

Henry was sullen as they left in the carriage together. The evening had finally ended in much laughter, and bonhomie, and the actor, for Maya had not revealed her identity, had been greatly appreciated, and won much applause. Henry refused to look her way, as she answered Twain's questions patiently. Olivia looked tired, and Clara tried desperately to follow the conversation, looking confused as she looked between Henry and Maya, realizing something was not quite right.

After they had dropped off the Clemenses at the

hotel—and neither Twain, nor his wife and daughter were in the least put out by the fact that Manuel, the servant, still hadn't returned from his evening out—Henry saw Maya home. It was already too dark for Maya to try any more adventures on her own. He told her that, and she burst out, angrily . 'You are obviously upset I tried out that stunt?'

'I don't know what you are talking about?' he said coldly, tapping on the walls in a signal to the coachman to drive a bit faster. 'Yes, you do,' she said fiercely, then she leaned forward, and turned his face towards her. He gave a startled gasp of surprise, her fingers felt cold, and firm against his scratchy, rough beard. 'Look at me when I talk to you, Henry. What is it that has upset you? That I do as I wish always?'

'Yes, always. Always. But that is your wish...,' He looked at her, shook his head, before the words burst out of him. 'You embarrassed your host, by doing that. Do you think with all that he tried...,' he stopped for she was already smiling at him, and her face in the feeble light of the lamp inside, looked paler than ever. 'I asked him, in fact I talked him into it. He was unhappy that the police were milling around, for there were reports a gang of jewel thieves was on the loose, mingling with the servants, and planning to rob the guests. And he had gone to a lot of trouble to arrange the play and dance. We just added this bit, as part of the act. It had to be hush-hush, for you know Vincent.' She looked out the window, turned back toward Henry, 'He's such a policeman always, and can be such a spoilsport. He would be against the dancing, the play, everything that is fun...'

'And you took lessons from Freddie?'

'He's not what you think...'

'He is,' Henry broke in furiously, 'one of these days, he is going to get into trouble. His hobnobbing with all the shady, devious types, just so he can pick up a magic trick or two.'

'Really, Henry,' Maya began, but just then they heard Abdul knocking on the carriage door, and realized that it had come to a halt. They had reached Colaba, and even at this late hour, the smell of drying fish assailed them. 'You should not believe the rumours about him. He is quite talented and wants to learn more.'

They had stopped on the short driveway, and the bleary-eyed Pathan watchman peered at the carriage window, his lantern held high, his stick tapping the pebbled path. 'Good evening, miss. I thought it might be you. Charlotte memsahib still isn't back.'

'Thank you, Ahmed,' she said, jumping lightly down from the carriage, and stepping onto the tiled portico. 'And never mind about Charlotte memsahib. She must be with McClelland sahib.'

She glanced back quickly and caught Henry's expression of disapproval. It was no secret that the British engineer, William McClelland, who had business interests in Jamnagar and other places in Rajputana, had been wooing Charlotte Ellaby for a while, especially the times he happened to be in Bombay. There was already a lot of speculation about them, and from Maya's smile, directed toward Henry in some reproach, it appeared things were finally working out between them. 'You should be happy, Henry. You've known Charlotte a while.'

'I am,' he said, very clipped.

'You don't look so.' They stood on the portico, as the coachman turned the horse around for the return journey. Abdul patted the mare in affection, before he jumped up next to the driver.

'I am just tired,' Henry said, suddenly longing to go. It had been a long day, and Maya's unpredictability sometimes added to it. 'I think McClelland may be leaving soon for England. A little bird told me. But I'd be really happy if there's one story with a happy ending at least.' The words slipped out of him, and he stared at her, wondering why he had said those words. 'Good night, Henry,' she said, and she reached up, and ran a gentle finger along his cheek, as Ahmed, the watchman, waited by the open door to the bungalow.

As he rode home, he realized what it was that had so upset him about Maya. A thing that had troubled him so much that he couldn't even bring himself to talk about it. That she had dressed like a man, had behaved unashamedly like one, almost, and he couldn't even bring himself to think this way: it was as if she were really more comfortable being a man. Or maybe, with all her love for magic and the Eastern arts, she had taken a fancy to Freddie Bancroft. Henry opened the window a notch, for a breath of fresh air, and it was as if the night had conjured up the very man he was thinking about.

There was Bancroft walking alongside his carriage, looking down at him, and then passing him with a careless wave of his hand. Henry gaped, not just at Bancroft's sudden appearance, but the fact that Bancroft was on stilts, several feet above ground, and he appeared to be walking effortlessly on them. Bancroft was a tall man, six feet and a bit more—a fact that always annoyed Henry no end—and with the stilts, his height seemed to have doubled. A mist formed outside, and Henry closed his eyes briefly, but when he looked out again, leaning out of his window this time, he heard the squeaky soft noise as Bancroft walked on the cobblestoned road, and Henry knew it wasn't an illusion, even a magical one, and he wasn't under the influence. He shook his head, in irritation at his own disbelief. Bancroft teetered, a stick like figure in the wind, but managed to regain balance in seconds. He looked back, aware that Henry was watching him. Henry closed the window, more sharply than he intended, thumped on the carriage walls, indicating that he wished them to drive faster. He couldn't wait to go home, to the Byculla Club, to his rooms there. He had seen one too many strange things. The last thing he wanted to remember as he yawned, giving in to his tiredness, was the sight of Bancroft reaching out an arm, to playfully run it through the palm tree fronds nearest him. It annoyed him, for he'd rather think of Maya. Her hair trailing on her forehead the way it had only a day ago, and this time, he'd push it away. Then he would reach down and kiss her full on the lips.

'Abdul, tomorrow begins early,' he told his man asking him not to wait up for him, as they reached his rooms. 'So, you must get some sleep. Any news of the case, about the murdered girl?' he asked casually.

'No, sahib. It seems the room in that lodge where she stayed is haunted now. There will be a puja there. The husband, they say, has been weeping all the time, refusing to return to work, and his wife has had to be with him always.'

'His wife?' Henry looked startled, 'isn't she…?'

'No, no, sahib, the first wife. She felt sorry for him, and later took him away to the chawl. He was crying piteously, thumping his chest and sobbing.'

Henry tried to remember what he had read just some days ago, but there were just too many confusing things happening in this city. Tomorrow, he would have to see the Clemenses, first thing in the morning. And then he would try and work out some appointments for his own work. The electric fan, he knew he could get some of the businessmen, especially the cotton mill owners, interested in it. A future investment for when the city ran properly and efficiently on electricity. Tomorrow, he thought last of all before flopping back against his pillow, he would get his tie back from Maya. He did want it back, he had bought it at one of New York's best stores.

How on earth had she gotten her hands on his tie? The thought jolted him out of his drowsy state. Had she worked her magic on him, in the same manner as with everyone else, earlier the evening? Henry just couldn't remember. She had been such a clever thief.

V

Small Disappearances that Tell the Real Story

Early that second morning of the Clemenses' stay in Bombay, there was nothing to indicate that in a few hours, Mark Twain would disappear. To the police, he would be reported as missing, right from his hotel room, where, before daybreak, according to a couple of very reliable witnesses, he had been seen asleep on his bed.

Henry had waited more than an hour before he reluctantly came to the dreaded conclusion that Mark Twain was indeed missing. He was not in the hotel, and no one knew where he had gone, or when he had left the hotel. Henry knew he should not have overslept, nor arrived late at the hotel. He knew too that he could have called the hotel earlier, just to check in on Twain. With a sinking feeling, Henry knew he would be blamed for the time he had wasted unnecessarily, just lounging in a chair on the hotel balcony, just waiting for the writer to wake up and emerge through the door of his hotel room.

At first, Henry had idly looked at the vendors passing by. The coconut seller who carried the green, pulpy fruits all over him, making him look like a mountain on the move; a couple of fishmongers who drove by in their small donkey carts; the birdman, with the birds raising a cacophony in their cages, hanging on poles slung across the man's shoulders; and then the workers crowded onto carts, headed towards the cotton mills of Girgaum, the heart of the city.

Henry still felt dazed by the events of the previous days. The story of the murder in the guesthouse, the suspected jewel thieves, and then, Maya's prank that had so left them all dumbfounded. That morning, even though several hours had elapsed, this thought made Henry smart more. He still couldn't bring himself to smile remembering Maya's act of the previous night, and how indignant it had made him. This was a place half a world away from the one he had known; the familiar things he had wanted to get away from. Here things were different, even upended in every way. What left a lingering irritation in him was also the fact that Freddie Bancroft, having won over Maya, could just as easily work his way into Twain's attention. And that was just what Bancroft had always wanted: attention from the right people, in the right places.

Bancroft and he had come to the city within weeks of each other. Bancroft claimed he had travelled across the seas, from Japan, the Dutch East Indies, Ceylon, and then, Bombay. And he, Henry Baker, had taken the train from Paris to Constantinople, sailed across the

Mediterranean, and then the crowded, tiresome journey by steamship down the Suez, across the last sea, the Arabian, the dry wind stabbing his face, leaving him with a piercing thirst, and an itchiness.

They hadn't endeared themselves to each other from the very beginning. Bancroft had wanted him, as a fellow countryman and trade consul, to intercede with the customs men to get his stuff in—Persian carpets, camel skin robes, ivory sceptres from Africa, and various other stuff for his magic shows—without paying any customs duties whatsoever. Henry had put his foot down. It just wouldn't do to get on the wrong side of the British. They made the laws here, and it was important to respect those. He didn't want to start a small conflict in one corner of the world, when bigger conflicts were raging elsewhere, in the Caribbean, in South America, and these could always get out of hand.

Bancroft had thrown a tantrum, raged out of the club where they had met. And Maya coming up just a few minutes later had offered him, Henry, a handkerchief. He had hated his own perspiring self then. It was sometimes hot in the club, when there were too many people in the billiards room, and in the smoking room. Henry knew the electric fans would be immensely helpful in this matter. But he forgot all about the fans, his plans for them, when he remembered the way Bancroft had flushed, had pulled a rose seemingly out of Maya's hair, and presented it to her with a charming bow, before leaving. He had won her heart with that sleight of hand, and no matter what he, Henry, subsequently did—the trips to Elephanta and Mahakali, and to the forests beyond Raigad, the raid on an opium train—nothing really measured up in Maya's eyes.

Maya and he would always have their arguments and differences. And yet they had so many things in common. That they were both outsiders in a way. He, a commoner from America, with no connections, except for a Yale degree that helped open some doors for him, and she with the rumours of her past and origin that followed her wherever she went. It only added layers of mystery to her. Being outsiders, Henry knew, gave them a fluidity, an ease to mingle with everyone, especially in high circles, and not really belong. He was from a land of moneyed men, as the belief went here, even if he had little of it himself, and she had those unusual looks that stood out, most times, except when she was in disguise. Of late though, Henry sighed, she seemed to be doing too much of that.

It was that book of course, the one by the Swedish visitor to India, more than a hundred and forty years ago, Carsten Niebuhr, that had so impressed her. Of all the five members of that ill-fated expedition, Niebuhr was the only one who survived. He adapted to the local customs, and dressed like the natives wherever he was, and that got him through an otherwise arduous expedition, but Maya, Henry worried, sometimes took things too far, and much too literally.

~

As morning advanced and sounds and activities around him in the hotel rose by notches, Henry rose from his lounge chair and strolled along the balcony. There were men watering the saplings below. At one corner, some boys had begun an impromptu game of cricket, and a man sat with a stringed instrument under a peepul tree. The tune he was playing seemed hauntingly familiar to Henry. He tapped his fingers on the railing, trying to place the tune, his memory hovering around it in circles, and he knew he had to hum it to finally place it.

Only later did Henry realize that all this had made him miss a lot else. He had been there for some time and Mark Twain still hadn't appeared. Then, at the far end of the balcony, he saw the two ladies, Olivia and Clara, come up the stairs, having done with their breakfast on the first floor. Moments later they blurred in view for suddenly there seemed to be more movement around. Servants and other attendants rushed around, looking busy and harried. Some carried carefully pressed clothes in their hangers, one rushed by with a carafe of water, spilling some of it on the way, and one servant, perhaps one of the hotel staff, was polishing the banisters with a sad dull look on his face. Meanwhile the snoring sounds from another room, muted earlier, had distinctly picked up.

'Mr Baker...' Clara touched him on the elbow, and then stepped back, a look of alarm on her face. She must have seen his dazed, drowsy look. Later, he would believe it had been a hypnosis of sorts. It had to be. It was precisely at that moment that he knew the tune playing in his head, Edward Elgar's *Salut d'amour*, and that it wasn't what the man, seated under a tree, a floor below, had been playing at all. He had listened to Elgar in a London music hall, some years ago, and the tune had stayed in his head, and he had remembered it all this time later. Perhaps the musician with the stringed instrument had been playing something similar, and that was what had brought back the memory. He felt his head with his hand, and turned to Clara with an embarrassed laugh.

'The sun is right on your face, Mr Baker. Do come away.'

Something had made Henry turn back to look at the musician again, who this time was looking up directly, right to where they stood, and Henry recognized him from the theatre troupe the night before. Henry's attention returned to Clara and Olivia who looked now, it seemed to him, somewhat flustered. There was a frown on Olivia's face, and it wasn't in worry for him. Just then, a door, a couple of rooms away, opened and a tall, hefty, red-faced man emerged, looking very annoyed.

'There is just too much noise, too much noise,' he said. His voice boomed, loud like a foghorn. He rubbed his ears, and eyes, and the women turned away quickly, averting their eyes for his robe had fallen open to reveal a thick hairy chest. He stopped short on seeing them, and he lowered his voice, but only by a notch.

'There is too much noise. I am not able to sleep,' he said. He sounded petulant, an overgrown child, and his accent was thick and guttural. 'Too much noise, ladies.' Olivia and Clara, with her their eyes rounded in alarm, looked at Henry, unsure if he was blaming them for it. There was a scurry of feet from the other end of the balcony, and one of the servants, his dhoti well over his knees, his turban askew over an eye, came running up. 'Sahib, already late.'

The loud-voiced man cuffed him on the ear, looked around once more, nodded at everyone and went back in, shutting the door behind him. The servant rubbed his ear, and looked at them, smiling foolishly.

'And where is Mr Twain?' asked Henry, after this little episode.

'Isn't he in his room?' Clara asked, glancing toward the door to their right. 'In his room?' Henry looked puzzled. 'No, there was no one inside when I looked in, just when I got here, and so I waited. One of the servants said you two were down at breakfast, and I...'

'You should have joined us,' said Olivia. She looked preoccupied, the frown on her face more pronounced. She glanced toward the door through which Henry himself had looked in. It seemed to him that he had spent far too long in the lounge chair, and the worry writ large on the women's faces now spread to him. He remembered seeing a neatly made bed, but no sign of Mark Twain. He had assumed he was down at breakfast too.

'No one...,' said Clara under her breath, and she ran some paces ahead, away from where they stood. She stopped abruptly, ran ahead toward the room where the sleep-disturbed guest had just emerged from, then retraced her steps to the door on the right. Looking back toward the landing, Henry caught a glimpse of the servants, a couple of them, long mops in hand, who looked on curious and nervous before they went back to their work. Clara turned the smooth brass handle, looked in through the door, and stepped back the very next moment, the alarm on her face now even more pronounced.

'Mama, he's not there!'

Olivia rushed forward, and Henry's arm caught the small of her back just as she was about to fall.

'But he must be there! Clara, you really mustn't...,' said Olivia, her voice dying away, her face flushed. 'We did see him, all covered up, and we were so glad he was finally sleeping.'

She rushed in, toward the bed, Henry and Clara behind her. Olivia patted the bed, first one end, and then worked her way up. Henry and Clara patted and thumped the bed too, echoing Olivia's every move, though it was obvious to them that there was no one on the bed, that the bed looked neatly made, and that there was no evident sign of disturbance in the room. The patter of feet sounded at the door, and several curious faces, each one at a different height, looked in. 'Amrikan not in.'

'Amrikan gone.'

'Amrikan lost.'

And from hushed lowered tones that rose to more urgent decibels, the news was passed on, all along the balcony, down the corridors, past the rooms, humming and buzzing till the sounds rose and fell against his ears, like a distant roar.

'He's not there, you say?' said Henry foolishly, looking at Olivia and Clara and the blur of faces behind them. He felt a blankness, as if the action was unfolding some distance away. Henry wanted to be distracted, to be pulled away from what was happening almost in slow motion around him. Any moment he expected Mark Twain to appear at the door. To his left, the door to the bathroom stood slightly ajar, moving on its hinges, and its louvered panels at the bottom creaked in a slight wind.

'But where is he?' Clara asked, her lips trembling, and her mother stared fixedly at the bed, a frown drawing two straight lines across her forehead. 'He was here. Mama did see him,' went on Clara, speaking fast. 'And we were glad. He had been unable to sleep almost the whole night, moving around in the balcony, and we heard the strain of the lounge chair as he sat on it. We thought he was finally getting some sleep.'

'Yes, we did think so,' Olivia said in a faint voice. 'And he was here, for I checked in on him early in the morning. I drew the curtain apart first so I could see, and then I pulled them back together again for even the faintest light has always troubled him. He just snuggled into his blanket.'

Henry took a quick look around, nodded half-reassuringly at the women, and waved a hand, dismissing the faces at the door. He looked at the women again, trying hard to mask his own bewilderment. Twain could have just stepped out and would be back soon. Henry had dozed off for a bit, of course, and he felt guiltier, the more he thought of it. The curtains swayed in the breeze, and the panes rattled faintly. Most houses kept the windows open, especially in the early part of the day, when the breeze was cool, and the insects weren't particularly bothersome. Henry glanced down, placed his hand on the bedclothes again. He lifted the blanket to feel the sheet, and the pillow, and drew back startled. The sheet felt warm, and there was a clear dent on the pillow. Someone had clearly been sleeping there not too long ago. 'See,' he said, pointing, his voice rising in momentary triumph. 'This means he has to be somewhere around. We will just have to check.'

Henry rushed out to the balcony, and for several moments, looked blankly around. The balcony wasn't wide. Lounge chairs rested against the wall, the servants moved past softly, as they had been instructed to do, and anyone walking by would have made some noise or the other. He was certain he would have noticed Mark Twain if he had walked past. Twain wasn't an unobtrusive kind of man in any way. That shock of hair, the ambling gait, the curious gleaming eyes, and of course, that unkempt moustache.

'Have you seen the sahib?' Henry asked the men gathered around outside the room. The way they huddled reminded him of ants, their heads butting around something sweet, and then quickly dispersing.

He pointed to the door to Twain's room and asked again, miming Twain's appearance to be more helpful. But the hotel servants looked back at him, some uncomprehending, others expressionless. They shook their heads, moving their heads side to side, hesitantly and then with more firmness. 'No. No, sahib.' 'Not seen sahib, sahib.'

Henry glanced down, alerted by something. The music wasn't playing any more, and the musician was no longer visible. 'That man,' he pointed down, and the men came nearer, some leaning over the balcony in excitement. 'I mean the man who was sitting there, playing some instrument.' He stopped. This would only confuse everyone, he thought. It seemed a bit far-fetched to be suspicious about a musician who was just trying to earn some money playing for the hotel's rich guests and visitors.

'You haven't seen him go out? Go out?' Henry repeated. He spread his hands wide, over the railings, to indicate the world outside, and the men watching him did their standard routine of shaking their heads dolefully. He glanced again at the door, and knew Olivia and Clara were inside, their panic growing every moment. He made his voice brusque as he asked the servants again. 'Amrikan sahib here. Did you see him? You can't all be blind. I shall complain.' They looked at him, looked at each other, then shook their heads again, very thoroughly. A couple of them held their ears in sheer horror of the thought.

Henry wiped his forehead with his hand. 'Can't get

them to understand anything,' he muttered, hurrying back to check again on Olivia and Clara.

~

Back in their own room, Olivia sat on a chair, her hands resting on its curved arms, looking shaken. Clara stood near, an arm around her mother's shoulders. Henry felt his heart sink, though he managed a reassuring smile. 'I am sure he can't have gone far. And the bed's just been slept in.' He bit his lip, feeling himself flush involuntarily. He had been here a good two hours, and had, for some time, dozed off, almost unthinkingly. The onus of it all, Mark Twain's sudden, inexplicable absence, his vanishing—for at this moment Henry really didn't know what else he could call it—lay squarely on him.

'Why don't you ladies make yourselves comfortable. I am sure we will find him.'

'Find him?' Clara wailed involuntarily. 'You mean he's lost?'

'No, Clara,' he said, a firmness in his tone that he did not feel. 'I did not mean that. I just meant that I will go out and look for him. As I said he cannot have gone very far.'

He stepped forward and pressed Olivia's hand. He hoped Clara would not mind his sudden testiness. He felt a bewilderment, a state of swimming in something unreal. A man couldn't disappear, or walk away without anyone noticing. He wondered if the women were tired, and needed more rest. It could be, he thought, a touch of the hysterics. They had after all, been travelling the world for several months now, and it could get a bit much. The East was a different planet altogether. If Maya had been around, he suddenly found himself thinking this, perhaps Clara and Olivia might not have felt so distraught.

He turned at a noise from the door. A couple of servants had appeared at the door again. They looked at the distressed Clara, and her mother who was wiping her forehead with a kerchief. They clicked their tongues, and their heads moved from side to side to show how much they commiserated. They folded their hands, gazed up towards the high white-beam ceiling and made those clicking noises again. Henry knew they were appealing to some divine power or another, hoping that the writer would return in a miraculous way.

'We were to go to the exhibition at the art school,' said Clara.

'And you will still,' assured Henry. 'I will just go down and ask the manager for help and some of us will go looking for him.' He patted Olivia's hand again and nodded to Clara as he left, leaving the door slightly ajar, for the morning air was sluggish, and the heat already simmered outside. As he ran down the stairs, he heard the tramp of several feet behind him. 'Stop,' he said, as he reached the landing. 'Stop.' He held his palm out, straight up. 'Go back to work. This isn't some tamasha, some theatre for all of you to watch free.'

The men scampered back, and Henry heard a resolute tread near him. A man in a plain dark suit, dark hair gelled back over a wide forehead, and sharp black eyes, looked up at him. He was thin as a reed, and touched his hair carefully, as if to assure himself it was all in place. 'I heard the disturbance, sir. I understand it is about the American gentleman.'

'Yes, Mark Twain,' said Henry who stood a step higher, as he looked down at the man. 'Have you...?'

The other man frowned, his hand was on his head again, and then over his ears. Henry saw the gold earrings in both ears, and he said, his voice rising sharp and impatient. 'Yes?'

'No Mark Twain in our books, sir. If you mean Mr Clemens, the American, that is how we made the registrations. We do not allow pen names, aliases, pseu...pseu...'

'Pseudonyms,' Henry finished, and the man smiled, and then looking up, he clapped his hands sharply. Henry followed his gaze and saw the servants still poring over the railings and banisters, following the conversation intently. 'Go, shoo. Go away.' He was clapping and gesturing with his hands. 'No work to do, or what?'

The men moved out of sight in a flash, and the faint vibration of the banisters as their hands fell away, was audible for a bit. Then the man cleared his throat, smiled, felt his hair again, and held out a hand, 'Peter Ronald DeSouza, manager of the famous Watson's Hotel since 1894. How may I help you?'

'Don't be...,' but Henry stopped himself in time. This was no time to show his irritation. 'Mr Clemens. That is what he must have registered himself as.'

'Yes,' said the man, lifting a finger. 'Samuel L Clemens and family. I insisted on putting down their names too. We do things properly here at the Watson's.'

Henry looked up, but no bobbing head now appeared over the rails. He could hear pattering noises somewhere, and the clink of cutlery from the breakfast room. A carriage or two rumbled past outside, the sounds rising and falling every time they passed an open window. When he looked down, DeSouza was already several steps ahead, his shoes making a clicking noise on the wooden floor.

'Where is...?' He raised his voice, as he made to catch up with DeSouza, who was already striding toward the atrium, bowing quickly to some of the guests, his head moving one way and then another, as he made for the black wooden desk at the far end. Henry was trying to remember the name of the servant that Mark Twain had only so recently engaged. The man with the untidy mop of hair, the broken smile, the trousers that came well above his ankles, and of course that singsong voice. 'Where's his servant?' he asked, panting, when he had finally caught up with Desouza, who had rounded the desk, nodding to a bespectacled, balding assistant whose eyes widened as he saw Henry lean far across the desk to get DeSouza's attention, and then DeSouza himself took a quick step back, startled to be almost nose to nose with Henry.

'Yes, sir. I am sorry,' DeSouza said, patting back his hair once again. He picked up a pen, and then with a polite smile fixed on his face, he bent toward the right, elbowing his assistant out of the way, 'How can...? Oh, it's you,' he said. 'Yes, about Mr Clemens.'

'It's his servant,' said Henry insistently. 'I don't see him.'

DeSouza put his pen down, raised his hands, felt his forehead, and then lowered them. 'Who is really missing? Mr Clemens or the servant? As per our rules, we have responsibilities only towards our guests, servants are not registered. We do not consider them guests at all.'

'I didn't mean that at all,' said Henry, gritting his teeth. 'The servant would know something about Mark Twain, I mean, Mr Clemens' whereabouts. And I don't see the servant? I don't even remember his name. A man with an...'

'Manuel, sir,' said the assistant speaking up loudly, looking at DeSouza in a somewhat frightened way. 'Manuel, he was there last night. Waiting up for the Clemenses. I do not see him now.'

He looked up at the much taller DeSouza who glared back, not liking the fact that the assistant had spoken out of turn. Henry extended his hand to the other man. 'Henry Baker, American trade consul. So, you say Manuel was here last night. So, he may know...?' His voice drifted away. He remembered not seeing Manuel even later in the night when they had dropped off the Clemenses after the party.

'Well, it does seem they are both not here. Not now anyway,' Henry said slowly, and clearly, as if the truth had dawned on him just then. 'And since Mr Clemens is not around, and no one has a clue, the hotel should do something.' He should have done a more thorough check of Manuel, the fact that Manuel had not been at the hotel in the evening before the Clemenses left should have sounded a warning note, and that Manuel was still not around, was even more alarming.

'But I'd like to be told for sure if Manuel was here last night when the Clemenses returned.' Henry looked at both men squarely in the face as he finished.

'It is not...,' began DeSouza again, and this time Henry glared at him. And the assistant piped in again. 'He was indeed here, sir. He wanted a sewing machine, some tear that he wanted to sew. We have never had one, not in this hotel. Our work...'

This time DeSouza interrupted with some asperity. 'We always have the best material. Even the cotton bedsheets, and covers are not from the mills here, but from America.' At other times, Henry would have seized on this information, it would have added to his business interests, but he looked impatiently at them both. 'We need the police to get here. There is a missing guest, and the servant may be...'

The men looked alarmed, and the assistant nodded and made to leave. He lifted the flap end of the desk, and DeSouza, a man who was beginning to profoundly irritate Henry, stopped him. 'Mehta, who gave you permission to leave?'

Mehta looked flustered, and Henry glared, leaning forward. 'It is a matter of great concern. The police need to be told.'

'We will do a thorough check of the hotel first. Mr Clemens may have wandered off and perhaps is unable to remember the exact location of his room,' said DeSouza. He stepped back, clapped his hands, and then rang the small handbell close to the register. 'It is a big hotel, you see.' He rang the bell harder, making the two lone guests at the far end of the lobby look toward them in some alarm. The noise of running feet came to them from every quarter. Standing in the atrium, its glass dome at a considerable height, the staircases at either end, the big swinging glass doors on either side, every sound appeared magnified, and the sound of rushing feet rose to a roar. Henry's ears throbbed painfully.

Some of the hotel servants appeared again, in their white uniforms and red turbans. They stood around the desk, and DeSouza raised his arms as if he were offering them benediction of some kind. 'Quiet,' he said. 'Have you seen Mr Clemens? The Amrikan. Guest on 3rd floor, Room 20.' He looked at Henry somewhat smug, pleased at how well he remembered every detail. 'And his servant too,' piped in Mehta, fixing his glasses, nodding to DeSouza, righteously.

The men were already shaking their heads, turning to each other, some of them fingering their lips, their faces, as they described once again for each other, Clemens and then Manuel too. 'This just won't do. You must call the police,' Henry broke in. He pointed to the instrument, gleaming and shiny, on its stand, and said in clipped tones, 'If you won't do, I can report you. For standing in the way of the law.'

DeSouza stood up straight, flicked a hair away from his forehead, and said calmly. 'We follow steps. The police must not be bothered unduly. In case...' And it was Mehta who pointed to the day's paper that sat on the desk, crisp, unturned, still smelling of ink. 'The murder, you understand.'

The headline read, *Strike Threat in Bombay Mills.* Henry felt a panic, recognized the swimming sensation in his head, one he had experienced only some weeks ago, the time the rainstorm broke over their boat just as they headed out of Elephanta Island. 'Mr Baker, sir,' and Mehta, the assistant's clammy moist hand closed over his, as Henry reached for the desk, trying to calm himself. 'The murder of the girl, Casi, sir,' Mehta explained, looking at him pityingly.

'A murder, and now a workers' strike, and you can see the police has its hands full,' said DeSouza, looking at him sternly.

Henry reached for the telephone, and Mehta, his fingers gentle on Henry's wrist looked at DeSouza in appeal. 'We must call the police if the gentleman so insists.'

'Mr Mehta,' the other man snapped. 'Please don't teach me how to run this hotel. I follow rules, and now since Mr Clemens seems to have well and truly vanished, we must call the police.'

Henry's eyes ran down the news item, as he listened to DeSouza talk to the police. Watson's Hotel was where the rich and the famous stayed. It was one of the city's most prominent locations and a recent one. A landmark that the city was justifiably proud of. Built entirely of cast-iron, the entire structure had been shipped and then erected on that open patch of ground opposite the huge grassy Esplanade, only some years ago. It had been among the first to have electricity. Though that experiment failed, and had not lasted long, the hotel was always well lit up in the evenings with gas lamps. It had been among the first hotels to get a telephone service in the city, a number that the operator at the exchange recognized, and so DeSouza had been put through almost at once.

The police, according to the papers, was truly weighed down with one too many things. In the afternoon just gone, the police had indeed arrested Tuka, on charges of murdering his wife, Casi. Since then, if the papers were to be believed, the city's cotton mills had seen considerable unrest. The mills were the city's lifeline; cotton exports brought in much-needed revenue and made Bombay, the thriving, cosmopolitan city it now was. There was another secret commodity, Henry knew, that was equally prized: opium, but its smuggling and consumption had in recent years, been widely condemned, in almost every circle. A far cry from the time fifty years ago, Henry had learnt, when opium had been the cause of friction and major wars between Britain and China.

Tuka Ram, as the news report from the *Bombay Gazette* had it, was an important man. He was the 'sardar,' the labour contractor for several mills in the city, responsible for getting the mills, and their owners, the valued and much-needed cheap labour from the villages beyond Bombay. The workers believed that the arrest and the murder charges on Tuka were an attempt to frame him. It quoted Gangaram Jamkhedkar, a local leader respected by the natives, on this matter. Jamkhedkar was known to be a close associate of Bal Gangadhar Tilak, and insisted that he spoke with the blessings of his leader.

The government, for its part, knew Tilak or any of his associates could easily spread disaffection among the workers with their version of events. The truth about the murder that he spoke of, Jamkhedkar said, was known by one and all: for Tuka was not even there when the crime had been committed. Many people had seen him leave the lodge several hours before. The police under pressure from the Governor and the city council had to arrest someone. And the workers who had struck work before on various matters, all in the interest of justice, intended to do so again. In one mill, the New Era Mill, workers on the night shift had walked out, demanding justice, and for Tuka Ram to be released.

DeSouza's call to the police didn't take long. Henry heard the receiver falling into place the moment he turned his head away from the door. Somehow, he expected to see Mark Twain. That he would return from a stroll outside, looking his usual, absent-minded, frazzled self. DeSouza smiled, a pleased, almost reassuring smile. A police deputation would soon arrive, he said, and Henry nodded, his lips pursed. He had had enough of the man, and his affected mannerisms. He wanted to think clearly. He walked toward the double-panelled wooden doors, and looked out at the street, with its vendors, the occasional carriages, a motorcar tooting its way among pedestrians, a seller of candy floss at the very edge of the Esplanade, and a newspaper boy holding onto a stack of papers, raising his voice often to shout out the news. There seemed no sign of Mark Twain, as Henry remembered him that first morning, in his brown sack coat, the pipe, the sailor hat, and that moustache that so distinguished him. Henry must have stood there a long while, looking out at the street, first one way, and then the other, and realized he was lost for answers.

As logic indicated, Twain had been sleeping late, and then he had simply gotten up and left. Maybe he wanted to see things for himself, explore the city on his own, and had taken his servant along. Henry shuddered as another terrible thought occurred to him. Manuel could have contrived to get him kidnapped. Or had delivered him to kidnappers. Henry was about to go back inside when he caught sight of someone standing under the peepul tree. A man, twirling his wide-brimmed brown sola hat in one hand, his black coat unbuttoned and swinging loose on him, looking toward the hotel with a steady, unblinking gaze. Henry recognized Arthur Pease, whom he had seen the other day at the docks as well. Arthur Pease, the persistent, annoying preacher who was always listing the city's vices, pottering around its brothels, music halls, and the opium dens located in Khetwadi, Grant Road, and Mazagaon. Pease who had family and friends in high places in the government in London and who wrote countless letters to the editors of the *Telegraph and Courier* and the *Bombay Gazette* berating the city's officials for their encouragement and lassitude in curbing opium smuggling. The two men looked at each other, and it was Pease who looked away first, pretending a sudden interest in the cricket game, and Henry, irritated at being distracted, dashed back upstairs.

Olivia, evidently exhausted by her worry, was dozing now in an armchair in Clara's room, her head on the armrest. Clara rose as he entered. 'Not to worry,' and Henry hated the way he said that for her eyes lit up. 'I mean the police will soon be here. But do you remember what he was wearing exactly, and if he took anything with him?'

Clara led him back to her parents' room. It was just like they had left it, the bed looked flat and empty. He noticed Twain's grey valise on the low bamboo table, and on the desk, a diary, black with a gilt edge. He also noted something that should have struck him right away. Twain's hat wasn't on its stand. Clara opened a panel of the small wooden wardrobe and stepped back to a soft creaking sound, looking startled. 'Father wore the same clothes as last night! See, the same brown coat…'

She was running her hands over the few coats arranged on their hangers, pointing to two pairs of shoes: a set of Oxfords, and the other, a pair of black rainboots, both arranged neatly on the wardrobe floor. 'He's taken his hat, his stick, and he didn't change. It makes you think…,' Henry mused.

'What?' asked Clara, and Henry replied, as calmly as he could, 'That he left in a hurry. Maybe he changed back into the same clothes and went out. He's absent-minded that way, isn't he?'

'But he always looks for the right clothes to wear,' said Clara thoughtfully. 'Not that he's fastidious, but he does care a bit. So, he must have asked the servant.'

'If he was around,' finished Henry for her, and then he remembered something about the servant, 'Manuel asked downstairs for a sewing kit. Would you know anything about that?'

'No,' Clara looked puzzled. 'In any case, I fixed some torn buttons for father only the other day. And father said nothing.'

'I see. Well, my dear, I think you should be with your mother. The police are here. I can hear…'

But he didn't have to say more. This time the tramping of feet was loud on the floor, and there was the sharp piercing pull of a whistle. People in the city were familiar with the sound. The whistling of policemen asking for right of way, for no one to intrude on their authority. Henry looked at the anxious faces of the two women, and he was once again filled with despair. He wished so very much for Maya's presence. Her calm efficiency, and ability to see things somewhat differently would have been so much help. Then, as if she had materialized at his desperate wish, he saw her, coming up the steps just a bit behind the policemen.

She smiled at the women, held their hands, kissed Olivia on the cheek, and told her it would be all right. 'It's not as big a city as New York,' she said, 'or London. And difficult for him to lose himself here.' She looked at Henry as she said that, and he instantly understood. An American, looking so out of place, would be easily found, and suddenly he wished for this to be proved true, almost instantly. 'Abdul came and told us. And I came here,' she explained to him.

'Oh, that is where he was,' Henry said, not admitting that thoughts of Abdul hadn't even crossed his mind.

Inspector Button, lean and scrawny looking, doffed his hat to the women. His hair flattened along the scalp gave him a sheared look. He exchanged a few words with them, before he turned to Henry. The three men who followed in his wake did so too, almost automatically. 'We will get to the bottom of this, I am sure. The manager downstairs told us Mr Clemens...,' Button looked at his notes, '...Mark Twain has been missing since morning. Who was the last person to see him?'

'I was,' said Olivia in a thin, reedy voice. Henry felt sorry for her, she did seem exhausted with worry. 'I saw him sleeping and thought not to disturb him.'

'Yes, we felt the bed and it was warm,' corroborated Henry, 'and he seemed to have dressed in a hurry and gone.' Henry detailed how Mark Twain had worn the same clothes from the night before, a grey sack coat, the white shirt with its upturned collar, the pair of pointed brown shoes that weren't there anymore. 'He is a writer, we understand,' Button said, his eyes scanning the length of the veranda. 'Did he go out in search of inspiration, something to write about?'

Clara piped in, 'He did intend to write something, but he's left his notebook there.' She pointed through the door to the table, and Maya leaned forward, her eyes now sharp with a sudden interest. 'The black notebook. It meant he did intend to write something. And he was talking of the case.'

Button took in the appearance of the room, casting a quick look everywhere, a stern, unsmiling look on his face. 'Look carefully. Right near the bed,' he told his men. 'Let no crowds gather. We must do our job.'

As he reached the table, he made a great show of taking out his kerchief and wrapping it around his hand before picking up the notebook, so as not to leave his fingerprints on it. Then he flipped it open, and Henry saw his eyes run down the first page before a brief smile appeared. 'He's writing about crows.'

Maya caught Henry by the elbow. He heard her low whisper. 'He had another diary last evening. Not this one but a smaller red one, with a pen or pencil tied to it. I remember from the party last night. He must have taken that with him.'

Henry looked at her and knew at once she was right. She was, most times, but he remembered his own puzzlement about the diary when he had seen Mark Twain bent over it the previous evening. He had been quite unable to understand his confusion then.

VI

A Long Sleep is Never a Restful One

The rest of that morning Inspector Button spent in talking to the servants, and the hotel staff. He inquired about the guests staying on the same floor as the Clemenses, the second floor of Watson's Hotel. He pored over the register, and his men spent hours haranguing the doormen and the few waiters, if they had noticed anything. There were two doormen; the older of them insisted that no one matching Mark Twain's description had passed through the door since morning.

The other was a tall dusky Pathan, with an impressively wrapped turban, who stood a foot higher than his companion. 'No one with a moustache like the one you describe,' he said, adamantly shaking his head. 'Think carefully,' said Button, wiping his face with his towel-sized kerchief. Already his patience was wearing thin. 'It does seem to me you are pretty useless at your job.'

The man's face darkened, as the three constables with Button tittered. They were men of the Ghats. They came from the coast south of the city and were shorter, more wiry people, and known to dislike the hardy, tough Pathans. The doorman stood tall, and said haltingly, thinking over every word, 'I keep an eye on everyone, sahib, even if one white man, in his big hat and long coat, is no different from the other. But I would notice. No one really goes out in the morning. It's in the evening the action starts.'

The other doorman, quieter and more watchful, but with a flamboyant moustache that curved almost to his ears, mentioned the sad-looking man who had come late the previous evening. He had waited for a long time to meet someone, a guest. 'He had a music case with him, sahib, but he didn't say much. Hardly anything.' The two doormen exchanged looks, and the taller one, with his impressive turban, became more animated, 'We didn't understand what he wanted. He said he had been here before. We spoke Pashto, and Urdu, and even Gujerati, trying to help him, but he only nodded, pointed up at the higher floor, and said he would wait. It was much later at night that he left. It was really late.'

'He must be the Serbian,' said Button to Henry under his breath. 'I wonder why he felt the need to come here. For someone who puts up at some seedy hotel at Kamati Pura, he seems to move around in some fancy company. He was at the party yesterday, and now he has to meet guests here. At unusual hours, mind you. There was always more to him, I thought. I think I should...,' But Button said no more, though he sensed Henry's curiosity. 'What were you saying?' he asked, but Button looked away. 'You will have to let us do our work, Mr Baker. The news is out, and our men will be sharp on their toes...'

~

'This is making me very anxious,' Henry said later to Maya when he had a moment with her. Maya had persuaded Clara and Olivia to leave the hotel for a bit, and to come over to her Colaba bungalow.

'I blame myself,' Henry said in a low voice, not looking at Maya, 'I was there the whole morning, and I didn't even see him.'

She patted him understandingly on the arm. 'You mustn't be too hard on yourself. That won't help you think with a clear mind. You would have heard him leave. The door creaks, and you'd have heard his steps. And he would have called out to you. He didn't strike me as too absent-minded. Absorbed, yes.' She was lost in thought as she looked out across the grassy Esplanade. A sadhu dressed in orange robes, with the vertical sandalwood lines on his forehead, sat behind clay vats offering water to thirsty passers-by. A fortune teller with two parrots dancing on his shoulder, aimlessly played with his dice. A few carriages passed, and labourers ran by, nimble on their feet, hauling along carts laden with sacks, and other goods from the port. It was almost noon, even the palm trees stood unmoving and still, and Henry felt tired, hungry, and irritable.

'Which makes you think,' Maya continued in a low voice, 'if he really did leave in the morning?' Henry stared at her and raised a hand to his throbbing head. Maya touched his hand reassuringly, 'We must think about this in a while. Everyone's hungry. Why don't you come with us too to the bungalow? Then I guess you have to go and give your statement to the police...'

It was then he told her about the musician. Not the Serbian, whom everyone kept talking about, but the man from the play. 'He was there,' he said, pointing to the peepul tree under which the fortune teller sat now. 'And he was playing the same tune over and over again. And I thought it was the Elgar piece I'd heard some time ago. I was really quite caught up with that.'

He looked unhappy, but Maya was looking at him intently, her eyes an intense blue in the sunlight. She was biting into her lower lip as she always did when thoughtful. 'The musician from the play. Eeshwar, he was here? That is really most interesting. And why didn't you tell the police this?'

'Because it all struck me later. I didn't realize who he was until much later, and then I found a lot of time had passed. I noticed Mark Twain not appearing, then Olivia's panic, and not till the police arrived and talked about the Serbian, did I remember that stringed player, and that he was sitting there, all the time.'

'Well, he played the esraj, and of late he has been causing trouble. Threatening to leave if he wasn't paid more and this is a busy time of year for the theatre,' said Maya, frowning. 'But maybe it was just a coincidence.' She pressed his arm. 'You've had a hard day, poor thing. Come along now.' And though he felt foolish, realizing he hadn't really given a good account of himself, Maya's reassurances were like balm, as calming as the sea breeze that wafted inland this time of year.

VII

What Ifs and Whereabouts

In the carriage, as he sank into the comforting darkness it offered, he let himself think over what Maya had just said. That, of course, he would have heard Mark Twain leave. He would have heard his steps tap-tapping away on the wooden floor. He wasn't really so mesmerized by the music. The door was just behind him, he had been looking out, staring out at nothing, thinking over things, about Maya and himself, and all the business plans he had. Had he been too distracted, or had he drifted away into some light sleep? And had Mark Twain crept out softly, not wishing to disturb him? It might have been difficult to see him leave the hotel itself, for these set of rooms were to one side, and one had to turn the corner to the right, to get a view of the hotel's entrance, with the carriages lined up along the road, the servants and porters sitting around waiting, some gathered in circles chatting, rubbing tobacco between their palms, as they exchanged the day's news, the gossip about the guests. But the police had questioned everyone, even those on duty in the morning, and no one reported having seen Twain.

Indeed, the writer had, as things appeared, just upped and gone. There could be a secret door he had walked through, or perhaps, as that terrible magician Freddie Bancroft was always claiming, a secret box he had climbed into and vanished. Henry shifted his leg, feeling it go numb, and felt a touch on his shoulder. Someone—it was Clara—was trying to gently shake him awake.

'We are here, Henry,' she said, and he realized he had dozed off, and for the second time, in just a few hours. 'I am sorry,' he muttered, glad to see the grey-stone small bungalow with the bougainvillea creepers around the archway that led to the front door. A small woman in a sari, the veil of her sari loose on her shoulders, shyly welcomed them. 'This is Indu,' Maya said in her usual efficient way, and she led them into a comfortable sitting room. With its low wooden divan, expansive cane chairs, colourful cushions stacked up on the carpets, and flower vases in every corner, the room emanated a serenity that Henry welcomed. He smiled with surprise when he saw Abdul appear at the door, holding a tray. He placed the carafe of coconut water and the glasses on the table, before bowing to the ladies. 'It's nice to see you here, Abdul,' he said, dryly. Abdul had always had a soft spot for Maya, especially the time she had insisted on getting him treated for an unexpected skin rash, that had turned out to be chicken pox. Dr Pechey had said he had gotten to the hospital just in time.

'Did the police speak to you too, Abdul?' Henry asked, after he had followed him out into the hallway leading to the kitchen.

'No, sahib, but I did not see anything. After bringing you to the hotel, I was outside waiting with the carriages, but not see Amrikan sahib.'

'Anything else?' Henry persisted, 'just think carefully. Or maybe he was dressed…' But he stopped mid-flow. Twain, as they knew now, had worn the same clothes of the night before, that he had perhaps slept in them for a bit before he left. 'And did you see Manuel?'

'There were people who saw him the last evening, sahib. He was at the hotel, brushing the sahib's coat, and then, at night, he had asked around for a needle and thread. Something he needed for a tear, he said, and one of the coachmen gave it to him.'

That was what the manager's assistant at the desk, Mehta, had also told him, Henry recollected. That Manuel had looked around for a sewing machine. The matter seemed to be urgent, for Manuel to ask around so desperately. 'Manuel's gone too,' he said, slowly. 'Did he say anything about what needed to be fixed?' But Abdul was looking lost. He scratched his head, and said, 'Manuel was there even early on, in the morning. He had taken up ice to the sahib, and the madams too. And then no one saw him go…'

'You must come back with me in the evening. When the police return to talk to the evening staff.' He spoke in as firm a tone he could muster, knowing Abdul would demur. Servants, helpers, those considered quite low in the social ladder were rightly wary of the police. They could always be rounded up on the slightest suspicion and pretext, defined as posing a 'disturbance to the peace'.

Henry wished, as he made his way back to the sitting room—from where Olivia's low voice could be heard telling everyone of the strange guru they had met in Australia—that all this had not happened. She was talking far too quickly; the strain of recent events was clearly telling on her.

'So, this man, he tells us all about the Hindu religion, and then was curious about our plans in India. Samuel was careful,' Olivia was saying, her words following each other too rapidly. 'He wasn't going to divulge anything, even to someone who looked so saintly. And the man said we must visit Benares. The city by the Ganges, where people come to die, where they find salvation by ending their lives in the holy river. They just float down like logs, and that seemed somehow profound, and also quite frightening.'

There was silence for a while, and then Clara talked of her father's next book. 'He is always saying that if he didn't have to write these pieces for the newspapers, he would write a new book about Tom Sawyer, and make it quite a mystery story.' She said it with a laugh, and then added more soberly, 'And now father has gone and given us quite a mystery of his own.'

'Isn't there another mystery that the city's quite excited about?' asked Olivia. She was suddenly talkative, but everyone wanted her to be so. It was a way to stave off tension and forget. Maya caught Henry's eye and she went on to tell them more about the unfortunate girl, Casi, who had been found dead in a native lodge in Sewree. 'It's a more crowded part of town, with shops, houses, and small jewel and shoe factories packed close together. And this girl had just come to the city, newly married, and quite excited by everything in the city. The manner of her death has made it so very sensational.'

'Someone's been arrested, the man you suspected rightly,' said Henry, remembering the headlines on the paper he had seen on DeSouza's desk.

'Yes, Tuka, the labour contractor, a supervisor of sorts. So quite a powerful man,' and Maya kept up the conversation with Olivia and Clara. It was all Henry, and she could do then to keep the stress at bay. 'Once you have an idea how things work here, you sense who has the real power in this city. The supervisor gets the workers to man the mills, negotiates their contracts, their work hours, and decides their wages. Of course, he gets a cut too, sometimes more than the workers bargained for. The employers too prefer it that way because they don't have to deal with the workers directly. This man, Tuka, is powerful, and his workers are very loyal to him. He's more than just a supervisor. Rather he's almost a father figure to them. For they have come leaving their village homes for a life in the city and Tuka is someone they can look up to. And then there's the Ganpati...you know, the festival of the elephant-headed god, that happens during the monsoons. Last year, Tuka and his men organized a big celebration in Parel, and that pleased big leaders like Tilak, Paranjape and others, and there were processions in the city. The police were saying that at one point, it really became difficult to manage.'

Maya stopped and laughed softly as she looked at their rapt expressions. 'Dear me, I do seem to have gone on for a while.'

'No, do go on,' implored Clara. 'I wish I could have taken notes, but I will remember it for Father.' She reached out and clasped her mother's hand. 'I am sure he would love to learn about this.'

'Well, so today's paper has this bit about how the workers are very agitated and calling for a strike because Tuka's been arrested. He was the last person to be seen with Casi, the evening before. His workers are saying he was at the mill all through the night, and even in the morning. When he turned up, the door to Casi's room wouldn't open and had to be broken open. It was locked, Tuka apparently told the police, and he wasn't a thief or someone who would come through the window to do such a vile deed...'

She stopped just then, and looked at Henry, for a similar thought had struck them. Henry felt a sudden disbelief. The thought of Mark Twain, his homburg or fedora in hand, descending a pipe to make a getaway from the hotel appeared not just incongruous, but downright impossible.

'But surely father wouldn't climb down a shaft,' laughed Clara, nervously, as though she had read their thoughts, 'and why would he?'

'No, not...,' Henry said slowly. 'This is about Manuel. No one saw him after the morning. But why would Manuel want to leave via a window, disappear suddenly, unless he had something to hide?'

'He seemed a nice sort,' said Clara, and then she turned to her mother. 'He was asking around for a sewing kit, as Henry told me. Do you know anything about that...?'

'Was he?' Olivia looked down at her hands clasped in her lap, as she thought. 'I think he asked me too, and I said, I still had things to unpack. When I asked why,' she looked up and stared at a small statuette of the Buddha on the corner table, before continuing, 'he mentioned something about a coat. That Sam's coat needed darning. But then he just saluted me and walked off. I really thought that was rude, but in a new country, one doesn't know what to do.'

'And this was the evening before?' asked Henry, leaning forward, for she spoke in a low quiet voice. He thought this matter of the sewing kit vis-à-vis a needle and thread, something Manuel had evidently obtained from one of the coachmen, was a red herring of sorts.

'I think so. It was just as we were getting ready for the party, and I was distracted,' Olivia's slow measured reply made Henry think hard. Manuel had been around later that night too, when the Clemenses were back and yet neither Olivia nor Clara had seen him. He saw Maya's attentive face, her eyes never veering from Olivia's face. 'I got up later that night. Maybe like Samuel, I couldn't sleep too,' she said. 'And I was taking a turn on the balcony. I saw his door closed, and I was relieved. For as Sam had complained, it was the crows that kept him awake, calling away at night, and they had awoken me too. But yes, I remember this now...' Her eyes darted to catch Henry's. 'Manuel, he was pacing in the hallway, murmuring to himself, and when I asked him about the sahib, he looked startled. I asked, is he sleeping, and he nodded. I got back to Clara here because she sleeps badly too in a new place.'

'Did you see him then?' Henry had leaned forward in his chair, his voice insistent.

She looked set to cry, and Clara reached out and hugged her, placing her mother's head against her waist. 'No, no, it's all right, Mama.' She spoke in a low gentle tone to Henry, 'She didn't have her glasses on that time, and some things and even people, look kind of blurry...'

Maya offered Olivia water again, patted her hand, and said she wasn't to worry. They would find him soon. It was clear Manuel knew a thing or two. 'It's from the small innocuous questions someone asks that you find the right answers,' she said, and this amused Henry. Maya and her aphorisms. He asked lightly as she glanced his way, and caught his slight smile, 'You had more to say about this man, didn't you? The one arrested for the murder?' Olivia still looked shaken, and he hoped a change of subject would help her. Later, she could think through things more carefully.

'They have the right man, but they haven't the right evidence. It's all on suppositions,' Maya said, very matter of fact. 'Tuka was indeed the last person to see Casi. He was the husband, there was the noise of talking and conversation, but then the door was bolted from inside, and the window was closed, not bolted.'

'Where do you get these details, Maya?'

'From the police,' she said, blandly. 'I wanted to do an article on her. A young woman who wanted to be a nurse, even a doctor. She had come to meet us, I told you that.' She looked at Henry, her blue eyes intent on him. Strands of her hair, loose, golden, and wavy streamed across her cheeks. She brushed them aside and continued. 'And we were going to do everything to help Casi. Charlotte and I were planning to raise a subscription for her, so she could stay on here, and go to the school run by Ramabai. We had...' And it was Maya's turn to look startled. She looked quickly at Henry, and then at the women, before she smiled, ran a hand over her hair, and Henry knew she had remembered something, and was saving it for later.

'You must rest,' she said gently to Olivia. 'Please, you must. There's a spare room, and it will be most comfortable. Henry and I are going to do everything we can.'

~

'What was it that you didn't say then?' Henry asked when they were alone. Olivia had looked tired, her face drained of colour. She needed rest, Clara insisted, and it would do her good.

'That there's a photo of Casi I have to pick up from Mr Shapoor Bedwar's photo studio. He does unusual photos, in a very artistic way, and trains his students too in a similar way. One of his promising assistants, Dinyar, took Casi's photo. It was a long process, and he had to wait till the light was just right, and develop it carefully.' She stopped, abruptly, her face flushing. 'This is so unlike me. You can tell I am nervous.'

'I am too,' Henry said, 'I am glad to say this to you. Just too much has happened.'

'Maybe I shouldn't have spoken so much about Casi, in front of them,' she said, tilting her head to indicate the hallway through which Olivia and Clara had just left.

'You were trying to distract them, and that's such a sad, tragic case, really,' said Henry thoughtfully.

'Someone came in through the window. I mean in the lodge she was in,' Maya clarified quickly. 'I keep thinking about it. The newspapers all describe Tuka as a stout man. I can't envisage him climbing up to the first floor, or even leaning across from another balcony to get in. He would be seen; he would make a noise. I wonder how it all happened...'

Then she grabbed Henry by the sleeve. 'She wore some jewellery the last time, when we went to Bedwar's studio on Grant Road. Do you remember the police commissioner warning about jewel thieves at the party?'

'Oh, how can I forget the party,' said Henry, and Maya flushed as she responded. 'The magic trick seemed to have been quite a diversion. But the police were there because the alert had gone out. But if I hadn't done the trick, would you have known about

Mark Twain's other diary? The red one with the pen tucked in it. That's the one he has with him.'

Henry for his part was thinking that the police never really needed a pretext to snoop on anyone, or gatecrash a party. Vincent had spoken of the jewel thieves, and his eyes had been on the violin player with the saddest expression ever. 'A Serbian musician,' Vincent had said, correcting the information Henry had had from Button at the port earlier. The police had been keeping tabs on him at the pier too. And then the violinist had, as per one account, turned up at the hotel too.

'I should go back to the hotel,' he told Maya. A late afternoon sun was drifting through the slats, leaving gentle sunny lines on the stone floor. There was a breeze outside, for the shadows of leaves, long and forlorn appeared occasionally too.

'I wish I could come,' said Maya. 'But I will wait here till Edith comes by, as she might, or Charlotte returns, and then there's that piece on Casi I must write. The *Bombay Gazette* will just have sensational details and forget the person behind the story. I wish I had remembered that photograph before.'

She looked thoughtful, her mind far away, and Henry was prompted to say, 'Maya, I hope...'

She looked at him fiercely, and he stopped himself. He had been about to warn her to keep away from danger, and Maya had sensed that and bristled. 'No,' he said hastily. 'This isn't censure. But you must be careful. Jewel thieves, for instance. They could be a murderous lot.'

VIII

Tall Men Can Look Through Windows

Henry's heart sank when he saw the police carriage still stationed in the hotel portico. The vendors were back in place at the Esplanade. He had passed crowds of boys leading horses by the rope, offering rides to guests, or those walking along the road. A painter had set up his easel and was looking across at the hotel. Henry noted his traditional native turban, a maroon cloth twisted into neat folds around his head. The servant who stood beside him held a tobacco box in one hand and an open umbrella in the other that dipped this side and that in the slight breeze. Finally, the man looked up, took off his turban and swatted the servant with it, before wiping his own profusely perspiring forehead.

Soon the umbrella was lowered and quietly folded up. Henry saw the painter's majestic moustache, the bald pate, and instantly recognized the artist, for he was really very well-known: M.V. Dhurandhar, a respected artist at the School of Art. He had been appointed especially at the urging of John Griffiths and Lockwood Kipling, whose son Rudyard was already winning acclaim as a writer of several well-received novels. Henry knew Mark Twain and Rudyard Kipling had met some years ago in New York for Kipling had memorably described this meeting.

It would have been nice if they had met in India too, Henry thought. That would have made the picture complete, and he, Mark Twain, a stranger from America, would have found company. Maybe he wouldn't have vanished quite like this. Henry caught himself as he thought such thoughts. He still believed Twain had wandered off. That was the safest thing to believe. But Olivia had mentioned the man they had met in Australia, the strange guru who had talked of Benares, the cave temples in India, of sages immersed in meditation for years and years. And with a murder, the threat of a strike, the jewel thieves at work, and the impassioned, irascible supporters of the leader Tilak, always ready to whip up native sentiments, Bombay suddenly seemed a dangerous place.

He went up the steps, past the lobby where the manager's assistant Mehta raised a hand to his forehead in the traditional greeting. There were more people in the lobby at this time, and in the atrium as well. Some, Henry presumed, were guests, for they were dressed in a distinctly formal way. Some in sack coats, others in the long robes the Chinese preferred. Henry skirted around a small circle of confabulating guests as he went up the stairs. Inspector Button was still there, seated a a low table at one end of the balcony. His men, about four of them, strode around in their boots, holding their batons in a menacing way, as they bade the hotel's servants and workers to fall in line. 'Answer questions as sahib asks,' one of them shouted. 'Understand?'

The men nodded, and some of them folded their hands, and mumbled about their work, their errands. The constables thumped their batons on the floor, and asked for quiet. 'It was last evening or maybe only some hours ago,' said Button, 'and all of you were here.' He pointed a finger, and stabbed it repeatedly in the direction of the men lined up. 'The American on this floor, a great writer, a visitor to this city, walked away, and you saw nothing.'

Some of the men had already begun shaking their heads, and the constables marched past again, rolling their batons on their palms in a clear threat. 'Listen to the question first.'

'Do you remember anything? Did you see anything? Anyone entering the room? Anyone who shouldn't be here in the first place.'

A man at the very end, a heavy set Pathan, the ends of his turban bobbing on his shoulder, nodded, 'I did see him, sahib,' he said, in a quiet, slow voice, 'my master has the room three doors away. I saw the Amrikan sahib enter his own room late at night. But I did not see him leave. I then accompany my own master to the graveyard.'

Titters of laughter followed, and the man smiled too, as he enjoyed the momentary confusion and look of fear that passed the constables' faces. 'Silence,' said Button. 'It cannot be that you did not see a man leave. You are supposed to be out here. You must be sleeping on the job then.'

'Sahib,' said the Pathan in a voice even quieter than before. 'We are working for our masters. My friends and I, all of us, work hard. Fanning our masters, fetching water, ironing the clothes...lot of work, sahib, little rest.'

The heads of the men around him bobbed in profound agreement, and in predictable reaction, the constables swung their batons again. Henry watched it all, knowing such questioning would not lead anywhere. Besides, Button well knew, that once the servants' duties were done, when everyone had gone to sleep, they too retired to the servants' room, a room kept aside for them on the first floor. The questioning was sheer braggadocio, for as far as all accounts went, it was in the morning that Twain had left the room, or when he was last seen. The warm bedclothes, Olivia claiming to have seen him sleeping, after a sleepless excitable evening, were all known facts. For the first time, Henry admitted to a cold fear. It had already been several hours. He hoped the writer had come to no harm.

'We did not see him, sahib,' all of the servants had begun talking at once. Button blew his whistle and a sharp piercing noise broke through the cacophony. It was then someone emerged from the room three doors away, the one in front of which Henry had been lounging that very morning. The same tall, hefty man emerged, still dressed the same way. An untidy pair of trousers, a long blue robe, and flappy loose slippers. He was red-faced and breathed heavily as he lumbered toward them, reminding Henry of a hulking frigate he had once seen in the turbulent Mediterranean.

'There is just too much noise, all the time,' he hollered just as he had done in the morning. 'What kind of a hotel is this?' He spoke in a thick, guttural accent, and Henry guessed now that he was European. Probably German, he surmised. It had been just a year or so that he had travelled through Europe to reach Bombay, and some recollections remained clear. He suddenly wanted to return to those seemingly happy, less worrisome days.

The Pathan servant turned towards the new guest, his hands folded, and as the taller man made to cuff him on the ear, he ducked neatly out of the way. The Pathan was clearly more attuned to the German's ways. 'The Amrikan, sir,' he said. 'The big writer. They are asking about him.'

'I don't care. This is a hotel,' the burly guest said, striding down the corridor toward Inspector Button's table. Henry noted the momentary look of alarm on Button's face, but he rose to his feet, adjusted his trousers, and tapped with his pen on the table, as the man advanced. 'You cannot have a police station, a thana on a hotel's premises. The guests here need their peace and sleep.'

Button stepped back so he did not have to lift his

head to look at the guest. 'And who may you be?'

'You do not...' But the other man stopped, caught his breath, and answered, his tone dropping but only by a notch. 'Gustave Boehme. I come from Germany, to make cinema. Cinema, you know?' He linked the fingers of both hands, raised them to his eyes, and moved his head left and right, so to give a more effective demonstration, and Button, standing arms akimbo, said slowly, 'Well, you make your cinema, and let us do our job.'

'This hotel is for guests,' the man called Boehme said, leaning down, placing his hands on the desk. 'And your job for questioning is in the police station.'

'Listen...'

'No, you listen to me. Since morning, I have been trying to sleep. I have had no sleep last night, because of my work. I make cinema. Creative work. I am an artist. And I am also a guest.'

'You have already told me that,' said Button clenching his teeth. Henry stepped forward, realizing a situation of this kind could easily get out of hand. An Englishman and a German arguing over something could develop into a full-fledged diplomatic fracas, especially if the men came to blows, or Button threatened the man with arrest.

'I am sure,' said Henry, forcing himself to smile pleasantly, 'this can be resolved. The questioning is almost over. No one saw Mark Twain, apparently. But the policemen need to be here, till he is found, or returns of his own accord.'

The German looked Henry up and down, but he stepped back, nodding, and rubbing his eyes. 'Well, I should never have made the mistake of staying here. And everyone said it's the best hotel in town. But just too much noise.' He shook his head, and his voice turned wobbly. He looked like a big infant ready to cry. 'Noise in the corridor, and at night, noise outside. The crows too, and then the people looking in, through my window. This isn't a hotel. Just a crowded railway platform,' he said, turning as he made to stride away, back to the comforts of his room.

As his words sank in, Henry started. He picked up pace behind the man. 'No one could be looking at you through the window. You mean in the corridor?'

Boehme stopped abruptly. He looked surprised to see Henry a step or two behind. 'No,' he said slowly, drawing out every word. 'Someone outside. He was at my window looking inside.'

'But how can that be? You are on the second floor. And the windows face the grounds outside.'

'Yes,' he said nodding calmly. 'As I said, the man looked through my window, and he frightened me. He peered through and when I walked up, my face almost against his through the glass, he turned on his long sticks and walked away.'

A man on stilts! Henry's mouth must have dropped in amazement, before he collected himself, 'And this was at night?'

The man Boehme nodded patiently, 'At night, just when I was planning to set out. If you think that it was a ghost, come to warn me about my work, you can think again.' He guffawed at his own joke, rubbed his lips where the spittle gathered, and said, 'That was no ghost.' Around them they heard a flurry of steps as the servants left for their various errands, having finally been dismissed by Button and his men. He was still at the table, writing up his notes. Henry waited, trying not to appear too eager or anxious. Boehme went on, 'The man was on sticks, a lean faced man with a thin moustache and long curly hair. English, he seemed to me. Rude man, he walked off with a strange smile, making that noise. And I, I know how to behave in a hotel. I didn't shout, but I did have a mind to complain.'

'And what did the man do?' Henry's mind was racing fast. Boehme could only mean Bancroft, the magician, whom Henry had seen the night before as well. Clearly, he had learnt to walk well on stilts, after all his studies of hypnosis and illusion. A lean faced man with a moustache and atrocious manners, that could only mean Bancroft. 'He walked away, and then looked into the windows to my left. I just told him to be careful before I shut my window. I didn't want to catch a cold, even before my night at the graveyard.'

Henry smiled thinly, and extended his hand toward the other man. Boehme's hand engulfed his in a firm, hard grip. Henry felt relief and excitement. After several hours, at the end of a long, frustrating day, there seemed to be a lead. Late at night, Bancroft had been walking on stilts—Henry had seen that for himself—

and quite possibly, he was the last man to see Mark Twain at night, or even later. Henry just couldn't wait to get to Bancroft.

~

An hour passed as Henry, back in his rooms at the Byculla Club, waited for Abdul to return from the doctors' bungalow. He had taken a message from Henry to Maya. He would not be back to have dinner with the Clemenses that evening. 'Don't give Maya memsahib the message in front of them,' Henry warned, and Abdul gave him his usual long-suffering look. He really wasn't an idiot, Henry thought to himself ruefully. 'And if she asks more, tell her some urgent business came up.' Henry's face darkened, for he wouldn't tell her about his intentions of tailing Bancroft, even accosting him. 'And come back fast, we need to...'

Abdul looked at him expectantly, but Henry paused, pursed his lips. 'I will tell you when you are back.'

He looked toward his desk, where his prized Colt Bisley lay in the locked second drawer. A brand-new model, with its five-inch barrel, that he had bought in London. Henry didn't want to use it, especially on Bancroft and he hoped the other man wouldn't make it difficult for him. Freddie Bancroft had quite a reputation, one that preceded him. He had first trained as a dentist and then worked as an insurance agent in Philadelphia before he had set out to make a magician of himself. It was an ambitious hope, and Bancroft could be impatient. The time when the

New York papers had reported unfavourably about his show, when his illusions had not worked, and his card tricks had bored much of the audience, Bancroft had thrown a tantrum, throwing his magician's props on the seated audience. He had then burst into the offices of the *New York Journal*. He had accosted the editor on the late evening shift, accusing him, and the paper, of favouring the other magician Alexander Hermann, and insisted that the next day the office itself would vanish into thin air.

A portion of the office was indeed found ablaze early the next morning, but Bancroft had an alibi. There were many people who had seen him on the return train to Philadelphia. And the culprits were found to be two workers who were part of the union of newspaper workers. But Bancroft later bragged about it, that he could indeed hypnotize people to do his bidding.

He had made sure people in Bombay knew about this too, and he was determined to stage his own show at the Rippon Theatre on Grant Road. Bancroft had dropped flyers all over, had demanded advertising space for himself in the *Gazette*, and was also soliciting funds from the likes of Albert Sassoon, Shapoorji Bengalee, and the others, to build those elaborate sets he so wanted. But, of course, Henry, his fellow countryman, hadn't been of much help, nor had he pulled his weight with the customs people.

Henry sighed. He was letting his jealousy get to his head. Bancroft must have added to his skills in the months he was in Bombay. For he had impressed Maya, and in a far shorter period of time, Mark Twain too, it would appear. And perhaps, Henry thought, Bancroft wanted Twain to write about him, an entire piece in the American papers about the magician's immense popularity in the East. And now, it would appear that Bancroft may have been the last person to actually see Mark Twain, for he must have peered into his room, as he had Boehme's, and it was likely, he did know a thing or two.

Henry looked at his notes on the table, and realized with some consternation that he had forgotten a meeting. With a man he disliked as much as he did Bancroft, but when business mattered, Henry knew he had to be quite the professional. Arthur Pease, the tireless campaigner against opium, the vices of drinking, and prostitution, had expressed an interest in the electric fans. They were needed, Pease had said, for the big meetings and assemblies he called every once in a while, in the Parsi meeting halls, and the town hall, and especially at the Reformatory Institute that was a particular favourite of his, for he always found a willing and suppliant audience here.

An hour later, Henry felt there was little point waiting for Abdul in his study. The longer he was on his own, the more he would fret over Twain and think sullenly about Bancroft. So Henry resolutely set off first for the police headquarters, and then to meet with Arthur Pease in Khetwadi, that lay a bit after Crawford Market. This was where Pease lived in a small bungalow, part of which doubled up as a healing centre for addicts.

Henry left a note for Abdul by the table near the hat stand, next to the silver embossed tray that usually held the keys, messages, and letters. *Come to...*, and he wrote the address. *House next to Daji clinic. Crawford Market. Come as soon as you see this.*

He called for a carriage, from the many standing aimlessly by the club. The coachman, a Pathan judging from his build and turban, saluted smartly as he jumped down from his seat to hold the door open. 'The police station first,' Henry said in a low voice, 'and then someplace else. I will tell you later. You do have the time, I hope?'

'Good, sahib, very good,' the coachman said, nodding to his helper who would ride with him. The boy resting at the foot of the statue that everyone called the Standing Parsi, came running up, and the carriage shook momentarily as he jumped up behind. 'Go fast, all right?' Henry said, looking through the window.

The man nodded, gently tapping the pony, a young, spirited brown animal, with his whip, and then, looking over his shoulder said, 'They are sending a lot of the police toward Sewree and Parel, the workers are angry. They really anticipate trouble, and they are stopping us from going there.'

~

At the police headquarters, Henry caught sight of Button, looking even more haggard as he talked to two policemen in the shaded corridor. He moved away as he noticed Henry and the two men walked toward each other. A patchy late sun poured in from the high glazed windows, and it was cool inside the grey-stone building. Designed in the Indo-Saracenic style that borrowed elements from the country's history—with minarets, filigreed windows, and domes—the building had been recently refurbished to make it a spanking new headquarters for the city's police. Though parts of it were still being renovated and improved on, the police had begun moving in since the year began. It was clear the city's policemen were proud of this new building.

'There's still no news, I am afraid,' Button said, apologetically, and Henry noticed the dark shadows under his eyes. He felt sorry for the man. He decided he wouldn't tell him yet what he intended to do about Bancroft. He felt his waistband where the Colt lay snugly. 'But we have been questioning the fisherfolk, the seamen at the ports, and even the boys at the docks, and by the seafront. There's been nothing. No report of any...,' Button lowered his voice before finishing, 'accident.'

Henry felt himself tremble. This was just what he didn't want to think about, but of course one had to consider every possibility. He thought about Mark Twain the last time he saw him, in the carriage as they rode back home. He had listened attentively to Maya, had laughed heartily at her prank, and hadn't looked upset or disturbed in any way. Olivia had not expressed any worry either. 'Do you think...?' He wasn't aware that his voice shook as he spoke to Button. The other man took his time, and his eyes were calm and direct as they rested on Henry.

'We just have to be open to all possibilities. It's not a safe time to be in the city. Or rather a city like this can never be truly safe.' Button thought over what he had just said, rubbed his chin, and then added. 'We are trying our best. No one saw him, that's the most surprising thing.' His voice dwindled away, and he was almost speaking to himself, as he went on, 'You would think a lot of people would have seen him, though it was early in the morning.'

And Maya, Henry remembered, had been doubtful about this. He couldn't well have climbed out of the window, nor walked out on a pair of stilts. It made finding Bancroft even more urgent. Henry smiled thinly, trying on his own part to reassure Button. He felt a sense of futility but was determined not to give in to that. There was something about Twain, he thought; that curiosity in him, the glint in his eyes, and the funny, droopy moustache. Henry couldn't imagine him coming to any harm. Any great harm, he added to himself, darkly.

IX

Unpleasant Meetings are Rarely Avoidable

'Did you want to meet Superintendent Vincent?' Inspector Button asked. Some of his earlier bravado had gone, Henry realized. The strain of recent events had evidently gotten to him.

'I am sure he has much to do,' said Henry, wanting to be on his way, 'I just wanted an update.' Arthur Pease could be crusty if kept waiting too long. Then almost as if he had read his thoughts, Button spoke up, 'We are dealing with the situation with the utmost urgency. We have stopped allowing any boats out. No sight-seeing boats, or sailing yachts to Elephanta, and beyond. But there was Pease's...' Button stopped as he saw Henry's expression change suddenly. 'Yes, an excursion that he had taken permission for some days ago. A boat outing with some people. The people in his healing centre. A raggedly lot, he said he wanted an outing for them. And that was to be the last excursion boat out for some days now, till the governor gives permission.'

'Thank you for telling me this,' Henry said. 'I need to send my reports too…' His voice died away, as he let the despair sink in. He had to write to Mark Twain's manager, Robert Smythe, who was expected to join the Clemenses in a few days, having finally wrapped up some business that had delayed him in Melbourne. Henry wondered if he could keep the news of Twain's disappearance under wraps for a day or so; after all, it had been just a few hours. Henry frowned, an absent look on his face as he did a quick calculation. 'Twelve hours, at the most,' he muttered, knowing it felt longer, and that he had been on his feet since then. But he couldn't let up, not right away. Pease first, and the telegram to Smythe could wait. Henry tipped his hat and Button clicked his heels smartly to indicate their meeting was over.

The carriage was waiting patiently for him. The helper was feeding the horse some thin straggly looking carrots, and the coachman sat on his haunches on the patchy ground, smacking tobacco onto his palms and gazing into the distance. Henry wondered if it had some opium mixed into it, but this wasn't the time to ask. 'It's getting dark, sahib,' the man said getting to his feet. He rubbed his palms on his stained loose kurta and patted his turban. 'Never mind,' Henry said. 'But there's still someone I have to meet. Khetwadi.'

They rode up Cruikshank Road, and then took the right to Esplanade Cross Road. He passed the high school and the Gokaldas hospital to the right. The palm trees rose in the darkening evening sky like sentinels, the lamplighters were out in their one-horse carriages, the temple bells sounded, and he could see the spire of the Babulnath temple through a gap in the trees. From someone's house, there came the faint strains of a man singing. Henry got off just as the road took a turn into the narrow Khetwadi lane. This part was always congested with carts and wagons, and a carriage would only hold things up. He dropped some coins into the Pathan coachman's hands, patted the horse and walked fast toward a house that he knew stood a bit away from the main road.

Arthur Pease stood, hands in his coat pocket, nervously looking down the road. He was already frowning as the carriage halted in the distance, and he saw Henry emerge through a small crowd of people. Pease leaned against a rickety wooden gate; a cat hunched on the wall right by him. Both looked on, watchful and sullen. The single-storied house that also housed his healing centre for opium addicts was at the end of the gravelled path. It was masked in grey, with only a faint light flickering through a window. A neem tree gave off a slight bittersweet smell, its branches shook and rustled, and Henry caught the cheeping of starlings nestling in it.

'Mr Pease,' he said, taking off his hat, and inclining his head. 'I remembered our meeting.' The cat mewed and glared at Henry before it jumped down the wall and disappeared in the bushes.

'Meeting?' The other man looked around, as if Henry had spoken to the cat, then frowned again. He peered at Henry as if he had suddenly become short-sighted. 'Meeting, oh yes,' he rubbed his hands on his trousers, fiddled with the gate, but he did not pull aside the latch, nor did he invite Henry in. 'I forgot about that,' he said, laughing jerkily, as Henry looked at him non-plussed.

Then Pease crossed his arms about himself, 'Well, I did forget, too many things on my mind. This city is going to the dogs. In every way.' He glowered, leaned on the gate, and said again, his nasal twang more pronounced than before. 'Going to the rats, I should say. With all the problems it has. I believe there's a plague outbreak in some quarters. Rumours, I admit, and the government is saying nothing yet. Not yet, no sirree, it's got too much on its hands.' Pease laughed darkly, and the gate shook with his weight on it, 'And all this while I have been asking them to take the problems a little more seriously. Bad habits make for bad living conditions, and then bad diseases take over. Whatever this illness is, plague or anything else,' he paused to look at Henry very intently, 'it will really get big in a few months' time. Mark my words.'

Henry felt a shiver down his spine. Was Pease being prescient in an evil, virulent way? 'Maybe the electric fans will help. They will certainly help in the near future,' he said, tentatively. He was a man of business, and this was a chance to wrap things up quickly. One meeting done, a deal closed, and he could return to the more urgent matter on hand. At the thought of Mark Twain, now gone missing, he felt cold sweat on his forehead, a sudden clamminess in his hands, and Pease's words seemed fainter amidst the other noises that surrounded him. People's voices rose and fell around, cymbals sounded from one house, there was that restless moving in the branches, and Henry caught a flash of something moving swiftly and the cat's baleful eyes were once again on him.

'Fans, eh? Oh yes, fans,' said Pease. 'We were to have a meeting...'

'Yes,' said Henry puzzled. He had met Pease before, and he had been brusque and crusty all times, but not frazzled, even vague like this.

'Here, look now,' said Pease, coming up. 'We sure can have a meeting. I have been meaning to have a meeting with you.'

Henry put his hand in his pocket and felt the rough touch of his gun against his arm, and then found the paper he was looking for. 'I have a pamphlet here,' he unfolded it, cringing at his own perspiring fingers as he held out the four-page newsletter that detailed how the new fans made by the Crocker-Wheeler company worked. 'These are,' he cleared his throat, and began enthusiastically, 'different and much improved from the older fans. And they certainly won't need one of those punkah-wallahs to operate them. The blades are covered with the steel net, and so there is no chance of their causing damage and harm. And the wiring too is concealed in a most clever way.'

He stopped, for Pease was looking at him, his lips narrowed, his eyes shrewish and unblinking. Henry felt that Pease considered him a particularly repulsive species of humankind, and that, at this moment, he didn't particularly care much about fans, electrical or otherwise.

'You did want a meeting about the fans?' Henry said then, looking him squarely in the face. 'In that case, shouldn't we move inside? I would like to also tell you about a possible demonstration. A fan, Mr Pease, or should I say, Reverend Pease, will be a decided advantage when you speak before the public. It can make things comfortable, for you and your audience. No one will perspire or want to leave early.'

Pease had shuffled closer, his hands in his pockets, and Henry took in a strange medicinal smell. Something that was bitter and sickly sweet at the same time. Pease took out a handkerchief, wiped his hands, and placed them back in his pocket. 'I did intend to give a lecture, to give you a proper lecture, Mr Baker, and I hope you will be all ears too.' He stood looking up at the taller man, who flushed red in anger, at the presumption in Pease's tone and how he had cut him short mid-flow.

'May we go in then?' Henry asked. He felt cold as things got darker, and in the light of a nearby streetlamp, Pease's face looked a spectral yellow.

'No,' the reply was quick, abrupt and panicky. 'No. You will not step inside my precincts.'

'I did come here for a meeting,' Henry said tersely.

'No meeting, not today,' said Pease lifting his hands. It looked as if he would push Henry aside before he paused. Henry noticed a swift cunning look pass over the man's face. 'Your conduct has been most abominable. You, Mr Baker, have no sense of morals. And you know what I am talking about. And that woman…' His face turned red, and he wiped his mouth on his sleeve, before he began again. 'Miss Barton,' he stepped back, a furious look in his eyes. 'Miss Barton…' he stressed the word, 'do you know the scandal you both are responsible for? Dressing like a man at that very important party, and then the two of you…'

He did not finish, for Henry grabbed him by the collar and pulled him toward himself. 'What was that you said again?'

Pease's hat fell off, and the light fell purple and grey on his thinning strands of hair. Henry saw his nostrils narrow, and then flare, and the rheumy mist gather in his eyes. 'Let me go. Let me go,' Pease hissed.

'What did you just say?' Henry let him go suddenly and the other man tottered on his feet. On the other side of the road, a window had opened on an upstairs floor, and Henry knew a crowd could gather all too soon. 'You are a nasty conniving devil. I fail to see how you call yourself a man of god, since all you see is evil everywhere.'

'Ha,' said Pease, a smug look on his face. 'You got it. That is precisely why I am one. Because I see…'

Henry balled his hand into a fist, 'If I hear you say a word more about Miss Barton, I will…' He took a step back, and forced himself to stay calm, 'Consider this a warning.' Pease raised his hand to his throat, and then very deliberately, shrieked, a thin, shrill sound, almost like a bleat. 'You have threatened and abused me. I will take the matter up, and will report you.'

'Sure, you must, and I will too,' said Henry sneeringly.

'And, I have witnesses,' said Pease looking across the road at the open window. No one appeared, but through the bars, the light of a lamp now showed and flickered. It was a grey-walled house, a portico on its first floor, with green doors, and columns supporting a blue painted veranda. Through the open window, they heard an accordion and the thump of drums. 'Those actors,' Pease said, rubbing his throat. 'Veritable scums on earth. They pretend not to hear.'

Henry laughed, scornful and abrupt, 'Your audience too has deserted you.' He brushed his hair back again. 'This has indeed been a nice meeting. You produce your witnesses, and I will see you in court.'

Pease looked to make another remark, his lips curling. He stopped, when he saw the expression on Henry's face. 'I mean it,' Henry said. 'And maybe they will have my fans in the courtroom. That will be the perfect irony.' He looked at him determinedly, his breathing fast, for no matter what he felt about Maya, how much she intrigued him, and remained mysterious, he would always defend her.

X

Encounters at the Magician's Place

Henry was still breathing hard as he walked back down the way he had come. Carriages slowed down as they neared, hoping he would avail them. But Henry walked on, lost in thought and in fury. He had never been so angry before in his life, not in Chicago, not in Yale, nor in his years in London, or during his travels eastward.

The road sloped and zigzagged in places, as he headed toward Breach Candy Road. Bancroft, the eccentric that he was, lived off a lane somewhere close to the graveyards, the Muslim and the Christian burial grounds that lay adjacent to each other. A place many avoided at this time, but Henry didn't really care. He was still indignant, and mortified, at how his meeting had gone. He didn't regret his behaviour one bit, but as the breeze lifted and he smelt the sea salt in the air, there were some things about the meeting that struck him as distinctly odd.

Pease had not even called him in. In fact, he had

hung onto that gate, as if afraid that he, Henry, would barge his way in. And there was his frazzled appearance. Pease was a man who liked to impress others. His clothes, though not Oxford Street tailored, were always practical, no nonsense and dour. He took himself seriously. But he had been perspiring, there was his crumpled shirt, and the muddiness on his trousers, and boots. Henry stopped short abruptly. He was at a part of the road where a gap between houses showed up the sea, grey and purple in the half-darkness, framed by thick mango trees and beyond that the taller palm trees. He heard the slow-moving rumble of the sea, the rhythmic swishing of the trees, and felt mesmerized. Pease, he remembered, had been out. Button had mentioned he had received special permission to be out with his patients to sea. He wondered if this was a usual practice with Pease, and the people in his care at the healing centre.

He heard quick running footsteps behind him and turned quickly, his hand feeling for his gun. The next moment, he laughed and felt relief unclamp his muscles.

'You walking too fast, Mr Baker,' Abdul said as he came running up. 'Too fast,' he repeated, panting, trying to control his breath.

'Yes, but we must,' said Henry, as Abdul fell in step beside him. 'It gets dark suddenly, and then the houses are difficult to make out. You aren't afraid, are you?' Henry asked, as the trees swished lower in the breeze, their branches trailing the walls, making an odd whistling noise.

'No, never,' said Abdul. There were few people on the street at this hour. Not too far away, they could hear the jiggle of the occasional carriage going past, the bells ringing loud, and in unison in a nearby temple, a drumming noise from a house they passed, for this city, as Henry had learnt, liked its music, and then just as suddenly, things would go quiet.

Bancroft's house was behind a grey bricked wall, cracked in places, where a jasmine creeper crept through like a sinister wild creature. The wall reached up to his shoulder, and Henry looking over it, whispered, 'We need to climb over this.'

The old bricks shook as Abdul gave him a leg-up, and Henry heaved himself over the wall. Abdul, lighter and smaller on his feet followed a minute or so later. A quick jump, a short pause as they squatted on the crumbling wall and then the soft thud as they landed together on the wet damp earth on the other side. It was a wild untended garden, with grass growing tall in places, and sudden dips in the ground that tripped them up as they advanced gingerly, picking their way through the untidy and unkempt bushes, the thorns at times vicious on their unguarded faces and arms.

'You never told me what Maya memsahib said,' Henry whispered, irritably. He had hoped Abdul would speak about it, rather than his having to broach the matter.

'Yes, sir,' Abdul stopped short, peering over a branch to look ahead. A wide portico with empty long benches was visible, with a lounge chair at the far end, next to some potted plants.

'She said...' Abdul hesitated, and then the words came out in a rush. 'She said that was fine, and that she would be out too, at night. And that in turn, you were not to worry.'

Henry looked at him quickly and looked away again. He didn't know what to think. He had to concentrate on the present. The house had a low thatched roof, and its louvered windows were shuttered. A thick peepul tree hovered over the front of the house, and on the right some way off, was a shady grove, some mango trees again, and the fragrant coral jasmine tree, its white-orange flowers that looked purple in the faint light falling on it. The light came from a fire burning low, at one side of the building hidden by a small parapet. Wisps of smoke rose and were swept away in the branches of the looming trees. Henry nudged Abdul and gestured in the smoke's direction with his fingers. They were to approach from different directions, and he pressed his finger to his lips. Abdul nodded, he understood they had to be absolutely quiet.

Henry heard voices clearly as he moved in slowly. Voices that were faint, reedy, and sometimes excitable. There were four, or at least three of them. 'How long must we wait, Balram?' Henry heard someone ask in a thin tired voice.

'Till that magician comes,' came the answer in a rough, hoarse, equally tired voice. 'We have to teach him a lesson. Coming in the way, just when...'

He broke off, and a third voice spoke up, 'So what do we do with him? Kill him?' This was a voice that sounded younger and had a lilt in it. Then Henry heard a shriek; evidently, he had been cuffed on the ear by the second man. 'No, you idiot. Just...use what you have. You do have it, yes?'

'Yes,' said the man, sounding sullen, 'here. I hope he doesn't have a gun.'

'That is why we wait, and catch him. I can't think why Sardar sent you. He has done so much, our jobs, our homes, the money we take home, everything is because of him. Do you have any...?'

His voice had broken off, and Henry hastened to move in quickly, unable to contain his curiosity. The next moment, he heard a sharp loud crack and stopped short, gasping involuntarily. He had stepped on a twig. He froze, hand resting on a branch, leg poised foolishly mid-air, and cursed himself silently for his clumsiness. A hush descended, the men fell quiet, and nothing moved. Henry heard the rough stamping sound of feet erasing the fire. 'Maybe he's here already,' the man with the thin voice whispered, his voice sibilant in the darkness.

Henry stepped to his left, and as he let go the branch, it creaked agonizingly. He waited, hoping his eyes would soon get used to the darkness. The fire had been stamped out, stray embers rose and quickly died away. It was a night with a thin moon, and all he could make out were the flashing lights of fireflies buzzing several feet away. As he peered, narrowing his eyes, he felt something steely and sharp against his waist.

'Quiet, not a sound.' Henry made to look to his

right, but felt a hard fist ram into his face. A cold wind wheezed past him with the force of the blow, and his elbow brushed against rough cotton as he was jerked forward. He heard a soft jangle, something metallic striking a branch, and the voice behind him was raspy and broken as he alerted the others.

'He was listening. Sahadev, I found him, this white man. The *gora* was listening to everything.' Henry was pushed forward roughly. He stumbled, hating his helplessness for he couldn't see a thing. He was yanked up by the shoulder, and he heard the click of a match, the flash of light, the smell of phosphorus, and he was looking into the sharp, intense eyes of a man with a thick moustache and an untidily tied turban somewhat askew on his head.

'Who sent you?' Henry flinched, as the man shouted the words at him.

'Keep your voice low, Sahadev,' said the man with the raspy voice Henry had heard earlier. 'We don't want attention.'

'Who are you?' he said, stepping into the faint flickering light. Henry, thinking fast, realized this was the one called Balram he had heard earlier. 'Ah, a friend of this magic-man. We thought he didn't have any friends.'

A hand yanked him by the collar, and he was looking straight at the unblinking dark eyes of a square-faced man, who spoke in the hoarse voice Henry knew well now. 'You cannot be the police,' he said, and his face stretched into a thin cruel smile. 'They aren't as stupid as you seem to be. You heard us, and you must pretend you have never seen us. The Sardar's men are everywhere. Everywhere in this city.' He stepped closer, and Henry held his breath, forcing himself to lock eyes with the other man.

His head was jerked back, and before he could let out a yelp of surprise, he felt the cloth, hard and painful against his mouth. He heard himself make soft, guttural noises, before he was pushed to the rough grassy earth on his knees, his hands pulled back and bound with twine. The jute strings were harsh against his skin, and a throbbing pain flashed across his wrists, and spread over him. He felt a hand slam against his back, and he fell, sprawling ignominiously to the ground, furious and also afraid.

'Not a word, and don't get up, understand?' said the raspy voiced man, kneeling on the grass, his voice hot against Henry's cheek. 'We are sparing your life because Sardar doesn't want lives taken. He wants to teach all of you a lesson. Putting him in jail won't stop him, like you thought.'

The men surrounded him, as Henry lay supine on the ground, the grass tickling his face. He smelt the leather on their feet, and the smoky dust still lingered from the fire. The man with the lilting voice spoke up, 'Now the American. We don't really know if he has the gold...'

'Shh...,' came the third voice, the one who had been quieter than the rest, 'don't speak too much. And remember, he has to pay for the insulting things he has done too.'

'There are three of us,' said the first man, sounding impatient. 'Can we take him on?'

'Three against one? You have to ask this?' and this time Balram sounded angry. 'No wonder the British could rule over us. We are three, and he is one. This one on the ground can't do anything.'

There was a silence, they moved around restless, stamping on the grass, breathing heavily. 'And the gold, the jewels, Sardar said, was to be brought back to him. We must force the magic man to give it to us. He must have it. And no killing, all right. Just the threat. He must not insult our gods, enter our temples and graveyards. Never again.'

Someone flopped down on the ground just beside Henry, and yawned. 'I am hungry. The kitchen, let's break in and get something?'

But the man with the raspy voice had still not finished. 'Remember the Sardar's orders. He has not told us anything about that.'

The other man—was his name Sahadev? Henry wondered—sulked, 'Well, he should take care of our hunger too.'

'Listen,' said the third man, 'it is just a matter of some more time.' He stopped, and Henry heard the rustling around him momentarily stop. He sensed that whoever had just spoken had raised his hand, and was asking for silence, 'Can you hear something?'

The insects buzzed, the crickets called, the frogs croaked, somewhere there was the slow bending of twigs, and in all this came the distinct sound of steps advancing decisively down the driveway, the thwack of stick hitting tree, and then a piercing whistle. 'The police,' said the man on the ground, startled. The grass moved roughly against Henry's face, as the man got to his feet hurriedly, and only Henry noticed the sharp metallic object that fell from his pocket and dropped with a soft hush on the grass close by him. Henry buried his face in the grass, feeling a quiet shuddering relief that the knife hadn't grazed him in any way.

The other two men stood completely still, listening intently. 'Anybody there?' The shout that came was loud, clear, and confident. Henry held his breath, unable to believe the evidence of his ears. It was Abdul, doing a very good impersonation of a policeman. The slapping of feet, a thump in between, the whistle again, and then the perfect impression of a watchman's voice. Boorish and brooking no nonsense. 'Anyone there?'

Henry rolled over, for the grass felt scratchy and abrasive against his face. The three men remained utterly still, and he could hear their ragged breathing, the way one of them pulled at his long shirt sleeves betrayed his nervousness. Henry remembered the knife he had seen, falling out of the other man's pocket, and knew he had to get it. The darkness made things difficult. The man nearest him dragged his feet on the grass, making a rustling noise, drawing a low hiss from his companions.

'Anyone there? A message from the police, about your Sardar. Answer.'

'Balram,' said the one closest to Henry, 'we must speak up.' His voice sounded strangled, and broken.

'Wait,' said the raspy voiced one softly. He cleared his throat and spoke up loud and sharp. 'What do you have to tell us?'

There was a silence, a pause, the cheeping of the nestling birds sounded louder than before, and the grass brushed Henry on the face again. He sneezed hoarsely through the cloth binding him, and the heel of someone's shoe struck him on the shoulder in warning. His wrists chafed, and he felt the firm nudge of the toe again on his shoulder. Abdul's voice came again, 'I hear you. First tell me your Sardar's name.'

'Tuka,' came the response in a reedy tone. ' What does he say now?'

'He needs you to go to the police station,' said Abdul, thumping his stick on a tree trunk, and giving another sharp whistle. There was a jerking in the branches, and the sparrows cheeped in indignation, a couple of crows broke past the branches, cawing boisterously. 'He needs you to go right away. To speak of his innocence before the superintendent. Else…'

'Else?' the man's voice sounded more strangled than before. 'Else what, sahib?'

Henry felt some of the tension leave him. He wanted to laugh, but the cloth felt rough over his mouth and skin. He moaned, and one of them kicked him savagely. 'Else he will be hanged.' Abdul paused and then said slowly, 'Midnight.'

The thin-voiced man shrieked, 'Midnight!'

'Midnight,' came Abdul's voice, clearer and sharper than Henry had heard it before. 'What kind of men are you? I came from the thana for your Sardar said he had witnesses. Men who would give their lives for him, and speak for him. Where have they all gone?'

'We must go,' one of them spoke up.

'No, wait,' said the raspy voiced Balram, more cautious and watchful than the others. 'We do not want trouble for ourselves,' he said in a low voice to the others. 'Why would the police come with Sardar's message? Think fast.'

He cleared his voice, and said again, 'Who are you?'

'You don't believe me,' Abdul sounded surprised. He thwacked the tree trunk again, once, twice, and said, 'When the time comes, and one of our own is threatened, should we not stick together? He will be hanged for murder, and you will have his blood on your hands.'

'We have to go,' said the man quietly, looking at his two companions.

'What do we do with this one?' asked the second one, looking down at Henry, nudging him with his shoe again. 'Go fast,' Abdul's voice came again, 'and maybe you will get a share of the gold.' He paused, and then his voice came sharp and clear in the darkness, 'Go, and you may still save a man's life. A man who says he's innocent.'

Henry made a harsh gargling sound; he felt the cramps in his leg. He was not prepared for the stick that came down on him, a hard thwack on his shoulder, and as he rolled over, wriggling in desperation and pain, he heard the thudding of feet as the men scampered away, through the rough grass, in a direction different from where Abdul had shouted from. He waited till the sounds had died away, and he heard their faint shouts as they scaled the wall, and as they slipped a few times. He waited a few moments and then struggled to sit up, feeling foolish and sorry for himself. His shoulder hurt where the stick had struck him. He rubbed it against the grass, but that gave little comfort. He heard running steps again, and then a voice called out, low and urgent. 'Sahib, say something, where are you?'

Henry groaned. He kicked the grass with his feet and moaned again. His throat was dry and raspy with the effort. Then he saw a flash of light, and Abdul's face appeared, shimmering in red and yellow. He smiled, and Henry had no time to think how spectral that made Abdul look, for he was running toward him fast, stepping into a puddle, so a speck of water caught Henry in the eye. Then Abdul was near him, lifting him by the arms, and feeling for the cloth tied tightly around his mouth.

He breathed in big gulps of air as he felt the cloth give way, and then Abdul snipped off the cord around his wrists with the small knife he always carried. Henry looked up at the sky, staring at the stars as if seeing them for the first time, and only then did he manage a thank you. He wanted to say more, that Abdul had pulled off a good impersonation of a constable, but his lips tasted metallic and dry, and his arm throbbed terribly. The pain, now that he was untied, had increased manifold.

'We must go, sahib. The magic man is not at home, not anywhere here.'

'Yes,' he whispered, then he tried to get up and his legs felt wobbly. He felt something hard in the grass, and as he bent down to retrieve the knife, a pain shot through his shoulder, and he fell over again. Abdul placed a hand around his waist, and helped him to his feet. 'It's my shoulder,' Henry whispered, gasping in pain.

'Let's go, sahib,' Abdul said softly, 'we will take it slow.'

Their eyes now well accustomed to the darkness, they made out the greying trunks of trees, the gravel pathway, and the overhead branches, above which thick white clouds thudded past. 'What was all that about?' he whispered hoarsely. 'How did you…?'

'I heard them talk as I hid,' Abdul said, 'and made up things as I went along.' Then he stopped so abruptly that Henry who held onto his hand for support lurched and would have toppled over again, had Abdul not grabbed him in time. 'Am sorry, sahib, am sorry. I was near that outhouse,' he pointed to his right, and Henry saw in the half-darkness a brown-walled shed, with a door standing askew. 'I hid there for a bit, and that's where I found the stick. It scared them off. But, sahib, look what I found too…'

They had stopped under the jasmine tree, the fragrance of its flowers redolent around them, and Abdul pulled out something from his pocket. Henry leaned closer to look, and saw a circular paper-wrapped object. He breathed in a distinct sickly-sweet smell, and with his finger, felt for himself the gluey, gummy substance that crackled through the paper. 'Opium,' he said, and Abdul nodded. Henry's eyes widened, he tried to sniff it again, but a piercing pain shot through his right shoulder, making him wince. 'Opium,' he said through his pain, 'I wonder what Bancroft does with it.'

Abdul found them a carriage once they were out on the road, and Henry sank into the cushions, and finally managed a smile. 'That was really smart acting, Abdul. Maya memsahib would indeed be very impressed.'

XI

Climbing into Hotels and Walking on Water

Maya came to see him the next morning. Henry, fretting and in considerable pain, heard her through the netted door. Behind this was the small balcony, filled with flowering plants he had only just learnt to name: hydrangeas, dahlias, and the sweetly bitter smelling marigold flowers. She tossed her hat neatly onto the table, and Henry wincing with some exaggerated pain, lifted himself to sit with his back against the headboard. She shook her head, as if she anticipated his question.

'The police are out on the streets in force. They have been there for days now, but I've seen increased numbers outside Watson's, and along Queen's Road.' She busied herself for a moment more as she brought the cane chair closer to his bed. This time her blue-green eyes met his, he read the concern in them, and he did not want her to look away. Her smile eased his pain somewhat before his mind returned to the immediate, the prosaic, and the worrying.

'I didn't hear Abdul let you in,' he said at last, knowing Mark Twain hadn't reappeared miraculously the previous night. Maya wouldn't havc looked so pale then, and her eyes would have had joy mixed with concern. For a moment, he had been filled with a wild hope. That Twain had returned on his own from a long walk, as if this were something he did as a daily habit, a matter of routine. Venturing out into new, strange cities entirely on his own. Maya shook her head imperceptibly, sadly, as if she guessed his thoughts, and Henry sighed too, in pain and frustration.

She must have come on her bicycle, for he noted the pair of red divided skirts she wore and the creamy plain shirt which did little to dispel the fatigue on her face. But he felt a strange, quiet happiness, the pain too seemed to ebb, and he knew it was the mere sight of her that made things this way. All he wanted to do then was to lie back, close his eyes, and listen to her soft voice fall over him in waves.

'You seem to have been in a battle of sorts,' she said She was holding his bruised hand, her fingers tremulous on his own. He knew his shirt was pulled away from his bandaged shoulder, and there were scratches on his face where the grass had cut him. His shirt was unbuttoned almost to the waist, and as he struggled to pull it together, she waved a hand impatiently. 'Can Abdul get me a cup of tea?' she said looking toward the door again. 'I didn't see him as I came up the stairs.' She yawned then, a genteel sound, that made Henry smile.

'Everything's been such a floorer,' he said slowly. 'And you,' he looked at her appraisingly, raising an eyebrow, 'look jammy, as always, but seems you had a bad night too.'

They heard running footsteps then, and Abdul looked in through the netted door. 'Come on in, Abdul,' Henry said, reaching for the glass of water near him. He grimaced as he turned, and Maya handed it to him, still looking at Abdul as he emerged into clearer view. He smiled at Maya, salaaming her smartly, then looked at them expectantly, his eyes moving between them. 'Well, Abdul,' Henry said, 'what is it?'

'At the police station, sahib,' he began, and paused, looking at Maya, 'As you may not know, madam, we were at...'

'No need to get so chatty, Abdul,' Henry snapped, impatient and irritated. He wanted to tell Maya himself, and as he well knew, Abdul's stories could get long-winded. 'Just tell me what happened there?' he asked, for he had sent Abdul on a special errand. It was related to events of the night before, but he wanted to tell her all the details himself, especially the bits about the opium being found in Bancroft's outhouse.

'Big crowds there, sahib, madam,' Abdul said, his head nodding at them both. 'I tried to get in, but two constables roughed me up. See,' he pointed to mud brown stains on his loose shirt. 'They pushed me, so I fell right near a cake of horse dung, and they all started laughing. But the police stopped that at least, even shooing the crowds away.'

Henry and Maya exchanged quick looks. Abdul looked very sorry for himself. 'There must be trouble at the mills,' she said, looking with sympathy at Abdul, 'with the arrest of the Sardar, Tuka, isn't that his name?' Abdul nodded, pleased to be part of this conversation. 'They will go on strike,' Maya went on, 'Though I don't think many workers would want that too, and so near the Shiva festival at...'

'Babulnath, memsahib,' Abdul completed for her. 'And there will be theatre there too. The different drama companies will perform.' The words rushed out of him, and Henry didn't like his loquacity one bit. He struggled to hold onto his composure and rubbed his shoulder where it hurt. 'Er, Abdul, just tell us what happened. Maya memsahib wanted some tea, please, and don't put in too much basil, as in the morning.'

'No, it's all right. Just let him tell us everything in detail,' Maya smiled indulgently at Henry, in the way she did when contradicting him. 'Why were there so many people at the police station? And what were the police doing too?'

'Memsahib, yes, lots to say, and lots to see,' he began again. 'I heard from someone there about a break-in at the Sardar's house. The people were protesting about that. That the Sardar was in jail for a murder he didn't commit, and the police was trying to plant evidence by breaking into his house. At the chawl where he stayed. Opium packets or something. His wife,' Abdul paused before he explained, 'the one not dead, the first wife, had got quite a few men from the chawl, and they were raising slogans.'

Abdul's arm shot up in the air, as he shouted the words he had heard, 'Hai, hai. Down with the police. But the police were also waiting for some experts from Calcutta. They were coming by train. Some men who can do their own kind of magic. Yes, believe me, sahib'—as he caught Henry rolling his eyes—, 'They study these lines and marks on the fingers, and can tell you if you did something bad.' He looked at his palms, held them out for their general inspection, and his voice wavered and fell away, 'Not like the palmists. But these people are experts in their own way, and their train was late. It was held up because of some landslide on the Bhor Ghat track. Though I heard some people saying something about a tiger on the tracks. Very much alive, and very menacing too.'

His voice died away, and Maya spoke up then, 'So much excitement,' but her voice was dry and quiet, 'some tea then, and only a little of that basil, like your sahib said.'

'That's his new concoction,' Henry explained to Maya as Abdul left, looking a bit downcast, for his tiger story hadn't unnerved them enough, 'Holy basil with all its medicinal properties. He just overdid it in the morning, and I felt everything in me had turned into one withered old log.'

Maya laughed in spite of herself, but once they were alone, with a slow whirring fan for company—the club had its own small electricity grid set up by an eccentric Parsi engineer—Maya said, 'We were worried about you. And what with Mark Twain still missing, and with everything else, this seems a city that's going mad.'

She reached out to feel his shoulder, and touched his face. His breath froze, and he stilled his body, amazed, and moved, wanting these moments to last forever. 'I should get hurt more often,' he said unsteadily, looking into her strange eyes. In the light straying in from the window, her eyes appeared to him a hazel green, and she let her hand fall away. She straightened the bit of sheet that lay crumpled between them, then her hand lay still on it, then moving away, as Abdul materialized again, holding up a tray with a steaming pot of tea and cups, and Henry began telling her in detail the events of the previous night.

He had the satisfaction of seeing Maya's eyes widen when he told her about being ambushed, the man coming up behind him in the dark, and she barely managed to thank Abdul who lingered, even after he had placed her cup on the teapoy near her. Henry told her, as Abdul toyed with the curios on a nearby shelf, of the other man's heroism, his rescue, and the act he had put on, all of which made her smile, and Abdul managed a low bow, flushing in pleasure. The smile brought a glow to her face, and Henry decided to tell her about the opium bit later, and only after he had figured out Bancroft's role in the whole matter.

'So that was where you were,' she said, putting her cup down, and Abdul finally withdrew, saying he had clothes to wash and iron. 'Abdul came to me with some kind of mysterious message last evening.'

'And you gave him one of your own if I remember.' He sat up straight, suddenly his shoulder didn't hurt as much as before, and he longed for a shave, and a bath. He saw the room as she might see it, and it looked a bit dismal, even cold. The wooden Kashmiri chairs with their colourful cushions, some with holes where sequined mirrors had fallen off, the tapestry depicting a Mughal hunt from Patiala that covered one end of the wall, the low tables, the shelf with the bric-a-brac he had collected during his travels, the portrait of the Elephanta caves, with its giant head of Shiva that his friend, the artist Edwin Lord Weeks had done, and the twin portraits of his parents that stood on a shelf next to a low divan. None of it added up to the cosy cheeriness of Maya's sitting room in the doctors' bungalow.

'Yes, I was delayed,' she began, rubbing her hands, 'Olivia was in a bad shape, and Clara, the sensible girl she is, took her in hand. They went for a ride with Charlotte in her carriage, and she took them to the night school. That was a distraction, Clara enjoyed teaching the girls...They made some lovely drawings.'

Maya was rummaging in her bag as she spoke, before she pulled out some papers. Crisp and yellowing, she unfolded them carefully, and pressed them flat against her skirt. He saw the large black print, the uneven lettering, and Maya was rubbing the ink off her fingers as she looked up. 'Guess where I found these?'

He whistled, as he leaned closer. He could see they were pamphlets from the Healing Centre, the clinic managed by Arthur Pease and a few other missionaries. The writing was insistent and urgent.

Save your souls now.

Pay us a visit.

In faith, and in the God we trust.

We promise a cure, and a better you.

The address was the very place he had been to the evening before. The meeting that had turned out to be a confrontation of sorts, with Arthur Pease making all kinds of vile allegations. Henry's face flushed with the memory, and his voice was rough as he asked her, 'What business did you have with Pease?'

She folded the papers and sat back, looking at him in a calm, unruffled way. 'I found them in Mark Twain's pocket.'

He gasped, and she smiled mockingly and in delight. 'It's time I tell you of my own adventures too.'

'I am all ears,' he said, smiling, knowing she was enjoying this moment, and was going to milk it for all it was worth. But he liked looking at her preoccupied, animated face, as she told him how she had dressed up once again. This time as an official on behalf of the American consul. 'Yes, I did. They didn't even ask questions,' she explained airily, before going on. He knew his jaw had dropped in surprise, and he pulled himself together as she went on. 'I told that man in the hotel, the manager's assistant, Mehta, who is otherwise nice and helpful that I had to go to Mark Twain's room, and check things for myself. And that there were things his daughter and wife wanted.'

Henry listened transfixed, to Maya's narration. At times, he was in an agony of suspense, and then he was plain amused at her audacity.

'Two rooms next door, there was a man playing the violin. I had the key, but still Mehta came with me up the stairs. I told him in my best officious voice that he was to leave me alone. I was here on important work, and his presence could only be construed as an interference.' Henry had to chuckle at this. 'Come to think, you would make a pretty good official.' He sobered up at Maya's mock-stern expression.

'What I was really curious about was the sewing and darning that Manuel kept talking about. You remember the accounts? How he kept looking around for a sewing machine, and then a sewing kit. And it made me very curious. Of course, I thought it had to do with Mark Twain's clothes, and that he needed them mended. But then Olivia and Clara had looked so puzzled, and Clara told you she—or was it her mother?—had stitched on some torn buttons herself. There was the matter of the diary too. I do know this, for I had pocketed his diary only the other evening.' She fluttered her fingers in the air, and Henry shook his head, rolling his eyes briefly. 'Quite a sleight of hand you pulled off.'

'It's called the art of distraction. I made you look at other things,' she said. 'That particular diary was red, with a sort of gold border, and the one left on his table was clearly another one. It was just plain black. So, I wondered about the other one, and if

Mark Twain had written anything in it. I intended to look through his room to get some ideas. It is just very strange that a man is sleeping one moment, in clothes he had worn the night before, and the next moment, he just ups and goes, with no one noticing him. With all your vagueness, Henry, I don't think you would be so oblivious.'

'Thank you,' Henry said, 'for that vote of confidence. You really have all my attention now.'

'So, I went into the room, and everything seemed just as before. I mean it was all untouched, and undisturbed, so really no one had broken in, he hadn't been threatened or anything. One does have to discount all possibilities. I checked the table, looked all over the bed, straightened the mattress, held the sheets in my hands, shook them hard, patted, and beat on them, quiet as possible. That's when I heard the jingle, something sounding clearly metallic. A part of the quilt near the feet, and just under the bedcover concealed something. I knew something had been hidden there.'

She stopped, and stared at Henry, 'Can't you guess by now?'

'Don't hold me in suspense, Maya, this really isn't one of your plays,' Henry sat up, the bedclothes slipping to the floor, but he was totally riveted by Maya's story.

'Do you remember me telling you about the photographer Dinyar, and the jewellery Casi had worn?'

'Wait,' Henry interrupted, his voice rising as he suddenly remembered. 'The men in Bancroft's house, they mentioned gold too. You mean, Casi's jewellery...'

'Yes,' she said, but her eyes had a doubtful look, 'yes, but what role would Bancroft have in all this? But never mind, let me finish first. So, the papers, as you would have read, quoted Tuka as saying she had only a little jewellery, but there is the photo of Casi, wearing quite a bit. I really must get that photo back from Dinyar. She had worn her jewellery when we had taken her to the studio. She was so excited. Poor girl. But yes,' Maya noticed Henry's impatient expression and quickened her pace, 'I managed to rip the quilt a bit, using the pen from the table. Mark Twain won't like it, and the hotel too. Then I put my hand in, and there were the jewels. Not a hoard,' she said as Henry looked on, totally speechless. 'But there was the necklace, the earrings, and some bangles. That would be enough to get one started in life.

'Here they are,' she said, dipping into her long shoulder bag, and pulling out a velvet cloth bag, tied up with thin string. The bangles jangled, glinting in the slanting light from the window, and Henry pursed his lips in a whistle. A moment later, he looked grim, as he asked Maya, 'You do understand what this means, don't you? That Manuel is the one? The killer?'

She held up her hand as he made to speak, 'No, listen, there's more to this. The danger bits, and the real excitement begins now. There was the violinist playing away in the other room, and he sounded terribly sad and loud. I didn't really hear the other sounds, of something, someone slithering and scratching. If I had looked up at the window, I might have saved myself time. Besides, it was really dark, except for the slit of light through the door. I had to feel my way around the room. But the darkness was a good thing, for whoever it was that slowly opened the window never saw me. I realized it only from the gust of wind that burst in, making the curtains move, and these papers that,' she pointed to the pamphlets still on the bed between them, 'fluttered and flapped, right where they had been dropped carelessly by the bed.'

She paused; she was suddenly breathless. 'Someone was at the window, that had a clear drop to the ground, two floors below. They have such high-ceilinged rooms at the Watson's. I was just stunned looking at that shadow against the window frame, the movement against the curtains, but I couldn't waste my time standing there. So, I reached for the wardrobe by the wall, hoping there was space for me to squeeze in, and it was just in time that I managed to shut the door on myself before I heard the sound of feet jumping lightly on the floor.

'The wardrobe had a long rectangular space for coats, put up on hangers, and when I felt around, I counted about three. That gave me some breathing space, though it did smell musty and moth-balled inside. The suits needed plenty of airing. Someone was moving around in the room, and as no one spoke, or whispered, I surmised there was just one person. And moving around lightly too, stealthily like a cat. Where I was, my back against the wooden wardrobe wall, I could still hear the violin next door. Someone played on, and quite musically too. It seemed distractingly beautiful, and sad. When I snuggled in deeper, there was a slight jangle, of the jewels in my pocket touching wood, and everything stilled.

'I could see a bit through the keyhole, and I saw whoever it was, light a match, and move the stick—yes, he had a kind of long stick with him—everywhere around, in a swirling motion. The flare lifted and dimmed as I looked on. I haven't seen Manuel, and all I could make out then was a thin, wiry body, intense burning eyes, and the long, wavering shadow his body made on the wall. Then the match was snuffed out, and we waited in the darkness, in quiet, except for the sad strains of the violin. He was playing some Mozart, and I knew for sure who he was then. The Russian, or the Serbian musician, at Mr Bengalee's party that day. The man in the room with me waited, and then as the music became louder, he hit and thumped the bed with the stick, and then again. I realized he was beating in time to the music, and every time it got louder, he brought the stick down on the bed harder. The wooden stick they keep in the room to beat away snakes and scorpions. It made the dust rise, and brought a mustiness into the room.

'It was obvious he was looking for the jewels, and when he didn't hear the jangle of metal he expected, I could hear him slapping the bed in some desperation. He had begun whimpering, panting, and sniffling. He was crawling on the floor too, I could hear the hollow drumming as he beat the wooden floor, not too hard, and then the bed too, the slithering noise he made as he crawled on the floor, and there was always the whimpering. Then we heard the shout from the next room. A harsh, booming voice, asking about the noise. The man in the room fell quiet, I couldn't see much in the darkness, and the man from the next room shouted again, "Stop that noise. Stop it at once."

'I heard the thud of a stick against the wall, a quieter voice speaking up too, all in the other room. And the man in the room with me, separated only by a wardrobe door, scurried to the window. I could hear a rattling, and he opened the window, rather hurriedly, and I saw him leave, lightly, expertly, almost as if he had been doing this all his life. The shouting continued. The man in the next room—I later found out he's the German who walks around with a camera—Boehme?—was in a real foul mood. He shouted about the hotel being the noisiest place in the city. He threw something around, it hit the wall behind me, and then the window closed, and a door too slammed somewhere. And it was all quiet again.

'I waited before emerging, and every sound appeared magnified. The man next door was still having a tantrum. Outside my window, things were dark. I could hear the sea not far away, and the doorman singing on the other side. I saw the men then under the tree, clearly, in the light of the streetlamp. Two men looking right up toward my window, and their sudden shout as they spotted something. It sent a chill down my spine. I knew then that the man who had vanished from the window was a marked man. The man next door heard it too, and while it was nothing compared to all the beating and whimpering that had gone on before, he seemed to totally lose his head this time. He opened his window, and I saw him throw out the stick. The same wooden stick kept in every room.'

Just then the phone rang. Henry and Maya glanced toward it, equally startled. It lay on a low stool just by the bed, and its prolonged trilling brought Abdul in from the balcony. He stared in fascination at the instrument, as Henry knew he would. Maya had stopped mid-flow, looking annoyed, and Henry nonchalantly reached for the telephone. Instantly a pain gripped him on the side, and he flopped back on the bed. Abdul was still goggling at the phone, and it was Maya who rose, and walked around the bed, to where the phone was. Her face was turned away as she spoke into the receiver. He heard the scratchy notes that came from the telephone. 'Vincent here. I thought Mr Baker...?' The voice at the other end broke off, clearly surprised by a woman answering the telephone.

'Yes, it is.' Maya answered, and Henry noted the heated flush on Maya's face at Vincent's initial peremptory tone. She mouthed the words, 'police' to him, and then proceeded to mime Vincent who must have had his pipe in his mouth as he spoke, and Henry bit back a sudden urge to laugh. But Maya had turned back to the phone, and her voice was serious and low when he heard her next, 'He's here all right. Is there a message I can take?'

Maya's eyes widened, as she listened. Her tone changed to a soft murmur, and Henry noted how grave she looked as she nodded, 'Yes, Mr Vincent, I'll make sure he's there.' Then she paused, bringing a firmness into her tone as she spoke next, 'This is indeed Miss Barton. Is there something he should know right away?'

Vincent's scratchy voice came once more through the receiver. He was speaking quickly, and Maya frowned. She nodded, then replaced the receiver with a quiet, 'I understand, and thank you.'

Her expression was serious as she remained looking at the phone for several seconds. Abdul threw a quick glance at Henry before he discreetly disappeared. 'It wasn't about Mark Twain. At least he said that. But he wants you to come to the police station, immediately. Do you think you can manage it?' She spoke in a low tone, trying not to give anything away, but they both knew what such a summons could mean.

'I hope it's not...'

She replied, 'I hope not too.'

He nodded, rang the bell for Abdul, and dressed in a jiffy, as Maya waited in the anteroom.

In the carriage on the way to the police station, she read out bits from the newspaper to him.

'In the strange murder of a young girl in a native lodge in Sewree, the suspect, her husband Tuka Ram, still asserts his innocence. His first wife stands by him and says he was at the mill and later with her that evening.'

'Casi, she didn't know he was already married; that

he had a first wife,' Maya said, looking up from the paper. 'She was just so excited coming to Bombay.'

Henry sat leaning to his left, to ease the pain on his right shoulder, his left elbow also had a deep, purple bruise that was now lightening. He wished he didn't look so ungainly, but Maya and Abdul had been most reassuring. 'Sahib, you will soon be fit like a soldier,' Abdul had said, as he had folded a blanket behind him to soothe his back. And Maya had smiled teasingly, and said she was sure he didn't mind the extra attention he was receiving.

'And the workers have called the strike, for when?' He asked.

'In a day or two. It is up to their leader to decide.' It left Henry bemused. That a leader in prison, suspected of a murder, could yet command so much reverence.

'There's obviously more to it than meets the eye,' said Maya. She turned the paper and folded it again to read better. Henry ran his fingers through his hair and tried reading the paper upside down He winced for his elbow hurt terribly now, but a stray word in the newspaper had caught his eye. 'Khetwadi...that's the place where he stays, doesn't he? That terrible man. Pease.'

She thrust the paper towards him, indicating with a finger what she had been reading. 'Talk of the devil. Arthur Pease has appealed to the Governor and the council to stop the performance of Oscar Wilde's *The Importance of Being Earnest*. He says Wilde is a most...,' she paused, and her face reddened, before she went on, 'obnoxious person, with a way of life that would put every civilized and cultured person to shame. That he is allowed to roam free in our capital, London, does not behove our fine reputation, the high moral standards we have set everywhere in the Empire.'

'That man Pease,' she said, putting the paper aside, 'is really the most obnoxious person himself. I can't stand his hypocrisy, the sneering look on his face, his way of turning up in places especially just to be a spoilsport.'

He knew what she meant. Once Pease had turned up with an inspector and a constable to interrupt the theatre group's rehearsals at the Grant Road playhouse. It was a scene adapted from a popular epic, and the inspector had finally refused to intervene after hearing both sides out. Maya had described it to Henry a couple of months ago. It seemed ages ago, and he felt a sudden happiness at the realization that they had known each other for quite a while now. 'It will be a waste of my time and yours,' the inspector had patiently explained things to Pease. 'This is a very familiar scene, even if it does involve gambling. If I intervene, there will be a thousand others who will accuse us of interfering with native customs.' Still Pease hadn't let up. He believed it was his mission to cure this land of all its ills, bad habits, and customs. People like Maya and him, Henry knew, would appear especially distasteful to Pease, though the latter didn't know the whole story about them. Their relationship was always stuttering, so fraught at times, and that the world thought otherwise, bemused him no end. Still, he was glad he hadn't told Maya all that Pease had said the previous evening, and now he never would.

'You had gone to meet Pease, hadn't you?' she said, looking at him, the sun through the open carriage lighting up her hair in a manner Henry found particularly fetching. A strand of hair strayed across her cheek and Henry had a sudden urge to draw it away, behind her ear.

He nodded, tearing his gaze away, 'Turned out it wasn't a meeting at all. I spent all my time outside. A few minutes. And he harangued me about being a most dissolute American.'

'It's strange for it was he who wanted the meeting in the first place,' she said, slowly.

'I didn't even get in through the gate,' he said bitterly, 'and well, it's his loss. He had wanted the fans to get more people to his talks, to have a bigger audience. No one would have noticed the heat then. Not that it really matters to him.'

Maya still looked at him, a certain pensiveness in her gaze, 'Makes you think though. If he had something to hide…'

'Probably, he had reams of those same pamphlets stored away leaving him no space for entertaining guests.'

'He wants to open healing centres at Elephanta, Alibagh, and the other islands away from the city, that's what I remember. Islands away from the corrupting influence of the city.'

As the carriage gently slowed, other noises filtered in. The rumbling of other carriages, vendors' calls, a ship's siren from the dockyard, and a group of pilgrims out on the road, jangling on their tambourines, and cymbals. There were stray shouts too, voices rising and falling, and peering through the curtain, just as the carriage halted, Henry saw the rambunctious crowd that had gathered before the police station. *Free our leader. Free Tuka.* Their arrival was evidently expected for a couple of constables cleared a way for their carriage, and for two others coming up behind theirs. The constables dispersed the stray groups of people by charging at them with their batons. 'Do you want to be locked up too, with your friends?' a turbaned constable threatened with distinct menace.

A crowd of people moved across the road, drifted away, and only some remained, still raising defiant voices. *We are with Tuka. Always with Tuka.*

'The superintendent is waiting for you, sir,' said a constable. He inclined his head to acknowledge Maya as well. The room they were ushered into had a big wooden desk, and cane chairs. The bamboo slats pulled low over the windows made things considerably darker and cooler. A pitcher of water sat dewy on a low table, and a gas lamp hanging low by a thread from an overhead beam spread a reddish glow on the table. Vincent appeared, wiping his hands on the towel a bearer in a white turban held out. He gave Henry a quick look-over, taking in his injuries and shook his head once, almost in admonition.

'It's not usually like this, and it's quieter now,' Vincent said, jerking his head toward the door, with an ironic lift of his brow. 'The whole night, there was such a ruckus. And you seem to have been in some trouble too, Mr Baker. The trouble here came from some disorderly workers from the mills. So, to come to the point, it's that magician, your fellow countryman, we need you to identify him and then he's free to go.'

Henry leaned back in his chair, caught by surprise, and a burst of renewed pain. Of all things, he hadn't expected this bit of news. He knew now why Bancroft hadn't appeared the previous night, and why the men had been frustrated by their long wait. 'You mean he's here?'

Vincent's tone was clipped and brisk. 'For disorderly behaviour, and refusal to follow orders. There were explicit orders, especially issued last evening, for no one to be on the shore and by the Bunder and Queen's Road, as our search continues. For...,' he looked at them both before continuing, 'Mr Clemens. But our man was there, on stilts too, and drawing a crowd. Took three of my men to get him in. And those stilts,' Vincent pointed to a corner where two long wooden sticks stood tall against the wall. Long and made of some dark wood, the sticks branched in the middle, right where there was a foothold, and an elastic band for the shoulders. 'We had to keep him in a separate cell for all the noise he made.'

Henry glanced at Maya, who on her part was looking intently at Vincent. As they followed him out,

Vincent turned abruptly, and Henry took a hurried step back. 'The jail is rather crowded today. The murder suspect is in his own solitary cell, but there are his men packed into the others. We hope to crack the case soon.'

'The experts from Calcutta,' Maya asked lightly, not looking his way. 'Are they here already?'

Vincent looked at her sharply and nodded. 'Ah, so you have heard about that! Yes, that's why we are sure about cracking the murder soon. That room in the lodge will have the evidence our experts are looking for. You are not getting anything more out of me, Miss Barton.' They were walking down a short corridor that broke into a colonnaded veranda. To their right, they passed table-filled rooms and clerks poring over files, and on the left, a string of potted plants on the stone railing. Another turn to the right, and they were back in a corridor again, with the prison cells visible at the far end. At that turn, Vincent stopped, rubbing his chin. He turned to the inspector with him. 'Have him brought here. No place for a lady.'

At that moment Henry really liked the man. He would tease Maya later about Vincent's gallantry, but in the afternoon, after they had accompanied Freddie Bancroft to his home, the place where so much had transpired only the previous night. Henry found it difficult to believe that it had only been some hours ago. The previous day had stretched interminably, and in an utterly miserable way too. He thought of Mark Twain and his heart sank.

Bancroft was escorted from his cell flanked by two watchful constables. He looked sullen and tired, with dark circles around his eyes. He appeared very different from the man Vincent had described as bad-tempered, boisterous, and surly.

Henry, as American consul, completed the formalities. He identified Bancroft as was required, signed the necessary forms of assurance and Bancroft thanked him, mumbling something when they were in the carriage. Bancroft looked dishevelled, his shirt sleeves and collar were grimy with dirt and perspiration, his brown hair fell over his forehead, and a day-old stubble had appeared on his chin. 'Looks like I owe you a favour,' Bancroft said. He apologized in the same indistinct way to Maya, hoping she would not mind his slovenliness on this occasion. 'I would have used my stilts to get home and not troubled you,' he said with a lopsided smile, 'but really, I feel cramped. A night in a jail like that would kill any weaker man.'

'I look forward to your stilt walk, Mr Bancroft,' Maya said demurely, 'but you do need your rest.'

Even when Bancroft smiled, a tired lift of his lips, he could look charming. Henry rubbed his back, glad the pain was easing and asked him why he had to flout police orders especially at such a difficult time. Bancroft spread his hands wide, but there was none of his old surliness as he explained, in tired tones. 'I had done it a day ago, and even yesterday morning. I never knew when the orders came up. There were men who kept shooing away children and others, but I was trying out my stilts.' Bancroft went on to explain how much he had been practicing, that it took sustained effort, and a skill to balance oneself on those long pieces of wood. He had had the foothold specially carved for his feet, he said. 'The woodworkers of Ahmedabad do a fantastic job, even with the most basic of things. And the beach, any place on the shore is the best place to practice,' he said. 'Then a fall, though I have been getting better, is cushioned by the sand.'

There were many who came to watch him too, he claimed. The urchins, the vendors, and even the society ladies out in their carriages to get some air, watched him. The idea to do a show by the shore, all the magic tricks at his command had occurred to him then. 'The card tricks, illusion games, the rope trick, and then this one on stilts, walking right out to the sea on them, and doing some fancy juggling in deep water. It would be such a show,' he said, with his lop-sided smile.

'The thing is no one stopped me then. And yesterday, I was out there twice. In the morning, when the boats were still going out, to Elephanta, Butcher, Alibagh. That man Pease was there too, returning with a sorry-looking crowd. He really appreciated my performance, and the questions he asked me too.'

'What kind of questions?' Maya asked right on cue.

'He is usually kind of irritating,' Bancroft said, his eyes lingering on her in a way that annoyed Henry considerably. 'There was a time he wanted to do a joint show with me. He giving his lecture, and me doing the entertaining, but man, can he be preachy and boring?

That would bring many people in, he told me. But I want people to have fun, laugh, and make merry and not be worried about thoughts of sin, and punishment. That puts so many people off. But of late he has been so insistent. More people would write about it, about us both, he said. The newspapers, especially. It would be good publicity. The only way I could put him off was telling him I would think about it.'

Even Henry smiled at that, though he did glower inwardly, as he remembered his last conversation with Pease.

'But yesterday morning, that time by the sea, he watched me again, and seemed genuinely interested,' Bancroft went on, running his hands through his hair. 'He stood there, nodding and smiling. The sorry folks with him, all looked dull and pained and a couple of them even flopped onto the sand. I had walked along the pier, past a ship unloading material and was at the docks when Pease and his boat came in. About five or six of them, and they stood looking on with Pease, like unhappy schoolchildren. I did one of my stunts, something I have been practicing for the last few weeks. I balanced myself on one stilt, and twirled the other one. It was difficult, and there was cheering, a lot of it. Pease clapped, and those with him did too. I would have preferred a more vociferous cheering, but there was a man who did doff his hat toward me, at my act. He was wobbly on his feet, the hat almost slipping from his hand, and when Pease pressed his hat back down on his head hurriedly he was even more wobbly, and would have fallen over if Pease had not been there.'

Maya sat up suddenly, startling both men. Henry caught her eye, she shook her head. Whatever it was, she meant to tell him later, and not in Bancroft's company. The import of Bancroft's words then struck Henry too, and he was looking at her, and at Bancroft, speechless, his breath coming fast.

'Did you take a good look at that man?' Henry asked, as Maya feigned a polite interest in the conversational turn.

'Which man?'

'The one who waved to you, with the hat,' Henry scanned the other man's face. 'The one who as you say, went suddenly wobbly.'

Bancroft's eyes closed, he rubbed the corner of his left eye, and said, 'I don't remember clearly. I was looking down at them from a height. A great height, I must add. They all looked just the same. Dissolute-looking Englishmen, I thought. He made them all walk in a line to the carriage, really like a headmaster managing his lot.'

'You don't know Arthur Pease all that well, right?' persisted Henry.

Bancroft took his time replying, his eyes were closed, before he said slowly, 'I can't stand him sometimes. He's such an irritating chap.'

They said nothing till they reached Bancroft's house, and he straightened up in the seat, with some anticipation. He parted the curtains, the rings of perspiration on his ruff and wrists appeared stark, like untidy grey stains, and mud splotches showed up on his shoes and trousers. 'Can't wait to sleep.' He peered through the window, stiffened, and stifled a curse. 'Is anything the matter?' Henry's voice was deceptively quiet.

'Something's been broken in,' he said through clenched teeth. 'The place where I keep my supplies.' The short gravelly driveway skirted past the outhouse, visible now with its broken windowpanes, and a wooden door standing askew on its hinges. The night before with the looming trees, the untrimmed hedges, the outhouse had loomed dark and sinister. Now it looked a sad brown in colour, with lines of damp on its walls, and the tiled roof blackened in places. A bit ahead, where the main house began, Henry recognized the flat patch of grass, the place he had been held captive. The carriage slowed, but even before it had completely halted, Bancroft had opened the door and jumped off.

'Thank you,' he doffed an imaginary hat Maya's way, and nodded toward Henry. He looked back at the outhouse, and a frazzled expression appeared on his face again. 'I need to see what's happened, and then...'

'Do you want us to get the police?' asked Maya, leaning out of the window, with some concern.

'No,' he said hurriedly, 'no, not them. Not again. I will be fine.'

XII

The Violinist Sees Interesting Things

Two days had elapsed since Mark Twain's disappearance, and for Henry, things were getting more stressful. Maya and Charlotte Ellaby had the sensible idea of Clara and Olivia moving in with them for some time. Olivia's health was a particular cause for concern. She wasn't weepy or hysterical, though Maya let on that Charlotte had taken care of that with the poppy-seed tea she had persuaded Olivia to drink. 'A few sips before she slept, and then again the next day,' Maya told Henry. 'It dulls things somewhat, for some time.'

Henry's pain too had abated somewhat. The menthol and camphor balm Charlotte had sent him the previous night had brought welcome relief. The servant from the bungalow had arrived well after ten, the balm in a glass jar placed in a coir basket that he held up carefully for a suspicious Abdul to assess. It was late and Abdul had been locking the rusty grill door that led up from the staircase to Henry's rooms at the Byculla Club.

The balm had given him a few hours of restful sleep, but Henry was up early the next morning, much before Abdul appeared with his tea. He wanted to rush back to Watson's hotel where he was to meet Clara and Olivia again. Maya had promised to come along too. Things had to move faster, he thought, and his heart picked up pace with worry all over again.

As he waited for them in the high-ceilinged breakfast room, with wooden beams running across the roof, and petalled gas lamps over every table, Henry read the newspapers arranged on slanting desks placed at one end and held back by a long wooden scale. The papers were about a week old, but suddenly it brought the world closer to this, as his parents still thought, distant outpost, right at the other end from where they were. Henry read of Utah's admission as the 45th state of the United States, and of trouble brewing on Arizona's border with Mexico, whose dictator Porfirio Diaz sounded distinctly dangerous. In Britain, things were changing in a revolutionary way. A man called Marconi was working on sending signals via the wireless. If possible one day, Henry thought, voices could be transmitted in a similar way, and carry far beyond a telephone's reach. The women were campaigning for a right to vote. His eyes moved to an item about the continuing protests about Oscar Wilde's play. A group intended to petition the British government to lock him up for much longer because of his brazen lifestyle. Just the last year, Wilde had been sentenced to two years in prison when he had taken the Marquess of Queensberry to court over libel. Wilde had lost, had been left bankrupt, and with a battered reputation. The newspapers had made much of his affair with Lord Alfred Douglas, and there were all the allusions of his unspeakable acts with young servant boys. Henry wondered whether Maya was following the news about Wilde. He heard the door swing open then and he turned as the four of them—for Charlotte was there too, with Olivia, Clara, and Maya—walked in.

It was a good thing, Henry thought, that Olivia was in Charlotte's expert care. There would be no danger of an opium overdose—and one needed that to induce sleep—for Charlotte was on hand in case of any unforeseen aftereffects. The tea, the opium infusion in it, had evidently allowed Olivia some sleep, but it could never be a long-time solution. There was a grave seriousness on everyone's face, even his own, as they greeted each other. He noted Olivia's pinched face, and Maya, who appeared more distracted than before, exchanged a quick glance with Henry, before she led Olivia and Clara up the stairs to their room. They would simply gather some more of their stuff and leave again for the doctors' bungalow.

Henry ran a hand across his scratchy beard, stealing a look at the clock. In a couple of hours, he was scheduled to meet the Governor, the sad-faced Viscount Sandhurst. There simply had to be more personnel made available, the police were clearly overstretched, and more men needed to be involved in the search for Mark Twain. It had been two days already, and Henry felt the sweat on his forehead at that insistent and clamorous thought.

He turned away abruptly, rubbing his forehead. Mehta at the front desk smiled nervously at him. The police inspector, he came up to say, had been around earlier that day, questioning the morning staff. 'We hope he's back soon. Mr Clemens...,' he said, looking over his shoulder, as if he feared DeSouza's intrusion any moment. Henry suppressed his irritation. Did Mehta honestly think Mark Twain had stepped out for a walk, and would be back any moment?

He managed a quick nod for Mehta before rejoining Charlotte. She was taking off her gloves and looked poised and unruffled, as she placed her umbrella in the stand, and moved toward the table by the window that Henry indicated. Coffee, she mouthed, and Henry gave her a quick smile in acknowledgement. They seated themselves at the table, but now he found himself unable to make much small talk. A soft silence settled between them, even a fatigue they knew they had to stave away. Wiping his face quickly with his handkerchief, he asked for tea for himself and coffee for Charlotte.

The violin player, the one Henry had last seen at Cowasjee Bengalee's party, appeared at the door. He carried a battered old leather violin case, its rusty handle squealing as it shifted and moved in his fingers. 'Mr Baker, a word with you?'

It was then Maya returned, looking agitated. 'She's missing a pendant,' she told them quickly, her eyes barely taking in the musician who looked on apologetically, as if he regretted intruding on them. 'Olivia's missing a pendant,' she explained. The thin cotton curtains swirled, and the covered courtyard was visible, where a fountain played, and men in short dhotis watered plants. 'It could only be Manuel,' she said, echoing Henry's first thoughts.

Olivia appeared at the door behind Maya, looking shaken. 'You must sit down, my dear,' said Charlotte, sounding quiet and efficient, indicating the chair by her, 'and have some tea.' Olivia joined them at the table and took a chair. 'Clara's up, she'll be done soon with the packing,' Maya said, glancing at the musician, who mumbled, 'I'll come back.'

'No, please.' Maya and Henry spoke up together, startling the man, who gripped his violin case more tightly. The waiter had come up with a tray, and Henry insisted that Olivia have the tea he had ordered. 'It will do you good,' he said kindly. The silver on the tray's curved ends gleamed in the soft golden light cast by the lamps. It was always bright in the dining hall, and relatively quiet this time of early forenoon. Guests usually left early in the day for their respective destinations, and returned well after sunset. Bombay could be unpredictable despite it being late January. There was always a lot to do, and see. Some tables were occupied by men in traveller's suits engaged in conversation. A group of ladies sat at a corner table deep in conversation. They were Parsi, as was evident from the veils and embroidered cotton saris they wore, and time and again they would laugh at a sudden shared joke.

'We will soon find it, my dear. After all, we do know who could have taken it,' said Maya, patting her on the shoulder. Henry pulled a reassuring expression on his own face. He felt terrible seeing the misery on Olivia's face. He should rightly be running like a deranged man down the streets shouting out Mark Twain's name, describing him to all and sundry, but he had to stay sane, to ensure Olivia and Clara were all right too. He was beginning to think that the matter of Mark Twain's disappearance was tied to other things, or to other people. Bancroft for instance, and that terrible man, Arthur Pease. He saw Olivia nod as she took her first gulp of the tea, and the musician shifted his feet, his shoes squelchy on the shiny wooden floors of the hotel. 'I should come back later,' he said, shifting on his feet again, and his face reddening in embarrassment.

Charlotte sized up the situation, and the man's awkwardness perfectly. 'It must be an important matter.' She looked at Maya and Henry, her eyes, now a deeper shade of brown in the gently darkened room, resting on them in a calm, resolute way, 'Why don't you talk to him at that other table? Olivia and I will keep each other company.'

'It's really all right,' Maya said. 'You were playing beautifully the other day,' she added, looking at the violinist.

'You listened, madam,' and the violinist's sad face lit up with momentary pleasure. He bowed, the hat in his hand fluttered, and the violin case in the other drooped a bit more. 'Yes,' she said, inviting him to sit, 'though it was a bit sad, and the man...' She stopped abruptly, biting on her lip. Henry had instantly caught on, though the man looked puzzled, even a bit hurt. Maya of course was referring to more recent events when she had overheard him playing in the hotel, in the room next to Mark Twain's. The man placed the violin case against his legs, and said in a voice, as low as before but somehow firmer, 'I played at Mr Bengalee's party two days ago. And I am now a part of Anna's theatre group.' His eyes had a sudden shine as he added, 'I play in the rehearsals too. Maybe you heard? The police thought we were making too much of a noise. That man, Pease, is always complaining.'

That name made both Maya and Henry exchange quick glances. The violinist began slowly, fingering his collar in some nervousness. 'But I wish to talk about someone else, about the Ameri...the American. If I could have some of your time.'

'Well,' Henry said, drawing a chair away from the table, 'you were sure holding your horses then.'

The musician looked flustered again and he bent to lift his violin case that he had placed on the chair before Henry, while he remained standing. 'You really must sit and have some tea,' said Maya, 'and tell us what this is about.'

'Yes,' he said, smiling in some relief, and it made

him look younger, carefree, and happier. But a moment later, the same dismal expression returned to his face, 'I understand you are looking for him. And that,' his voice dropped to a whisper, 'he was here in this hotel.'

'I see, Mr...,' said Maya, and her smile faltered, as she realized, and Henry did too, that they didn't know his name. 'My name,' he looked eagerly at them, 'Bozidar Karadordevic.' He waited for their reaction before relenting. 'That is indeed a long name so call me Bozi. And I play,' he patted the instrument case next to him, 'the violin.'

Henry hoped his wariness didn't show on his face. This was also the man the police had been suspicious about, his presence linked to the gang of jewel thieves in the city. It seemed far-fetched to think this nervous-looking musician could have anything to do with Manuel. In the mystery over Mark Twain's disappearance, only this much was clear: Manuel's thievery, and that he, Henry, should have been more careful in the matter of a servant. As the American consul, he held himself totally responsible. As for the matter of Olivia's missing pendant, that was one mystery easiest to resolve. They had simply to look through the jewels Maya had recovered from Mark Twain's bed to see if Manuel had secreted it away among the other jewellery.

He caught Maya and the musician looking at him expectantly, and he knew he had been lost in his reverie. He smiled, apologizing. 'I was just thinking. I remember you at that party, and as Miss Barton here said, you did indeed play beautifully.'

Bozi smiled and bowed. 'Thank you, Mr Baker.' His voice dropped and his eyes darted around the near empty room one more time. 'Yes, I do know your name. I asked at the desk about you. I had to speak to you, and so they told me. You see, I was here that night.'

The waiter hovered nearby, before Maya looked him in the eye and told him they didn't really need anything. 'Except for some quiet,' Henry muttered, as he looked back at Bozi.

Looking at the waiter's retreating back, Bozi began to speak. 'I am here to play music,' he said, 'the only thing that matters to me. I left my home far away, to play my music. Sometimes I paint too.' He gestured with his hands, and Henry noticed the square-shaped emblazoned ring on his right finger. He waited for him to go on and stopped himself in time from drumming on the table. 'This is a peaceful land,' Bozi said, his eyes closing dreamily over long curling eyelashes. He had a thin pointed face, reddish-brown hair fading around the forehead, and deep brown eyes that flashed open, looking straight at Henry this time.

'Peaceful until all this happened,' he laughed. 'I was here that night, after that party to meet the German man. The man who has a room just next to Mr Mark Twain. He wanted me to meet him at night, to make a film on me, out by the sea.'

Bozi said he had waited first, for Boehme, the

German, had promised he would meet him in the lobby. It was after nine, and fairly late. But the German kept odd hours, and Bozi could only get there after the party at Mr Bengalee's. So he had walked for a bit, and then hailed a carriage to the hotel. It had been difficult to find one at that hour. Bozi waited in the lobby, but even twenty minutes later, Boehme had not turned up. Bozi had wandered around to the front desk. Then he had the thought of going up to Boehme's room himself.

'The thing is, doing this can be a bother. There's my violin that I really cannot leave anywhere. And I didn't really want to ask the desk for his room number. They don't want to give out such information,' said Bozi. He looked the kind of man who would be too timid to go up to the desk and ask DeSouza anything. 'As I was standing there, I saw that man, Pease. I was just as surprised to see him as he was to see me. He had a satchel with him, his wide hat on, even at that hour, and the brown suit. I am trying to remember everything because I know this may be important. He said he was going up because he had a meeting.

'I was glad of some company. Pease and I took the two flights of stairs, up the red-carpeted steps, and he was telling me all about the evils in the city. This is the vice city, he told me, with its flagrant living, opium dens, the old customs. "What I am trying to do is just a drop in the ocean. I am trying to tell people about it. In schools, in reformatories,, churches." And then he gave me this...'

Bozi put his hand in his pocket and dug out a

pamphlet that looked just like the one Maya had found in Twain's room. A yellowing parchment showing two square boxes, with that alarmist message in one square.

In the second square was his address.

The Pease Home for Peace

Khetwadi. Bombay

'He saw me looking at it, and laughed, assuring me he would soon have a phone. Sometimes they, all those against me, and my good work, stop people from coming to see me, he told me. Since my violin was in my other hand, I put the note in my pocket and his voice wheezed against my ears. They know I have that power, he was saying. Very quiet, very insistent. It made me quite scared of him. He was telling me that he had the ears of the ministers and important people in London, and so his enemies, the men who feed this vice day in and day out, they did everything they could to stop people from meeting him.'

Henry leaned forward, his elbows on the wooden table. 'And did he say who they, his enemies, really are?'

Bozi looked at them in earnest. 'He was in such full flow that I did not ask. Nor could I interrupt. But I suppose he meant all the city's important people. For he went on to tell me that all the big people, businessmen, the British officials, even you, Mr Baker, wanted folks in London, and the world to think of Bombay as a big, thriving city. As big as London, New York, Constantinople, and Paris. It is indeed one, that man Pease said, when he saw my expression, but there is evil too. An evil I am trying to end, he told me. We were standing on the veranda on the second floor, and he was already panting. The rooms were at the far end, Boehme's a door or two after Mr Twain. He kept two rooms, one just for his camera equipment. I need men to speak for me, to write about me and my very important work, Pease told me. When he leaned forward, I felt his stale sweet breath on me, and it seemed he was putting a spell on me. When others talk about my work, speak for me, you will see how things change. He kept telling me. This city will change. For the better. He looked past me, and then he said there was someone he had to meet.'

Bozi said then how Pease had brushed past him, in a sudden hurry, as he made for someone who had just emerged. The balcony was grey in the half-darkness, except for the light scattered by two lone gas lamps across the road. They cast a flickering orange yellow light that strayed through the veranda rails, and streaked across the wooden floor, making a shimmering pattern, and Bozi could make Mark Twain out as he walked out of his room, the light angled sharp on his face.

'He kept scratching his hair, and rubbing his face. Then that man, Pease, and he began walking toward me on the balcony.' Bozi frowned, narrowed his eyes as he tried to remember. 'I heard him say that he just couldn't sleep, and that...'

Maya's fingers were taut on the table, and she fidgeted on her seat. She leaned forward, raising a hand to get Bozi's attention. 'Who was talking then?'

'Twain. I mean, Mark Twain,' Bozi said slowly. 'He said all this as he walked with Pease, and they both walked toward the stairs. "It's hot," and he paused, and Pease looked at me, with his funny half-smile. The other man, Mark Twain that is, was talking in a sleepy, irritable voice. "In the afternoon, they advised me to take a nap. Everyone does that, but the crows." He kept shaking his head, complaining at the cacophony they raised. Pease nodded, and I realized I had just been standing there, and very rudely, eavesdropping on them. As I moved away, to make my way to the room where Mr Boehme was, I watched them walk toward the stairs, his walking stick making a slow tapping sound. The stick had a shiny brass knob that caught the light, and I could see it easily. Then Pease caught my eye just as I looked back, and said to Twain, "A stroll will do you good. The fresh air and quiet will help you sleep."'

Bozi looked up at the chandelier as he finished, and his hands lay clasped on the table, the thumbs scratching each other. 'I should have told you earlier,' he said, 'but I really had no idea. Mr Boehme, I could hear him snore from two doors away as I neared. His servant was sleeping sitting up against the wall outside his room.'

Henry and Maya looked at each other, and both had the same thought. The servant hadn't noticed a thing because he had been asleep. Then as if he couldn't help it, Bozi smiled, a quick upturn of the lips that took years away from his face. 'There's more.

For around the corner of the hotel, I saw the man on stilts appear. It seemed altogether a strange night and it hadn't ended yet.'

'So did your German friend awake when you knocked on the door?'

Bozi laughed and brushed back the hair that had fallen over his forehead, 'Oh, he did, and he was in a bad mood. The Pathan, his servant, awoke and rushed to the door. The man tried to hit him, but the servant, anticipating this, was already bending to avoid the contact. There is just too much noise around, Boehme said, in a voice loud enough to carry down the balcony. But we soothed him, the two of us. We must talk inside, I told him.

'It was really dark inside the room, Bozi went on, the light from outside did not alleviate the gloom in the least. The window was open, and there was a calm breeze blowing in. That puzzled me, and Ali too. No one here sleeps with windows open. But Boehme, he looked out of the window for long moments, and said, "Can't see it now. Can't see it." "What is it?" I asked. He looked kind of embarrassed, turned away and then in a totally different voice shouted to his servant. He ordered him to fetch the stick that had fallen out the window. He had thrown it out, and wanted it back. And he would do it again, when I was in the room, playing my violin for him. I had my back to the window, but Boehme, he interrupted me a few times. Twice he raised his hand, saying there was something at the window. He really threw quite a tantrum. When the stick went out of the window, the servant had to go again. It was terrible, the way Boehme treated that man. But he wouldn't tell me anything. Not yet...

'It was only when he had the lamp on, and got his camera out, that he told me about the strange apparition he had seen. A face looking in, a face that had appeared through the window.'

Quite a lot of people then claimed to have seen Bancroft that night, and Bozi's account had been as detailed as possible. He had taken pains to remember every bit. Henry jumped up from his chair, startling the musician and Maya. 'We need to...' He began, and then gripped the table hard, as a sharp pain struck him in the shoulder. His knuckles turned white, and Maya reached out to hold him just as he almost fell. The chair under him fell over, and it got even more people by his side. Charlotte came up too, and between the two of them, Maya and Charlotte, Henry was helped back to his chair. He protested profusely, reddening at their expressions of concern, and told them in as firm a tone as he could muster that there really wasn't much time to waste.

'It's clear, isn't it? Where he could be, and we don't have a moment to waste.'

'Did you mean father?' said Clara, her eyes suddenly alive with excitement.

'Yes,' he said, wincing as he tried to make himself more comfortable. 'We have to be going.'

'I am afraid, Henry, you are really in no position to dash off into action,' Charlotte's voice was quiet, and business-like. 'If you trouble that shoulder of yours anymore, you will only aggravate it. A few hours' rest, and a massage might work, and the police can do the rest. You could rest at the bungalow.'

'No, no,' he said hastily, 'I will go back to my rooms. I will be fine…' He was embarrassed at the attention. DeSouza looked in through the large, panelled doors, and the stewards nearby stood at attention, trying to look solicitous.

Henry exchanged looks with Maya. 'I will hope you will consider the doctor's advice,' she said. That sudden demureness in her voice, the smile she flashed the musician's way made Henry suspicious. He didn't want her to go adventuring on her own, in some disguise or other. Pease and even Bancroft sounded like desperate men. He also felt the irritation that always came with his feelings of resentment and envy. All his chases, whether of Pease or Bancroft had been ignominious disasters. Maya, however, had had quite an adventure closeted in the hotel room, and he was certain Bozidar Karaderdovic wouldn't have been as forthcoming if Maya hadn't patiently and gently urged him on. He had taken almost half an hour to tell them about his encounter with Pease. Henry would have been well on his way to Khetwadi to the Pease bungalow by now if things had wrapped up sooner.

'You can't go there all on your own, you do understand, don't you?' Maya said, holding his arm as she led him out. If he held himself rigidly straight, Henry realized, the pain diminished somewhat, but he felt comforted in the way Maya held him gently, her arm firm around his back.

'To Pease's house, I meant,' she said quietly. 'You can't just barge into a man's house. You would need the police, and even for a search inside his premises, you would have to have a reason. And a permit, I might add. We must think this through.' She patted his hand, as Abdul ran up, two carriages riding along beside him. The women would return to the bungalow, and he was glad Olivia looked more hopeful, her face less strained than it had been in the morning. They finally had some news of a kind about Mark Twain, there was every possibility he was safe and well, and it was Arthur Pease who had to be tracked down. The questions still remained about Manuel, where he had been, and who had been actually sleeping in Twain's bed when Olivia went to look in on him in the morning.

~

'I think things are complicated, are they not?' the musician said, as Henry and he got into a carriage. It would take Henry to Byculla club, and the musician to another destination, the Sassoon reformatory school where he was to play for the students. Henry remembered with a groan his appointment with the Governor, the Viscount Sandhurst, and wondered if the Governor could be convinced to give him, Henry, special permission to search Pease's premises. Then, Bozi spoke. 'I think this man Pease holds the key,' he said ruminatively, his fingers caressing his moustache, before returning to the violin case, almost of their own accord. Henry was stretched out on the seat in front, wincing every once in a while, as the carriage jerked abruptly or took a sudden unexpected turn.

The windows were open, and there was the usual carriage traffic on the Esplanade as they headed northward, to Parel Road. Here they would take a left to Grant Road, so he could drop Bozi off at the Reformatory school before moving on. 'What will you be playing for them?' Henry asked softly, trying to forget the pain, Bozi didn't hear him. As they moved into Esplanade Market Road, they saw the police forming a barricade. Several purple uniformed men, in yellow turbans, were directing the carriage and cart traffic with their batons. Two bullock carts had been stationed on either side of the road, narrowing it further and making for quite some chaos. The crowds jostled on either end of the barricade, women looked out from their trellised balconies, and the cacophony was in total contrast to the quiet of their ride thus far up the wider Esplanade Street. A policeman looking harassed, repeatedly blew on his whistle to draw attention, but it was proving difficult. A bird-catcher played with his parakeets, drawing a crowd of children; a knife grinder sat on a stoop not too far away, sharpening kitchen knives and peelers as veiled women stood around him.

The police were looking into every basket, peering into every carriage, before letting anyone through the barricade. The bullock cart owner whose vehicle and animal had been commandeered for such an operation sat resigned to one side, smoking a beedi. He told them, in response to Abdul's query—an exchange with the hands moving quickly and arms that sweepingly took in the world around them—that some thefts had been reported in this wadi. The entire central part of the city had been barricaded in the hope that some of the stolen goods could be recovered before these were secreted out.

The carriage with Bozi and Henry, and Abdul standing on the footboard, zig-zagged its way past the small buzzing crowd. Agitated men and women stood looking for a way through, some of them clearly agitated as they were expected at the mills, and any delay meant a cut in wages. There were others, their baskets laden with wares on their heads. A sweet seller, his offerings displayed in the glass box swinging by a rope over his shoulder, rang a small bell that sounded forlorn every time the noise around him dimmed momentarily.

'They will never be able to catch a thief like this,' said Bozi, looking his usual lugubrious self.

Abdul leaned in through the window, looking excited. 'It's the opium thieves they are looking for, sahib. I asked the Pathan inspector there,' he said, pointing to the still harassed looking policeman with the whistle pursed in his lips. 'He was talking of a series of opium thefts. The Amrikan magician...'

'Bancroft,' exclaimed Henry, quite in disbelief. He seemed to be popping up everywhere.

'Yes, from his house, and then there was another

robbery in a house in Parel. The police aren't saying much, but it's the same house where there was a break-in just a day ago. Tuka's house. His wife is saying the thieves came in just to plant evidence against her husband. To make him out to be a smuggler of opium, and a murderer as well. The police are hoping to catch the thieves before they get away, since the theft at Parel happened an hour or so ago. The wife, Rukmini bai raised a fuss, marching onto the police station, and the mill workers are even more upset. Even the women. They are saying that the police are trying to frame one man just because he is so popular. They aren't really bothered about the thieves who have broken into the same house twice.'

It took Henry more than an hour to reach his rooms, which left him considerably irritated and tired. His pain had diminished somewhat, and he was certain, in an hour or so, he would feel good enough for his meeting with the Governor. After all that Bozi had told them, Henry knew he had to meet Viscount Sandhurst post-haste.

He had looked anxious as Bozi gave him a last understanding wave of his hand as he got off, just at the turn to Khetwadi back road. Bozi would walk past the rows of jewellers' shops, the silversmiths, the woodworkers, the small Jain temple, before he reached the reformatory school. The shops were all on the ground floor, and the upper floors were crowded with windows and balconies that jutted out into the road. Crows hopped on the red tiled roofs, and the sun was by then already so hot that it hurt Henry's eyes to look up.

'I will see you soon again, something tells me,' Bozi had said, with his quiet shy smile, and Henry smiled wanly in turn. He wasn't a bad sort, and Henry was honest enough to admit his jealousy. The man had had Maya's attention, and she had been kind to him. Just as she had been kind with him too, Henry, that morning. She was, he thought in tired irritation, just about kind with everyone.

He breathed a sigh of relief once he reached the cool, fragrant interiors of the Byculla Club. His room was in darkness, the coir blinds pulled down, and the running fountain in the small courtyard made a calming bubbling sound. He switched on the fan, helped himself to iced coconut water from the wooden icebox. He liked his creature comforts, he thought, as he lay back on the lounge chair, holding the iced glass to his head. Then he heard the phone ring and answered it on the third ring.

Maya's voice came quick through the line. At this hour, with the quiet all around, her voice had never before sounded so clear, and calm. 'I tried you some time ago,' she said, and then half-laughed, 'the operator will wonder at my desperation.'

She didn't wait for a reply, as she went on, 'It did take you a long time to get home. But Edith—Dr Pechey, right?—who was at Mazagaon to give a health talk to the mill women, told us about the blockades. It's very strange, what she had to say. There were a few women who complained about their crying babies.

That the babies wouldn't sleep, or remain quiet, and so the women couldn't work at the docks or the mills. Do you know what I am getting at, Henry?' she paused to ask sharply. Henry who couldn't bring himself to admit to his confusion, and who had been lulled to drowsiness by the comforting darkness around only said, that she must go a little slowly. 'Too many things have happened, haven't they?'

Maya went on as if his answer didn't matter. 'The women always give their babies a bit of opium. A paste mixed with water, so they are quiet while the women, their mothers, work at the mills. For some reason, the opium's been stolen, so there's just nothing they can give to their babies. Thefts reported especially from Sardar Tuka's house. Don't you think it all ties up?'

'Yes, it does. Of course, it does,' Henry said hurriedly, 'there can't be many sources of that stuff, or whatever it is they might want to call the drug. And it's gone, and the women are complaining.'

'Yes, Henry, you have it,' she said pleased. With a blinding flash Henry recalled Abdul's words, and what he had heard from the policeman. The thefts suspected at Tuka's wife's house—he was always forgetting the woman's name—and at Bancroft's, where a packet of opium had indeed been found. Perhaps it was indeed Tuka who was supplying the opium to the workers, and to the women workers who needed it for their babies. As a labour supervisor, he had the contacts for it. It was all connected, and to sort things out, Henry needed some sleep, and that was just what Maya suggested next.

'You rest, while I work out the puzzle. The one about Mark Twain leaving late at night, and then he was apparently back again, for he was sleeping in the morning, as his wife said. Well, I have been thinking about Manuel's strange behaviour, and I think he could help us with that.'

'Except that Manuel's not been around too,' Henry said.

'Yes, that's worrying,' she said, 'we do have an idea where Mark Twain could be. But not about Manuel. Did he just jump out of the window, and into thin air? Like the way he came in the other day?'

'Don't do anything dangerous, Maya,' he warned.

'Dangerous,' she laughed, 'it's touching you are so concerned. No, I won't, really. I just wanted to go to Dinyar, the photographer. And get Casi's photo. She had worn all her jewellery, and I wonder if what I have with me is all that she had. It's really quite a bit. Poor girl.' She paused before she said quietly, 'The pendant that's missing wasn't there, Henry. I did look for it among the other jewellery...'

And on that sad sober note, as they mourned a young girl, whose murder had thrown the entire city into chaos, and who was connected to a lot of other things, they hung up, promising each other not to do anything risky or foolhardy. Henry yawned, returned to his lounge chair, turned his head to a more comfortable angle and fell asleep, almost instantly. 'Just an hour,' he told himself, 'then to the Governor, I go. And bring the police to Pease, yes.'

XIII

Afternoon Intruders Make the Least Noise

The creaking sound, the streak of light cutting a sudden line across the wooden floor, through the darkened room, broke into Henry's sleep. His eyes, he had been told, were never fully closed even when he slept. A fact that made him quite a poor sleeper, and a light one, for he awoke at the slightest noise, the least disturbance. The French window was behind him, its louvered panes reached the floor, a grilled railing faced the back garden lush with tall grass, and thick trunked banyan and peepul trees fringed the walls. The sudden sunlight made him frown, the ribbon of light on the floor wavered and shook, as a shadow crossed it, and Henry turned in his sleep. But it was the soft sound of a footfall, a step on the wooden floor that got him fully awake. He blinked, looked flustered as an unfamiliar shape wavered, fluttered before him, and then fell at his feet, his hands folded.

'Sahib, I didn't do anything, I didn't,' Henry was alarmed to find a man's head near his feet. Someone who had prostrated himself on the floor and was speaking words that for Henry in those first few moments of waking up made no sense. He struggled to sit up, wincing in pain, and the man lying full-length on the floor jumped to his feet, a quick graceful move, his hands still folded, and Henry was relieved that he didn't fall over in alarm.

'It's Manuel, sahib,' said the man, salaaming him, before sinking down to sit on his haunches, his hands clasped in a piteous gesture. 'I didn't do anything. Not kill anyone.'

'What's all this then?' Henry said, looking warily toward his table that held his revolver in its top drawer. He should have kept it close by him, but then he had never expected to be accosted in such a way. Manuel sat at his feet, looking entreatingly at him. Through the netted door, he saw Abdul in the balcony, trimming the ivy on the rails. Henry nodded at him to come nearer and Abdul slid in silently through the windows.

'I see you at the hotel, and I know you are the American sahib's friend,' Manuel said, wringing his hands, rubbing them over his face, 'But I didn't kill him. Save me, sahib.'

'What are you...?' But Henry hadn't finished, for Manuel had turned swiftly, to take in Abdul's presence. He rose to his feet then, smiling ingratiatingly at the other man, and said, 'I can tell everything. But sahib, about the Amrikan sahib, Twain sahib, I know nothing. And there are people who will kill me. Please save me.' He repeated those words again, and his eyes misted over.

'Where is Mark Twain? Clemens sahib, I mean?' Henry said, his voice sharp and angry. 'He has not been seen for three days now!'

'I not seen him since the first day. Since he came back,' Manuel said, blabbering, his eyes shifting quickly from Henry to Abdul. 'Believe me, I do not know about him.'

'Look, why don't you tell me from the beginning,' Henry walked slowly toward his table as he said this, alert to any sudden move on the man's part. But Manuel did not move, his head swivelled as Henry reached his desk, pulled his gun out, and tossed it once in his hand. 'Please don't shoot me, sahib,' the man's voice broke, and with trembling hands he wiped his face, and then sat down abruptly, his arms wrapped around himself. He sank even lower to the floor and lifted his hands again, to touch his ears in a gesture of abject penance. Henry said in clipped tones, 'Start right at the beginning. And don't try to lie. It's very clear you are in with the jewel thieves.'

The man let out a strangled yelp, 'Let me tell you. The truth, you must believe me, sahib.' Then Manuel proceeded to tell them the details of that evening, and the days that followed, and Henry found it a truly riveting story.

~

Manuel had slipped into the city, with a few others from his village in the west Deccan. Some of them wanted to work in the mills, but he had come in with two others because they were thieves.

'Thieves, sahib,' Manuel said, pleading, 'not murderers.' His name was actually Manu, and as with their kind, he was expected to report to the police. 'Waghares,' Manuel said, pointing to himself and Henry understood. That was the name of a criminal tribe, as the authorities labelled them, and like other similar tribes, the police kept close track of their movements. They had intended to go to the police station right away to report their presence, as was required by law, but at their settlement in Mazagaon that first morning he was approached by a ponderous, respectable-looking man. 'A Maratha sahib, a dark fellow with a moustache like a brush, wearing a turban.'

It was he who had given Manuel a job, that of looting a room in a Sewree lodge. He gave Manuel an advance of two rupees, and said he knew quite a lot of his tribe. 'That we are quick on our feet, and that we climb easily and fast.' Then he went on to give Manuel detailed instructions.

'Listen to me,' the man had said, in a low voice, his dark eyes fixed on Manuel, 'the Raja Lodge, on the second floor, a room that looks right onto the marshes. In the morning, you deliver this package to room 12. Some sweets. And in the evening, just when you hear the temple bell ring, go back there, and get me the jewellery. Some will be in the almirah, but the necklace and bangles you have to take off her. And get it back to me right here. Got it?'

Manuel had nodded, and then to his surprise, the man reached out and pulled him by the ear. 'You idiot. When you go back there, the second time in the evening, you have to…' Here he stopped, and dragged Manuel still by the ear toward him, so that his words were low and hoarse with menace, 'You climb up the wall from behind. That's why I said, it's the room that looks right over the marshes. Do it, get me the jewels, and meet me here.'

The man had let go of Manuel abruptly. He mimicked that move now before Henry and Abdul, half-falling on his back, his face turned toward the ceiling. 'I would have fallen if the two other men with him had not caught me. "You got it, right?" One of them said, and I felt the knife against my neck. "Do exactly as our Sardar, Tuka says, or…," and he pushed the knife in a bit deeper.'

At this point Henry gasped, for the name was of course familiar. Maya's aspersions had been right after all. Tuka had definitely plotted something, there were just some blanks that needed filling up. Manuel remembered nothing about the man, except his eyes, and that moustache. The rest of his face Tuka had quickly covered up, and his voice had been muffled and hoarse, even as he warned Manuel not to try any tricks.

'"We will be watching you," he warned me. So, I didn't go to the Banganga temple with my two other companions. I don't know where they are now. And I went to the Raja Lodge, with the package the man Tuka had given me. It was neatly wrapped with sal leaves and tied with cotton. It had sweets. I tried to resist, but in the end, I had to take a peek, and took a bit of the soft fig sweetmeat I found inside. Quite unlike anything I've ever had before.

'It was easy enough to find her room. No one stopped me when I told them Tuka sent me. In room 12, I passed on the package to the woman, worrying already that she would notice I had opened it. But she was a small, delicate-looking woman, with a sweet smile. She took the package and gave me an anna. That tip was so unexpected, but she said I must take it. "It's what everyone does here, don't they?" she asked. Only after I had left, and was walking toward Chowpatty, I remembered what I was do. That I was to rob her, enter her room like the thief that I was, and steal her jewellery. I walked around aimlessly, trying to find my companions. Then I ran into the men again, Tuka's men. I met them again at the Big Market at Crawford. There was no way I could evade them.'

Manuel's voice shook, and his hands trembled. His words when they came next were quick and broken and Henry had to interrupt him several times to understand things clearly.

Manuel had moved through the crowded market, twisting through the narrow crooked alleys, trying to squeeze into the smallest of nooks, but Tuka's men were always a few feet behind. The alleys through the shops led one way in, and a certain way out, and one could get lost there, but not if someone didn't want you lost. Past the fake jewellery market, the fruit sellers, the meat shops, Manuel ran but if he took a turn to the left or right, he saw their red turbans not too far way. He knew then he had to run out straight, out of the market, and return, all the way back to Sewree. Strangely the moment he left the market, he no longer saw the men tailing him. But he did not dare look back again.

It took Manuel more than an hour, and the sun was setting, and in the marsh, the lights of the insects hovered, and danced, making him shiver. Just as he had been told, the back of the lodge was dark, with no lamp, not even a human presence.

There was just the buzz and hiss of insects and the marsh creatures not too far away, the sound of someone playing music—and here Manuel mimed the act of someone drawing a bow, as fingers of his other hand strummed some invisible strings—and the occasional sounds from inside the lodge, someone calling out, someone coming down the stairs.

It was easy for Manuel to get up to the second floor, shin up the ledge over the window, the columns, and the gaps in the bricks. The window opened with a light touch of his knife, and there was still light enough for him to see things, once he was inside. Though he bumped into the water pitcher that rocked a bit before he hurriedly straightened it. He could make out a human shape on the bed, and at last the almirah too, just by the headboard. The woman was asleep and did not even stir. The almirah was unlocked, the latch lying loose, making it all so easy.

Manuel had taken out a small wooden box in the almirah that contained the jewellery, took out all the ornaments and tied them securely in a pouch at his waist. He patted his waist, where his dhoti was tucked in neatly. He would have left when he remembered the necklace he was to remove from her neck. This is where he needed all his skills. But she seemed fast asleep, unmoving and still. 'Almost, almost'—and for the first time, Manuel had looked at a loss for words—'as if she had taken something.' He remembered the sweet he had had not too long ago, the one he had stolen from the package. That had made him drowsy, and he had fallen asleep under a babul tree on Chowpatty. He stood there, he said now, just looking at her, remembering her smile.

Henry interrupted him then. He had to ask Manuel to hurry, this was really no time to be poetic. Abdul sniggered, muffling his laughter with his hand, and Manuel, licking his lips, went on with his account.

Lightly, he brushed the woman's hand with his finger. She remained motionless. That was the thieves' way of checking how responsive a person was, or how alert, but he heard her gentle breathing and realized not even a mosquito's sharp nip would wake her. His finger touched her on the elbow, moved to her neck and then he brought out the small knife he always carried.

At this point Henry's grip tightened on his pistol, and he gave him a sharp look. Manuel smiled apologetically, and lifted his vest to show the knife tied at one end. A thin evil-looking weapon with serrated edges. It could snap off the thinnest of chains, the sharpest metal with ease, with no one hearing or noticing a thing. He resumed his story. His fingers fluttered over her neck like a fly, and she didn't stir. Manuel heard her take a deep breath, she turned around in deep sleep, and that made his work easier.

He made a motion with his fingers, they hovered, fluttered, and danced in the air, and Henry did not drop his guard. He impatiently gestured with his gun, asking Manuel to get on with his story. Abdul for his part looked on, mesmerized. As if—and this truth struck Henry with the force of a brick—Manuel was trying to hypnotize them. Henry dismissed the thought, blinked rapidly, and told himself that he was letting the magician Bancroft needle him too much.

His fingers were on her neck for the briefest of moments. They did not stray an inch. Not an inch below. Manuel insisted that even thieves like him had some principles they followed like religion. They had their honour too.

With the necklace and the jewellery now secure in the folds of his dhoti, Manuel made for the window, relieved that he had kept his end of the bargain. But a moment later, he had the fright of his life. His breath caught, and he felt someone had reached out through the window and grabbed him by the throat. For there, on the marshes, dancing with the lightning bugs, and the hissing insects, was a man, tall as a tree, shimmering like a ghost. Manuel knew for sure he was waiting for him. His face was turned toward where Manuel stood by the window, and he could make Manuel out easily. The man hovered in the wind, shaking like a leaf but not falling over. Manuel stepped back, but the man in the marshes did not move. He stood straight, like a shadow, waiting. Like the very god of death, Manuel insisted, his eyes large on his face moving between Henry and Abdul.

He had stepped away then. The darkness inside was less gloomy than what appeared outside. What happened next made him almost scream in fright. For he heard footsteps, and the slow crack of the door bolt being drawn. Everything was in darkness, and he could see things in the room only because he was familiar with it. And he knew he was already late and had forgotten his instructions. He knew he had delayed things for several hours. There was no light streaming into the room, and yet he saw that figure outside in the marshes, and closer too, he heard the noise at the door.

The door had opened just a bit, and a figure sidled in. Manuel slipped under the bed just in time. The sheets were loose, and had fallen over the sides, so whoever it was entering through the door could not see him. Manuel saw the slow advance of steps, a long figure that stretched like a shadow from the door to the bed. The door closed slowly, and he saw the man's sandals. Black sandals that squelched a bit as he advanced. Manuel's blood ran cold as the man drew near, for there was something so very certain, and evil, about the way he moved. Manuel tried hard to quieten his breathing, to silence everything, even the flow of blood in his limbs. He smelled the mustiness, the dampness on the other man's feet, and desperately scrunched his nose trying not to sneeze.

But the urge only built up. Manuel held his nose tight, he closed his eyes, in short, he tried doing everything he could to stop the sneeze from breaking out. A storm surged in him and he took deep, silent breaths, praying to his god Waghoba for succour. The image of the god, the big cat, with the fiery eyes, kept appearing in front of him. The bed creaked as the man sat down heavily on it, and began to shake and heave each time he moved. Manuel broke out into a sweat, his heart thudded fast and loud, and he must have indeed lost consciousness, or blanked out for a few moments, for when Manuel next opened his eyes, everything was darker than he remembered, and far more still than before. He realized that the bed above him was shaking no more, that someone was breathing heavily, and then as his eyes focused again, he saw the leather sandal close to him, with no foot in it.

Henry noticed Manuel pull out something again, from the cloth bag tied around his waist. He gasped as Manuel held out a sandal, somewhat scrunched up, and sorry-looking, but just as he had described. Black with straps that crossed each other. Manuel held it out, licked his lips, and began again. 'Get him some water,' Henry said, quietly, and Manuel looked at him gratefully as Abdul turned to do as bid. Manuel drank noisily and wiped his lips, before beginning again.

It was at that moment, as he lay under the bed, that he heard the distinct creak. It was the window opening, and the man still in the room, just above him on the bed, heard it too. Manuel rolled over on the floor, and saw the same dark shadow from the marshes. The moon came from behind, and the shadow stretched like a line across the floor. He saw the dark menacing head too. A man with dark fine curls, and a face as white as the moon itself.

Henry drew in his breath. The surprises, the twists and turns in this story never seemed to end. It was Freddie Bancroft of course, wandering over this strangest of all cities on his stilts, who had caught Manuel in the act of scaling the guesthouse wall, and was following through on his curiosity. Or was it something else?

Henry's thoughts were interrupted as Manuel rocked back on his heels, and told him of how he had heard the other man yelp in alarm and fright. Manuel saw his foot then, caught in the light of the moon. A bit of hair on the toes, a long curved toenail that looked purple in the light. But he saw no more. For the man got off the bed, ran to the door, and dashed out. It was all over in moments. Manuel still lay there, not moving. The man at the window looked on for a moment more but he must have been alarmed too, at the way the man had run out. The sound of footsteps hurrying away down the corridor faded after a while. The man at the window, Bancroft, moved away just as suddenly as the other man had run away, and Manuel remained in the room, under the bed, dazed and wondering if he had dreamt it all. It must have been a long time later, or maybe he had indeed fallen asleep when the sound of the window slamming closed got him awake. The moonlight lit up the room. He could even see the moon as he peeked from under the bed. The woman lay on the bed, so unnaturally still that it was then Manuel knew she was dead. That the man who had crept into the room through the door had done it, and that the man at the window and he were the only two people who knew he had done it.

He sensed then the danger to his life. For he came from a tribe of common thieves and who would believe him? He knew he had to escape, to try and get away from the city as fast as he could.

For a day, Manuel had stayed hidden, mingling with the temple crowds and the people on Chowpatty. He had even crouched amidst the Muslim graves in the Byculla burial grounds for a night. That was for him a less scary prospect than encountering the men who had been on his trail only the other day. Then he felt he would be safer in the more secure, better patrolled parts of Bombay. The open spacious areas in the south where a greater presence of police would ensure no one harmed him.

And later he found his way into the hotel, and that was where he found Abdul negotiating for a servant for Mark Twain and his family. Right away Manuel had offered his services. He had picked up a bit of English from working at the ports, where ships sailed between Goa, Ratnagiri, Raigadh, and Bombay. 'The Amerikan sahib was a good man.' This was what he kept repeating fervently.

There was not much work for him to do. The

German guest two doors away was always hitting the Pathan, his servant, if he was late with the tea by as much as a minute. Manuel had indulged himself in the most fanciful of dreams. That he would leave with the sahib and his family, and be their servant for life. That way, he could see so much more of the world. But only some hours later, his first evening on the job, he saw fate had caught up. The two men had reappeared, they were there, under the peepul tree, keeping him under watch. That was when he knew he had to give them the slip. But he still had the jewellery, and had to do something about that. The only place he found secure was the mattress in Mark Twain's room that already had a slight tear. It was only a matter of ripping it a bit more, slipping the bag of jewellery inside, and stitching up the quilt with a needle and thread he got from a coachman.

'Did you take anything else?' Henry asked sharply, remembering the pendant Olivia had lost.

Manuel's face went blank so quickly that Henry understood he wasn't even pretending. It could be that Olivia had dropped the pendant somewhere else, and it would turn up once the hotel room had been cleaned thoroughly. 'Never mind,' he said, 'get on with the story.'

Manuel had climbed out after stitching the jewellery into the quilt. He rubbed his arms now as if they were still sore from the effort of climbing out the second floor window, slithering down the water pipe, over the back stairs, and the window ledge. He again began his aimless wandering in the city, constantly looking over his shoulder for Tuka's men. But there were too many people at his heels. At Chowpatty as he joined a crowd listening to one of the church men speaking, he felt a tap on his shoulder. And while he did not seem as towering as before, or someone tall enough to look through a second-floor window, he was still tall enough for Manuel to know who he was. He had that long hair, his face, lit up in excitement, was aflush in the late evening heat.

Bancroft had made Manuel the strangest offer, one made up of entreaties, and mimed gestures. 'You must teach me how to do that, to slither up walls like a lizard,' he had pleaded. 'What you did was magical. You must teach me; it will make me an even better magician.'

Bancroft had offered to make Manuel his assistant. They would travel the world, give shows, and it would bring them fame and fortune. Manuel was tempted, till he remembered the jewellery he had hidden away in the sahib's room, and that he couldn't just leave Mark Twain's service without as much as a by your leave. That was what he explained to Bancroft, and they agreed to meet at Chowpatty within the hour.

The Clemenses, he thought, were at the party at Bengalee's house. But as Manuel came up to the hotel, he saw the two men skulking under the tree again, just where he had seen them the last time. He realized they hadn't cottoned onto the fact that he had left, that they believed he was still inside. He thought he could quickly slip in, retrieve the jewellery, leave a hurried explanation with one of the servants, before making his way out again. But he had lost sense of time entirely. He had no idea if the Clemenses had returned from the party. When he saw the light on in both their rooms, the shoes left outside for cleaning, he was struck with guilt and remorse and some inexplicable regret at the choices he was confronted with. He grappled with his conflicted thoughts, as to whether he should approach Mark Twain at such a late hour or wait till morning. But the choices were forced on him, for the magician Bancroft hovered outside, on his stilts, and there were those two men, their fatigue adding to their anger.

Manuel decided to wait. He had crouched against the wall, away to one side, where he was away from the light and thus likely not to catch anyone's eye immediately. But the man on stilts was drawing shrill laughter from those around, and Tuka's men were making wisecracks that irritated Bancroft. For he turned around and lifted one of his stilts threateningly. Manuel, crouched on the side of the veranda, could see it all. He shrank against the wall, hoping to become invisible in every way. He heard footsteps leading away, and thought it was one of the servants slipping away for water, or to relieve himself.

That was when Henry interrupted to ask if he was sure about this. It had occurred to him that it might have been Mark Twain he had heard, walking down with Pease, just as the violinist Bozi had said. Manuel frowned and thought for a moment. Slowly, he said that he had in fact heard the tapping of a stick on wood, and servants would never walk about in that fashion. They would never give themselves such airs. He shook his head decisively. It could not have been the servants.

When silence had fallen again, apart from the owls hooting in the trees, the crows still restless, the dogs in the cemeteries barking like they always did this late at night, and as the city fell asleep, Manuel rose. He heard the watchman on their rounds, calling out their warnings. He stepped back in surprise when he saw Mark Twain's bed empty. He saw the open cupboard, and knew the sahib had dressed hurriedly. The same coat Manuel had ironed earlier that evening was no longer on the hanger, nor was his hat. He would be back soon, Manuel surmised, and that left him just enough time to retrieve the jewels. Mark Twain had evidently tried to sleep for the bedsheets were rumpled, and it was still warm, as Manuel patted the mattress. It amazed him, the softness of it all, the comforts the rich could enjoy. He didn't envy them in the least. It was in one's destiny where one was born. You did not know where you would be born, into which family, and then one had to be extremely lucky to change one's destiny. Manuel believed he had been lucky just by keeping clear of the law. This time the lure of gold had proved too much. The more Manuel thought along these lines, he became increasingly morose. Moments later, he heard the sound of music very close. Someone playing the violin next door. It made him sad and sleepy, and he had simply turned over the bedclothes, and slid into the comfort the sheets offered. Only a little while, he said, and a dreamy look came into his eyes as he recounted this again to Henry.

Henry could guess what had happened next. Mark Twain had not reappeared, and Manuel had slept right on, in undisturbed comfort. The music had lulled him to sleep and even the appearance of Bancroft at the window, a sight that irked the German no end, had not roused Manuel. Instead, it might have been the burst of sunlight through the window some hours later, when Olivia had crept in, and pulled open the curtains, that made him stir. It had taken Manuel only some moments to come fully awake, and the sound of footsteps around him, the sight of the morning outside, in all its fullness, made him panic, and in a trice, he was out of the window.

'But you came back again, didn't you?' Manuel had begun nodding but Henry wasn't done yet. 'And the jewels were not there, right?'

A frightened look came over his face, his hands trembled as he folded them again before Henry. 'I really don't know how they disappeared. But...the pendant, it was on the table, I felt it with my hands, and picked it up. Sometimes these things happen,' he lifted his hands, took off his tightly wrapped turban and nonchalantly plucked out the pendant from its folds. As Henry extended his hand for it, he had the bemused thought that there appeared to be too many things Manuel carried around on his own self. But he was talking again, in earnest low tones, 'Sahib, please believe my story, I came looking for you once I heard about the Amrikan, that he was missing. I felt the men urging me to get the jewels had something to do with it, but not me, sir. Not us, sahib. Believe me.' He had fallen to his knees again, and Abdul scratched his head, in genuine puzzlement. 'Doesn't he get it that the more often he does this bit of drama, the less likely he is to be believed?'

Abdul had spoken in his own native Pashto, a language Henry too was just picking up, but Manuel looked at Abdul, shook his head decisively, and said, 'My tribe, we are never believed. Branded as criminals, we are seen as nothing else but thieves. No matter how much we protest our innocence. I just fell for the trap. And the thought of making some extra money quickly. I will be suspected of things other than stealing too. Sahib here, he is good man. He will not judge me for the taint my community wears. He will, I think, believe me.'

Manuel looked at him so piteously that Henry smiled thinly. His mind was racing ahead, a part of him wishing that Maya had been witness to Manuel's detailed disclosures. Mark Twain had still to be traced, but piecing together what Bozi had said, and what Manuel hinted at, it was obvious that Arthur Pease had taken Mark Twain somewhere that night. He had to think through everything, Henry thought, and he needed to tell Maya this. Abdul was looking at him expectantly and he said just the very thing on Henry's mind.

'You will then be going to Maya memsahib now?' Abdul asked, and Henry flushed, not missing the twinkle that flashed momentarily in Abdul's eyes.

'Not a moment to lose, Abdul,' he said in sharp tones. 'I will call the Governor too. Lives are at stake.' He pointed the butt end of his gun Manuel's way. 'This man's life too. There are men on his trail still looking for him.'

He placed his revolver securely in his coat, and looking at himself quickly in the mirror, he told Manuel, who now stood with a despairing expression. 'Your life is in danger, that's the long and short of it. You are safe here, and Abdul will be on guard. Just call me at the doctors' bungalow if anything urgent comes up.'

Abdul's eyes lit up at the prospect of finally being permitted to use the telephone. 'No one saw you come here, right?' Henry asked Manuel, though he knew the answer already. Manuel had used the window to get in. An unusual mode of entry could sometimes be the safest.

'Don't step out at all, even out on the veranda,' he said looking at them.

~

As he hailed a passing carriage on the road, Henry hesitated. It occurred to him to go along to Pease's house on his own. Khetwadi lay in a direction bang opposite to the doctors' bungalow in Colaba. But he had already had an unpleasant encounter with Arthur

Pease, and despite all the new evidence he had gathered, the testimonies provided by Bozi and Manuel, Henry knew, he couldn't barge into Pease's house without the police. And the police, strained on every level, with the protests about Casi's murder and Tuka's arrest, were always going to be slow. And three days had gone by since Mark Twain had disappeared. Henry shuddered at the thought of this bit of news leaking out and reaching London and New York. He blanked out all the terrible possibilities that could follow from this.

XIV
How Music Draws Out the Most Reticent

Henry didn't quite like the plan, and repeated his objections. 'It's madness. You can't possibly think to resolve everything this way,' he said, but despite his protestations, he knew there really was no other alternative. Doing things quickly was what mattered now, and one wasn't sure if the police would agree to storm Pease's cottage at short notice. Too many permissions would be required, and it could create quite a scandal. *American writer held hostage by British missionary*, Henry could already imagine the headlines.

Maya looked at him, midway through tying her turban. She frowned, peering into the mirror. Tying a turban was a convoluted exercise. There were pleats to be made, and folds arranged in neat layers, one over another. Maya had just secured a pleat, got it around her head, but an end repeatedly fell over her eye. An actor watched her, tried hard to stifle his grin, before he stepped forward to help. Ramu was slender, with a thin moustache, and a ready smile who was excited about his own prospective role in the impromptu plan Maya had thought up.

'You just need a little practice,' he told Maya reassuringly, as Henry watched the actor bundle up the cloth quickly around one fisted hand, pleat it with one hand raised high, and then arrange a fold neatly across Maya's forehead. Henry felt an odd pain in his chest, feeling that he had no simple way to ease himself into similar familiarity with Maya, as could Abdul, or even Bancroft. Then he remembered her fleeting kiss on his cheek from a time that seemed far away now. He had totally forgotten about it, and the memory made him turn away abruptly.

That morning, they were in a house that belonged to Cowasjee Bengalee on Grant Road, located close to several of Bombay's theatres. A house that Bengalee who loved the theatre sometimes lent out to travelling troupes. A damp-streaked, two-storied house, built in the traditional way, with a tall gate made in the wall itself, complete with twin cupolas on either side. The gate led into a courtyard, with a walled-in fountain. The first floor built on a raised ledge had rooms all round, and they were in the main hall with makeshift mirrors lining one side of the wall. Sometimes a crow or two would descend on the window ledge to look in curiously.

They were a troupe of six. Besides the two of them, Maya and Henry, there was Bozi the violinist, Eeshwar, the string player from Bengalee's party, with his baleful expression, and Ramu, who made up for the tension around with his chirpiness and easy smile. Henry greeted Eeshwar with a clipped nod, and remembered him playing outside the hotel the morning Mark Twain was last seen. Had Eeshwar been trying to draw Boehme's attention, and had been pipped to it by Bozi who had reached there earlier? He saw how the two men studiously avoided looking at each other and Henry understood it as a clear case of music rivalry.

Maya had come up with the idea of a play only the previous evening, and minutes after Henry had raced into the doctors' bungalow. Clara was keeping a careful watch on her mother, but Olivia's wan face showed some colour when Henry reassured her that they had a good idea of where her husband could be. Superintendent Vincent had also called earlier in the afternoon, Maya told Henry, and they too were following up on some leads. They had been certain about two things. That Mark Twain could not have left the city, and that he was still alive.

'Your mother does need some rest, and it'll do her good,' said Henry to Clara, kindly, in a soft tone.

'Yes, I was just finishing some illustrations,' said Clara, 'father might want to use them in his new book.' She ran her fingers over the old piano, and as the keys tinkled to life, she said, 'Father, I think I should tell you, does have this habit of wandering away on his own. It comes from his days on the steamboat, and that story of the runaway slave. He always said that was a true story.'

She flushed, wondering if she had spoken too much in her nervousness. Maya smiled encouragingly, and said she was certain her father would return soon. 'We would love to hear more of his stories.'

'The police said they had rounded up some criminal elements,' she told Henry then, turning back toward him, 'and they are satisfied they have nothing to do with it.' Maya's lips set in a stern line. 'Vincent looked very pleased when he told us that. About the police and their methods to get to the truth. He did not make it sound very pleasant.'

Henry remembered the checks and barricades placed all over the city, to catch the opium thieves. 'It did take me some time to get to Byculla the other day, and I was quite frazzled by then,' he said.

'So much else has been happening,' said Maya, sitting down on the meshed cane rocking chair. 'I need to remember to tell you in just the right sequence.'

She took a deep breath, and held out a square-shaped paper to him. He saw the diaphanous cover, the white-edged frame, the picture in it, and realized it was the photo of Casi that Maya had talked about. Casi, she was only a girl really, her hair pulled back across a narrow forehead, eyes wide and expectant. Her sari, neatly draped, came to above her ankles, and a nose ring fell in a half-circle over her lips.

Henry looked at it a long time, and shook his head. 'It's pretty upsetting, isn't it?' said Maya quietly. Her face was close to his, her fingers holding onto the photo of Casi. 'So much promise. And wiped out.'

He saw his own square shaped index finger against her slender thumb. Then he gently put an arm around her 'I know how you feel, Maya. I am sorry this happened.' She leaned her head on his shoulder and then she looked at him, her blue-green eyes flashing up at him, brilliant and determined. 'Dinyar told me something important. It bears out what Bozi said too, about Pease.'

Dinyar had been looking very unhappy the time Maya turned up at the photo studio. His face did not light up, nor did he show much enthusiasm when she complimented him on the photo. He had the shadows just right, and everything about Casi in the photo was so accentuated. The fine bone structure, the weave in the sari, and even the anklets, delicate on her feet. 'It's something to do with exposure, and how careful you are when placing the film in the chemical solution,' Maya explained to Henry.

Dinyar, however, had only nodded, and then Maya had demanded an explanation. Had Mr Bedwar, the man who taught him and who owned the studio been mean in any way? 'Then Dinyar told me about his uncle, and he jumbled up so many things that I had to figure out the order on my own. Dinyar's just been married, and he stays in somewhat cramped rooms in Kalbadevi. His uncle, he told me then,' and Maya's eyes had a light in them as she understood the significance of her next revelation, 'was sent home from the addiction recovery clinic that Mr Pease runs. The one at Khetwadi. The Healing Centre, Dinyar said,

Pease had dropped his uncle back himself a day or so ago, saying there was some work to be completed in the clinic, some cleaning up to be done.'

Maya paused, 'As a matter of fact, Dinyar gave one too many explanations, and I realized that it was Pease who hadn't had a good enough pretext on hand. Pease said something about a troublesome patient who needed all his time. He also said he was expecting an important visit, and he didn't want his centre to look overcrowded. Dinyar looked tired and miserable. His wife didn't want to be under the same roof with a strange man. This uncle has been in the healing centre for a good couple of years, so I don't blame her. So Dinyar has had to put up...'

She stopped, returning Henry's intent look with one of her own. 'Putting everything together, it's clear more than ever that we must go to Pease' place, find a way of getting in, and then, make a safe getaway with Mark Twain. You could never do it on your own.'

His eyes widened as she finished, the last sentence summing up everything he felt and had thought of too. 'The police,' he said.

'It'll be quicker this way. The plan I have,' she said, impatient. 'No, you must listen to me. I was cautious yesterday, but all we have is what we have heard, there's nothing more substantial, and Pease is powerful.'

Henry turned toward the low divan. He had a sudden desire to sit. Maya continued earnestly, 'Some of what I have to tell you about the plan will not please you, and you will disapprove, but it's the only way. Besides, the arrival of the police will alarm Pease and probably scare the poor men in there.'

In the end Henry had let himself be convinced. They would appear as a group of travelling artistes, musicians, actors, and jugglers. They would put up an act that would draw Pease outside, and then sufficiently distract him for enough time for one of them to sneak inside, spot Mark Twain, and run out with him to safety. 'Once that's done, Pease can't do much. He will bluster and threaten, but his guilt will be clear to see,' Maya had an oddly satisfied look on her face as she finished.

'There's little I can do about an act, though,' Henry said now, looking unhappily at his own turbaned self before the mirror. Maya had it all worked out and he hated being the odd figure, the one who didn't quite fit in. Bozi would play background music on his violin. Two people in the theatre group she was acquainted with, Ramu the young actor, who had played the king's son in the play the other evening, and Eeshwar, the sarangi player, would pitch in as well. 'Freddie will do something magical. A juggling act, or some illusionist trick,' she said last, a bit hurriedly, as Henry frowned in distaste. 'It will give him a chance to set things right, Henry. He really doesn't want to be on your wrong side.'

'You make me sound like some disgruntled old uncle,' said Henry. He felt unhappy, wishing there was some way he could impress Maya, as Bancroft evidently could with his devious magic, and Bozi, with his sad playing. 'Maybe he should play a more cheerful tune,' he suggested, as he felt Maya's appraising eyes on him.

'You do look good just as you are,' she said then, 'but Pease, of course, has seen you, and he'd recognize you right away. Tall with that frizzy hair that nothing can tame, and your taste for clothes. Maybe you should wear something darker, a thick bushy beard, and that long winding turban does do the trick.'

The thick woolly beard glued over his own pointy one, and his cheeks, made Henry feel hot and scratchy. He watched Ramu put on his own turban and step into the long curved shoes, and Henry stripped off his beard, wincing as the glue hurt him, and proceeded to fan himself with it.

'You can't keep doing that,' Maya scolded, flashing him a look from under her turban. She looked at herself in the mirror, and gave her moustache an extra twirl. 'That might make the beard loose, and it will slip off your face at crucial moments. So, have you got your lines right? It's something you can improvise.'

'I don't think I have it in me to be an actor,' Henry said to her again in a miserable undertone, and just that moment Freddie Bancroft walked in. He was dressed magnificently for the part. With a royal maroon cape that he unfurled the moment he stepped into the room, his hat and baton in place, and a coat with flashy gold buttons, Bancroft presented a mesmerizing sight.

'Don't be silly,' Maya cupped Henry's chin and turned his face towards her. 'You are doing it for Mark

Twain,' and then her eyes twinkled, 'and for Olivia and Clara too. Yes, I noticed how she flushes when she sees you.' He added slowly, 'I would give anything to have you look at me that way.'

Maya shook her head and looked into his eyes, clasping his hand with her own. 'Now about your lines. Remember, we,' she said, gesturing towards Ramu, who was looking in fascination at Bancroft, 'are the two natives, and you, Henry, the commander of the fort, will not let us in if we do not answer your questions. And you will ask us questions from your history, and we will provide you all kinds of wrong answers, from the epics, and local legends, and of course you won't let us in. And the music will play, as a signal. At the end of every answer, it will rise to a crescendo, the violin and sarangi playing in unison so you can ask us anything, any nonsense, because no will hear you. And then Freddie can jump in midway and begin his act.'

'Will you marry me?' Henry asked then in a low voice. Maya turned startled eyes toward him, and he improvised, his lips twisting into a smile. 'You did say I could ask anything. Anything.' Maya reddened, but there was little chance of saying anything more for loud animated chatter had broken out following Bancroft's entry.

'I wonder where he will keep that baton and crystal ball of his when he does the juggling act?' Henry said, changing the subject. He wanted Maya's gaze on him, not on Bancroft, but the conniving magician that Henry felt Bancroft was, everyone was indeed staring at him, almost enraptured. Bancroft tossed the hat, the crystal ball and baton up, in a neat circle, and caught them gracefully as well. 'The things in my hand, Mr Baker, I know better than to let them slip away,' he said silkily, and Henry knew that despite their recent friendship, they would never really get on. And Bancroft, because he couldn't resist showing off, slipped the crystal ball into his hat, and then flipped the hat over. The ball had well and truly disappeared. Maya smiled, Ramu clapped in delight and the musicians stopped playing in appreciation. Even Eeshwar, the man who looked so unhappy otherwise, managed a slow, thin smile. Only Henry noticed the becoming flush on Maya's cheeks. He had last seen it some mornings ago and knew it was there because of him. He felt then, a rush of wild, sweet hope, the kind he had never encountered before, and he wanted it to last and last.

XV

A Performance of a Lifetime

'Stop playing with your beard,' Maya hissed at Henry the second time as the carriage stopped, a few metres before the Pease cottage and his Healing Centre. 'It'll be okay, believe me.' He was still lost in what had happened some moments ago, and he heard Maya's voice, soft against his ear.

'Just don't look at Pease when he comes, please look at me.' He raised a quirky brow at that, and they were smiling at each other as they jumped down from the carriage that had brought them the short distance from Grant Road to Khetwadi. It was around nine in the morning and the road was already busy with men pulling two-wheeled barrows loaded with sacks, priests going door to door, holding up a plate with offerings and incense sticks, and a couple of carriages rushed by calling for passengers. Henry straightened his hat and stopped his hand from straying toward his beard again. It was the fourth day since Mark Twain had last been seen, and today, if all went well, they would find him. Henry had a good feeling about things, and in Maya's company, the day had begun well. His superiors in Washington DC would disapprove of his methods but he would worry about this later.

They stopped just before the gate to Pease's cottage, and looked at each other for the briefest of seconds before Maya nodded. That was the signal to begin.

Bozi fixed his hat, drew his bow over his violin strings and began to play. That was the cue for the young actor, Ramu, to launch into a soliloquy about travelling with his brother to the 'big and bad' city of Bombay. The windows on the upper floors flew open, and women and children looked out excited, pointing out the troupe to others. Henry suddenly felt self-conscious, his fingers longed to feel his beard one more time, to secure his hat firmly once again.

'In the big bad city, the big bad daroga, the commander of the fort, stood at the big gate,' Ramu wheedled in a singsong voice. 'Only some people could get in, not everyone, though we pleaded and pleaded. My big brother and I asked to be let in to see our father. He is old and ailing. The cotton mills are big bad places to work in, and the supervisor is...'

This time the crowd that had gathered around finished for him: 'Big and bad,' and there was laughter, and a rousing applause at the end. 'Good people,' said Maya, in a loud authoritarian voice, 'if you are so kind, will you help us with the, with the...'

'Big and bad city,' the children yelled again and the first coins were flung their way. Bozi and Eeshwar played a long-drawn sonorous tune, and then Bancroft stepped down from the carriage and onto the street. He was greeted with even bigger cheers, as he twirled streams of colourful ribbons in his hands. 'The big bad city,' went on Ramu, 'has its pleasures, it has a world-renowned magician, but it also has its share of many...'

He didn't have to prompt this time. The children once again finished for him—'big and bad things'—, though one of them yelled 'good' before he was outshouted and booed. Ramu raised his hands asking for silence before going on, 'And the big and bad daroga sahib decided to make it as difficult for us as possible, so he set a test for us. A big bad test, with big questions.'

This was the cue for Henry to come into the act. Swinging his baton, striding with purpose towards Ramu and Maya, he spoke with as much authority as he could muster. 'No one enters the city. Only I can decide such things in the...'

And this time, the crowd that seemed to be growing by the minute shouted in glee: 'The big and bad city.' Henry turned around and frowned as he took in their audience. Urchins in their short loin cloths, some women smiling shyly, holding their veils in the crook of their fingers, leaving their faces only half covered, and a few idling workers, wearing lazy expectant smiles. Some other entertainers had gathered as well. Henry saw the snake charmers with their baskets, and the sweets-sellers finding a place for themselves too, their rectangular wooden boxes at their feet, their bells shaking in concordance to their laughter.

'This is no big bad city,' Henry moved around threateningly, in character, his baton sweeping in a wide arc over all those gathered, 'but the greatest of all cities, as good as London, New York, Cairo...'

'What are these places, sahib?' asked Ramu, fingers on his chin, his face raised to the sky.

Henry thumped his baton on the palm of his other hand as he admonished. 'Cities. Don't just call them places. Cities, world famous, with dreams of gold, roads paved with...'

He had intended to say, 'streets' just as he caught Maya encouragingly mouthing the words, when the crowd chimed in again, 'big,' and after a pause, 'bad.'

'That makes no sense, you...' he said annoyed at this interruption, and with himself, and Maya for thinking him silly enough to be prompted. He strode toward one section of the crowd, where the grinning urchins and street boys jostled for a better view. They were repeating the words, 'big' and 'bad' ad nauseum and of course this way the words made no sense.

'Bombay city, we have heard, is a big bad city.' Maya had spread her arms wide, and implored the audience to agree with her. 'Isn't it?' And the audience responded with rousing yells. 'It is. It is.'

The musicians began playing again. Joyous, rambunctious music that Maya and Ramu began marching to, gesturing to the audience to join in as well. Taking their cue from Maya and Ramu who stomped around in a circle, the boys in the audience—for the women were far shyer—held hands, and stepped forward two steps and moved back again, as Ramu chanted, still very serious. 'In the big, bad city, the women are careful. There are big bad people everywhere.'

Henry was soon into the spirit of things like everyone else. He intoned in perfect synchronicity. 'There are big and bad people who come to the city to give it a bad name. That is why we...' He was interrupted by a booming staccato voice.

'The big and bad daroga sahib,' someone had shouted behind him, and Henry turned to where the sound came from, twirling his baton, 'Who dared call me that? I am no mere daroga, but...' He looked around the crowd, mock-threateningly, swinging his baton high, making Ramu move out of the way, his arms over his head, crying dramatically in fear.

'It was me,' and Henry did another complete turn, sharply and in annoyance. It had to be Bancroft of all people, who had a stellar role in this makeshift, impromptu play, and he bowed, smiling at the rousing cheers that came his way. Henry snapped, a feeling that matched the role he was in. 'You dare...'

Henry caught Maya's imploring stare, and he clamped down. For he saw what Maya had seen as well. Arthur Pease had appeared at the gate of his cottage, and he stood, arms akimbo, a frown on his face. Bancroft towered over everyone as he stood on his stilts. He had thrown several balls up in the air, each one of dazzling colours, packed with cotton and yarn, and there was a gasp as the colours melded into each other, and it looked as if he was twirling a rainbow that reached higher and higher, as he threw and tossed the balls up a greater height, his arms like a magician's batons. The crowd broke into loud cheers of delight.

'You must improvise,' Henry caught Maya's breathless instructions, as he stood somewhat unhappy and red in the face as Bancroft stole the limelight with consummate ease. 'He's looking on, and soon he could have the police here.'

'The big and bad daroga sahib stood looking on,' began Ramu who exchanged a quick look with Maya before he went on, 'as the world's greatest magician took the stage. This is what we have come to see,' Ramu went on, returning to the role of the seer in the play, as he informed the audience about how as his older brother began negotiating with the big bad policeman, he as the younger brother simply sneaked into the city.

The musicians played again. Eeshwar stretched his bow slowly across the strings, his eyes closed in ecstasy, and Bozi, not to be outdone, marched around in a circle, playing a rousing tune. Bancroft threw the balls up in the air again, and the crowd, like one giant fascinated creature, looked up, mesmerized by Bancroft's ribbons of light. Henry realized that what Bancroft was pulling off was something akin to hypnosis. Everyone in the crowd stared fixedly at the coloured balls, unable to look away. Henry saw Pease take in the scene quickly, and the crowds too, and his frown only deepened. He noticed Maya slowly edging her way toward the gate, trying to remain unobtrusive, hoping Pease's attention would be drawn to the magic Bancroft appeared to be weaving so effortlessly.

'There is no need to fear,' roared Bancroft to Ramu. He brought in a singsong intonation to his voice that grated on Henry's ears, but the audience lapped it up. 'Why fear when the big magician is here?'

The delighted crowd shouted in unison, 'Big and bad magician.'

And Henry having had quite enough, and hoping to draw Pease away from the wicker gate in front of which he stood with some menace, spoke up loudly, his voice quivering with pretend rage, as he walked up to Bancroft. He had to crane his head back to look at Bancroft who towered over him, and quickly stepped back a few paces. 'You cannot perform here without permission.' But Bancroft barely heard, for he was still tossing up his balls. Henry raised his baton, and was about to shout again, when he heard a hoarse voice close to him. 'You cannot do this here, in front of a clinic.'

Arthur Pease now stood next to Henry, and they were both looking up at Bancroft who had scarcely registered their presence. Henry held his breath, fearing he would be recognized any moment, but Pease's eyes were narrowed and sharp as he looked up at Bancroft. A musty cobwebby smell came from him. 'You cannot,' Henry heard Pease say, and he repeated the words automatically as well. 'You cannot...' He cast a quick glance around, and realized that Maya had seized on this momentary distraction on Pease's part. Pulling aside the wicker gate, she had slipped in. The actor Ramu noticed it too, and astutely turned back to face the crowd, breaking into a loud tremulous wail to get their attention.

'And so, this big and bad city where two brothers came to seek their fortune, it swallowed up one of them. And the younger brother went around town, asking everyone he met if they had seen his beloved older brother.' Ramu went up quite spontaneously to someone in the audience, a missionary woman in her long brown skirt who had just gotten off a carriage and had curiously edged her way in, and posed the question to her, 'Sister, have you seen my brother?' The woman stepped back surprised, then flushed at the attention as every head, some envious, others curious, turned toward her. Beads of perspiration gleamed on her forehead, and on her upper lip, and she brushed her long skirt nervously with her hands. The crowds leaning from their balconies tittered, and some small boys shouted almost in unison, 'Big, bad sister, have you seen him?'

Henry seized his chance to step back from Pease, as cautiously as he could. Bancroft tossed his balls higher, as he moved amongst the crowd. There were screams of delight, hisses of warning, as he came closer to where the women had gathered on the second-floor balconies; thin stone structures with wooden rails that overhung the raised platforms of the first floor. Climbing plants snaked through the rails, winding up the pillars, reaching right up to the paper lanterns that swayed from the wooden ceilings, or the clay figurines at the head of every column. In some places, clothes hung over the balcony rails to dry. Colourful multi-hued saris, plainer dhotis, and a flowing sheet or two. Ramu edged closer to the missionary who stepped back, looking over her shoulder for her carriage. But the coachman too was enjoying the show, smiling broadly as he took in the performance.

'Lady, please don't go.' Ramu was wringing his hands, a whiney note in his voice, as he mock-pleaded with the missionary. The crowd's attention was on Bancroft, who was, to Henry's annoyance, giving the performance of a lifetime. Bancroft pulled something out of his cuff, a wavering flat ribbon, and tossed it up, where it coiled around a balcony rail and as the crowd looked on, more streams of colour came gushing out from his cuffs, snaking and wriggling past Bancroft, and around him, flipping on the road like flailing fish, shivering like petals, curling up like big snails, and rolling along the street, winding through the people, Pease among them as well, shifted and stepped back. Some crouched low on the ground, laughing and dodging as they tried not to get in each other's way, scrambling to touch, even pick up the fluttery, wavy pieces of cloth. The balls fell randomly in their midst, and Pease almost stumbled on one, as he made his way forward. He moved, his arms outstretched, palms raised high, as if he were blindly feeling for anything that might come in his way. His face, lifted toward

Bancroft, tilted even further as he neared the magician.

With the crowd's attention on Bancroft, Henry quickly glanced towards the gate. He felt a momentary pang of relief. The latch was back in place, and he had a fleeting glance of the blue shawl Maya had around herself, and the darker hued turban she had on her head. Then she became smaller and was soon lost in the short curving driveway overrun with grizzled bushes and low hanging trees. He hoped Ramu would not do anything to draw attention to her, for he was standing, his hands clasped, before the woman missionary who in turn was standing before the coachman, and the latter, oblivious to all this, was absorbed by the performance unfolding around him, slapping his thigh now in delight as Pease tried to catch Bancroft's eye. Pease was within arm's reach of Bancroft who loomed over him, performing another trick with a sari. The orange and red sari shimmered in the air, as Bancroft unfurled it, once, twice, and then over him and part of the crowd. More balls popped out, some trailing long threads of yarn, and there were heightened screams of delight. Bancroft swung the sari around himself, it flapped in the breeze, and billowed the next moment. Bancroft made a pretend fumble, tried to secure some control over the sari, and smiled as he lapped up the crowd's applause.

Pease tried in vain again to get his attention. He reached up to tug Bancroft by the elbow but the other man high on his stilts barely noticed him. It was then that Pease, in some frustration, pulled Bancroft by his coat tails. Henry took advantage of all these distractions to slip in through the gate. He exchanged a quick glance with Bozi who moved across the crowd to shield Henry from Pease's view. As Henry looked back, he saw a disaster unfold on the street that only moments ago had resembled a wondrous makeshift stage.

As Pease shook Bancroft by his long coat tails, Bancroft first tottered, then flailed from side to side. The sari swelled, and fell over him, enveloping him and swallowing Pease too. Henry heard alarmed shouts as he made a dash for the raised porch of the Pease cottage. Bancroft must have fallen, unable to keep his balance. Henry glanced back one last time, hoping Bancroft wasn't badly hurt. But he heard only an inchoate screaming, and over the wall, he saw a horse rearing up in nervousness, the women leaning even lower from their balconies, hands to their mouths, and in snatches, he could hear Bozi still playing on. A collective rising cacophony from the crowd followed Henry in a jumbled wave, as he ran even faster up the driveway toward the Pease cottage.

He looked resolutely forward, intending to run to the back of the house. There might be, he hoped, a window open somewhere, or even a kitchen door. But right on the patio, the louvered double door moved slowly, as one end swung on its hinges, and Henry wasted no more time. He pulled aside the swinging end that winced loudly in protest, and rushed in, only to find himself engulfed in a thick jute curtain that smelled of mothballs, and something else he couldn't quite place immediately. An odd mix of a chemical and the kind of smell from fish hung out to dry on the docks. Henry pushed aside the curtain, sniffling in impatience, but the lobby, a small spare room with sticks of various kinds in one corner was suffused with the same smell too.

Next, he stepped into a sitting room, now in darkness with lowered blinds, wooden chairs with plain looking cushions, a rectangular writing table at one end, and an untidy shelf, packed with files. As he looked to the door on the right, a man in a pair of loose cotton shorts meandered in. His one hand trailed the wall, and he muttered to himself, evidently in a daze. His eyes barely took in Henry as he swept past. The next moment, the door at the other end, to his left, burst open, and Henry caught a quick glimpse of a vegetable garden, and clothes strung up on a washing line.

The man who entered next was taller, wearing a loose, flapping long shirt that hung over his knee-length dhoti. He had a wild-eyed look, and stopped short when he locked glances with Henry, who in some alarm stepped out of the other man's way just as he came rushing toward him, holding his arms out, as if he expected to be stopped any time. The curtains flapped against the man, who pushed them aside roughly, and as the wind swept in through the two doors, the one facing Henry and the other through which the man had just left, he heard the distinct sounds of someone banging on a door not too far away, followed by a shout. Henry recognized the voice instantly. A woman's voice, firm and unwavering. 'Let us out. Immediately!'

There was a pause, and Maya's voice, clear and somewhat tremulous, came again, followed by a pronounced rattling this time. 'The police are just outside. You cannot keep us inside.'

'Wait,' Henry shouted in turn. He was breathless, his words sounded strangled to himself, but he felt relief and a certain joyousness. He plunged through the door that led to the vegetable garden. The building had appeared smaller when seen from the front gate, and Henry saw that the garden was enclosed on all sides by green walls, the paint peeling off in places. A door in the wall led outside, and through this Henry could see part of the same wild garden he had run through once he was past the wicker gate in front. On either side, he saw brown louvered windows, some shuttered, others open with a ragged curtain stretched halfway across. There were a couple of doors in the walls to his left and right, and he heard Maya's voice again. 'We need help. Quick.'

It came from the side of the house that directly faced him. A barred door looked him in the face but there was an open window through which a face suddenly appeared. A man with dark tousled hair broke into a smile that revealed several teeth missing, before he turned away. Everyone in the house seemed most peculiar, Henry thought, as he ran toward the door, hearing Maya's voice clearly now. She was in one of the rooms at this end of the house. He passed patches of grass, and as he neared the door, he was assailed once more with the same smell, a pungent odour of a chemical, and rotting fish. He shook his head, as if beating away the smell, and lifted his head to shout in turn, hoping Maya would hear him. 'Maya, it's me. I know you are here.'

'Henry!' The lilt in her voice involuntarily lifted his spirits. One day, the thought flashed through his mind, as he glanced back at the circular pods of flowers on one patch right along the wall, he would tell her how she had sounded. How relieved, and desperate, and happy too. He stood, his hands against the door, his eyes still intent on the patch, at the bulbous green pods standing on reed thin stems, and the pink petalled flowers jostling each other, and knew instantly what he was looking at. This was a poppy patch, next to a small field growing tomato, and a pumpkin vine that trailed along the wall.

'Henry, he's here. Safe and well,' Maya shouted. 'They have locked us in.'

'Hold on, I am trying to get in.' Henry was desperately trying to devise a plan to get to them quickly.

He reached the door to one of the rooms. The door was evidently locked on the other side. Henry stepped back, hoping it wouldn't strain his back too much, and that it was just a simple latch that held it fast, the usual thin iron chain stuck on an overhead nail that a well-aimed kick could often loosen. He drew in his breath, took in the many more faces that had appeared in the windows around, all with a certain dopey look, and matted hair, before he lifted a leg and slammed it hard against the door. All the recent pain he had been through, the despondency he had found himself in, suddenly lifted. He could hear Maya's voice in his ears, as he lifted his leg one more time, uncaring this time that the beard stuck on his face had slipped a bit. He heard the welcome sound of something in the wood cracking, the shouts from farther away appeared clearer too, and Henry aimed another kick at the door. This time there was the distinct sound of something falling, a metallic clank sounded against wood, and a zinging sensation swept up his leg. He knew the effort had hurt him, but he had to keep on, and as he lifted his leg, the left leg this time, the door suddenly opened, and a man, skeletal in appearance, his eyes big in his emaciated face, and wearing only a dirty white dhoti stood there, his hands folded. 'Have you come to rescue us?'

The question startled Henry, and the man stood looking on, his hands folded. Then, to his alarm, Henry saw the man's eyes fill with tears. 'You must take me away. To my family. I am not an addict.'

Henry managed a shaken smile, and he heard the banging again, louder this time. He had to get in right then, and the loudness of the banging made him more desperate. He moved in the direction of the sound, but the man stopped him, his fingers closing over his wrist. Henry winced, subconsciously scrunching up his nose, for the man had a musty, unwashed odour about him. 'I will do what I can. Where is this noise from?'

He saw the tears on the man's face, but Henry turned away quickly. He ran down a short, narrow hallway lined with potted plants, past a table holding old newspapers, toward a door to the right. As he stood before it, gathering his breath, he allowed himself a last sigh of relief before he reached for the bolt. It squealed when he lifted it, and made a clunky metallic noise. He winced as his finger caught on the hook just as he slid the bolt across. The next moment, he forgot his pain as the door was pulled open, and he looked into Maya's blue eyes, her flushed face. Behind her, on a lounge chair, in a room that carried the same pungent smell that lay everywhere in the house, was Mark Twain. He was sitting in an odd way, his head to one side, his arm flopped over one arm of the chair, but there was little doubt it was him.

Henry stood against the wall, feeling Maya lean against him, and they stood there for long moments, feeling light-headed, tired, and also a terrible relief. Her turban was on the table, carelessly discarded.

'How did you know where to find him?' Henry asked her, with some admiration.

'I didn't,' she said. 'I walked in and was looking in at every door when another man suddenly appeared. I had to improvise then, telling him I was from the police. A detective. And he was suddenly scared. "Where is he?" I asked and he pointed to this door. But when I walked in, he pushed me and locked us both in.'

Henry surmised this was the man whose path had crossed his, right at the front entrance. He must have been running to warn Pease. Henry looked past Maya. Mark Twain was still unmoving on the lounge chair, showing little sign of coming to life. The sun filtered in through nets placed over the window, and Henry noted how sparsely the room was furnished. A flat wooden bed covered with a white sheet was placed in the corner, next to which was a table with a notepad, a photo of the Queen on the dank yellow walls, and damp patches appeared high on the ceiling. There was a three-tiered bookshelf with old issues of the *Bombay Gazette*, and a book he recognized as Rudyard Kipling's *Plain Tales from the Hills*, and then the Bible, the gold painted leaves on its cover glinting in the sun.

Henry lifted Mark Twain's hand, pushed back the cuff, and felt for a pulse. The relief on his face, as he felt a faint throb, gave way to disgust and anger. He saw the ring of dirt around Mark Twain's cuffs, the dust and sweat gathered like grey patches on his neck, his moustache drooped over his lips as he dozed. Then there was how he smelt, not just musty and dank, but reeking of that pungent odour that Henry now associated with opium.

He gritted his teeth, his hand bunched up into a fist, and he turned around, startling Maya. She held a small brass pitcher up. She dipped her hand in and gently ran her damp fingers over Twain's forehead, his hands, and then his face, murmuring in a low voice. 'We must get him out here. And fast.'

He understood what Maya meant. They couldn't carry him out on their own. It wasn't just that carrying Mark Twain out would be cumbersome, they could be challenged by Pease, in any number of ways. Henry understood the urgency, and he touched Mark Twain again, first on the hand a trifle gingerly, then patted him on the shoulder, leaning closer to whisper, 'Mr Clemens.' He gagged at the smell that arose from the writer and took a few gulps of fresh air before he turned back again, 'Mr Twain, Mark.' He stopped, for Maya had begun giggling in some high-strung relief, and he began laughing too, as he shook Mark Twain's shoulder gently again. In response, Twain simply shifted, his head lolling lower on his chest, and Henry looked for someplace else to nudge him. He was still calling out his name, looking at Maya with a hint of a smile, when he heard a commotion in the hallway. The next time he turned back to look at Mark Twain, it was to find the writer's grey eyes looking at him, dazed and lost, and for some moments, Henry equally lost, stared back at him. Then he heard the footsteps. He saw Maya calmly put away the pitcher, rub her hands on her turban that she then wrapped around one hand, and they turned to face a furious looking Arthur Pease, standing at the door, arms akimbo, his mouth working but unable to utter a word.

XVI

A Man Who Sleeps a Lot is Forgetful

Only in the carriage on their way back to the doctors' bungalow in Colaba did they let themselves relax and think calmly over the events of the past hour. Mark Twain joined in weakly, his smile faint, his face gaunt from his recent experiences. Henry still felt anger every time his eyes strayed towards Twain who sat at one end of the closed carriage. He was aghast Arthur Pease had acted the way he had, and was mulling over what actions he as American Consul could take. The safety and welfare of all American citizens was his responsibility, and while that made him feel very important, he knew he had to have answers for all that had happened. He mulled over whether he could file a complaint to the Governor, the Viscount Sandhurst, about Superintendent Vincent and his 'seeming inaction' about the case. And Arthur Pease? He had to write to his superiors in Washington DC about him, and they had to take it up at the higher levels. He would make sure of this. Then his eyes caught Maya's and suddenly they exchanged a secret smile, one that held relief and spoke of shared conspiracy too. Maya leaned forward and gently held Mark Twain's hand in hers.

'You must rest, after you've spent time Olivia and Clara. They have been really worried.'

Mark Twain nodded in understanding, closed his eyes, and appeared to doze off. But his eyes suddenly opened only moments later, and he patted his pockets. Then with an odd half-smile, he reached into his right pocket, and his hand emerged, holding onto a red notebook. Irritation flashed across his face, for the pencil attached to the string was stuck in his pocket. The coat looked frayed, and hung limp over him. The hem of the pocket gave way as he struggled, and when he pulled harder, the pencil swung sharply out in an arc to strike the carriage wall before falling back on his sleeve. When he spoke, his voice was faint, and still raspy.

'I made some notes. Some stuff they gave me had made me groggy, but I still wrote.'

He flipped through the pages, first slowly, and then quickly, and this time his fingers shook, his irritation with himself was plainly evident. When he looked up, his eyes had a blank expression, and then he said plaintively, to no one in particular, 'The pages, they don't seem to be there.'

Maya and Henry exchanged a quick look. She said gently, as if explaining things to a child, 'You really must not worry. Once you have rested, I am sure you will remember everything.'

He sighed, shook his head, leaned back on the seat, his head resting on its rounded edge, where the cushion tapered off towards the window. In moments, he was snoring gently, his moustache shifting with every breath.

'That man really has a lot to answer for,' muttered Henry, his hands balling up into fists.

'I think Pease might be well aware of the charges he faces,' Maya said in a low thoughtful voice. 'I just wonder why he had to do it.'

'I'd think the opium turned his head too.'

'And Bancroft's, and probably many others too.'

It was early afternoon, and heat swirled inside their carriage in drowsy waves. Henry could clearly recall the events of the last couple of hours. It had taken well over an hour before Maya and he could bring Mark Twain out of the cottage. Just as they had managed to get him awake, and were hurrying to get him to his feet, Pease had appeared at the door, his face blotchy and red in anger, wet with perspiration, unable to say anything for long moments. And it was Maya, as she held Mark Twain's hand in her own, while Henry picked up the writer's hat that had somehow rolled under the bed, who told Pease, in quiet, clipped tones that they were taking him away.

This was when Pease pushed the door fully open, and entered the room, spluttering in rage.

'You cannot do that. He came on his own, with no compulsion, or force. And there are still meetings.'

He was just an arm's length away and he reached

out clearly wishing to snatch Mark Twain away from them. Henry and Maya tried to fend off Pease and in all this, Twain fell back on his chair with a faint, startled 'oh'. Henry stepped up to Pease and said, 'As the American Consul here in Bombay, I am answerable for the well-being and safety of my fellow Americans.'

Pease drew in his breath raggedly, he blinked, and for what might have been long moments, Henry and he looked at each other. 'We must really be going,' Maya said. This time, Pease made no effort to stop them, though he still held out an arm, and spoke to them, in a voice that sounded edgy and panic-stricken.

'He came of his own free will. To know more about the evil trade in opium, and the habit it induces. I am the best person to tell him about it.'

'You seem to have left him in pretty bad shape,' Henry responded curtly.

Pease's hand was still stretched out, but he was noticeably trembling.

'As I said, he came on his own. It was as he wished. He wanted to write about it, for the American papers. He wanted to see how the evil habit has grown on people, how so many of them are still addicted to the drug.'

'Did you give it to him?' Henry enunciated every word, bringing in a menacing note as well.

Pease was reduced to a nervous wreck. His hands fluttered, flailed, as he struck randomly at the air around him. His face was sweaty, his mouth opened but he was clearly lost for words. At the door, some more men had appeared, and Henry recognized the man who had dashed past him when he had made his way in. Another man came in behind the first and both had demented expressions on their faces. Henry sized them up quickly, and then, in a flash, he produced the revolver from inside his coat. There was a dramatic change of expression on every face. The two men took a nervous step back, the one in front stepping on the other's toe, who bit down on a startled yelp of pain. In that sudden pause, they could hear the clamour, the raised voices outside, followed by the piercing sound of a police whistle. Henry saw the relief on Maya's face, and the alarmed glances exchanged between Pease and the two men.

The very next moment, the two men had turned on their heels, and rushed out of the room. Only Pease stood by the door looking out, glancing often in their direction. A low stool had toppled over, and no one bothered to lift it. To Henry's right, Mark Twain sighed, and when he lifted his hand to brush an untidy strand of hair away, Henry was assailed by the pungent smell again. 'We really can't stay on,' he told Maya in some desperation, looking at Mark Twain. With his revolver in a firm grip, he advanced, finding himself close to losing his temper as he neared Pease.

'You gave him the stuff, didn't you? And you have the opium here, don't you? Not just growing it in your garden, but the actual opium cakes. And you are now going to hide them.'

Pease looked fearful and belligerent in turn. There

was a rush of feet outside, and then Henry saw them, as they turned into the sitting room through the hallway. Inspector Button, with two constables in tow, came up. Button was quick and dapper as always, and the two men behind him were hunched forward, batons in hand, looking menacing and obsequious at the same time. Button looked Henry squarely in the eye, and raising his hand, he gestured to his men behind to stop.

'We came as soon as we could. There's a riot like situation you left there. If my men hadn't been in the vicinity, it could have been worse. More than just taking Mr Bancroft to hospital.'

Henry gasped. He had expected something of this sort, from the moment he had seen Pease come up to Bancroft to get his attention. But Maya spoke up, urgently. 'We have Mr Clemens here. He was reported missing, and he was here all the time.'

'Yes,' Henry said, placing his revolver back in his pocket, 'I am afraid we'd to take matters in our hands. We suspected Mark Twain was here but with no proof, it'd have been hard to convince you.'

Button frowned, tapping his baton on his palm. He looked at Pease, at all of them in turn, before he began again.

'We take all this seriously. And that there has been too, a serious disturbance of the peace. A riot like situation outside, as I have said. A man injured, a robbery or two has also been reported. And a missionary, Miss…,' he stopped, the name had suddenly slipped his mind. 'Never mind, never mind, she was harassed by a group of Hindus. Then your men'—he jerked his head in Pease's direction—'came and told us about a break-in here. We thought it was the same gang of smugglers trying to disrupt things.'

There was a low murmur of discomfort from Mark Twain and Henry stepped forward decisively. He would brook no further delay.

'Inspector Button, we were here to find Mr Clemens. As you can see, we have found him here, with no thanks to you. He was held against his will, helped by liberal doses of opium. I am the American consul here in Bombay and so responsibility for Mr Clemens' safety rests with me. I am taking him to be seen by a doctor, and that I think is urgent.'

Button opened his mouth but closed it just as abruptly, deciding not to contradict him on this matter. He turned and barked a quick order to one of his men, in Urdu. 'Get a carriage. Jaldi!'

~

And now Mark Twain was in the carriage, and headed for some comfort and respite. Pease had looked on sullenly, and it was only when they were almost at the door, did he speak out.

'I hope you will register a case against them, Inspector. For causing a disturbance, and for breaking into my house and centre with no permission. There is also some damage to the door.' Maya and Henry could still hear him shouting as they made their way down the driveway, toward the wicker gate. The two of them walked on either side of Mark Twain, holding onto his elbows, matching their steps to his, for he walked in a slow, gingerly way. 'You will pay compensation,' Pease shouted in a voice already sounding frazzled and cracked. 'I will make sure of this. I will.'

In the carriage, Henry discreetly moved the curtain, to let in some air from outside. The smell that emanated from Mark Twain was simply too overwhelming. They were now passing the Grant Medical hospital, where Freddie Bancroft had been taken for his injured leg, and still a good forty-five minutes or so to the doctors' bungalow in Colaba remained as they rode down Hornby Row with its clubs and newspaper offices, past Esplanade with its University Building and Watson's hotel, familiarly abuzz with life, then the wide half-circle around the impressive black stone statue of the Prince of Wales, on Queen's Road appeared to their right, before they crossed into Colaba Causeway. Henry could hear the soft roar of the sea in the distance, and he squinted to see a brightly coloured kite drifting through the palm trees. It reappeared again like a speck against the low white clouds. He heard the whistling sounds of a vendor, the chanting of musicians, and the clop-clopping of horses on the road. Mark Twain had been found safe, relatively unharmed, yet Henry felt oddly deflated. He knew it was part fatigue, but he sensed a loss as he leaned against the window. He felt the balmy afternoon air on his head, and closed his eyes. He wanted to think about Maya, how the last few days had gone by, with more strangeness and excitement than he had ever imagined, and knew he would miss them.

He was dreaming then, of the time he had travelled through Europe by train. From Paris to Munich to Vienna, then Budapest, before the final disembarkation at Constantinople. At night, just as they had left Strasburg, he sensed a ghost in his carriage. A woman who had got lost in the mountains. That was the story the night conductor on the train had told him. *Keep your curtains drawn, sir. You might see her, hear her singing, and that can make you forget.* He had wanted to forget so many things then, the life he was leaving behind, the new life he wanted for himself, and he had stayed up looking through the window, seeing nothing but the moon low on the shiny white land. In a couple of places, he glimpsed lone lights in cottages, and just as they passed a tunnel, he saw the light to his left. It seemed someone was holding a lantern up in the darkness. He felt someone shaking him, by the hand, and the shoulder, and brushed it away, thinking it was the conductor, and then he heard Maya's voice low in his ear.

'Henry, Henry, there's something. Listen.'

He rubbed his face, brushed his hair aside, flustered at having dozed off, but she was leaning close, her cycs intent on something else outside the window. 'The young man over there, he was shouting out something about a murder. A murder in the Grant Road area.'

He looked toward Mark Twain, oddly reassured he was still there. The writer sat hunched over oddly, looking at his diary, his pencil in hand. 'Mr Clemens, is everything all right?' Henry asked, and then he fumbled unsure what to call him now. After all they had been through, he wanted to drop formalities. On the other hand, calling him Mark Twain, the way he thought of him in his mind, made things appear unreal. Henry wanted things to be on easier, more relatable grounds.

Mark Twain looked up, smiled vaguely and unhappily. 'Oh, call me Sam. That will do very well. But as I was saying, there was this page here, that I had written up, that evening when I left with Pease. We had talked of many things...and now...'—he riffled through the pages, murmuring to himself, as he did so. The diary slipped from his hands as he was checking for his lost notes a third time, and Maya bent to pick it up for him.

'It does look as if they have been torn away, Mr Clemens.' She held the diary open and showed the ripped perforated centre where a paper or two had been hastily pulled off. 'That's strange,' Mark Twain was scratching his head, and looking most unhappy, 'I never do that. Sometimes even things that make no sense at first, do so days later.' His voice trailed off, he closed the diary, put it back in his pocket, and looked through Henry's open window, at nothing in particular. 'Have I been away long?' he asked then in a voice full of wonder.

Maya and Henry exchanged a conspiratorial look. They seemed to be doing a lot of this of late, Henry thought, and he would surely miss these days, as he heard Maya reply, 'You set us a whole big mystery, and it was terribly worrying, especially for Olivia. Clara took it all in her stride. But it's over finally, and you will have quite a story to tell.'

XVII

How to Avoid a Diplomatic Fracas

'Almost four days!' Mark Twain kept repeating that to himself quite in daze, even after they had reached the doctors' bungalow in Colaba where a big welcome awaited him. Clara rushed down the driveway, remembering in time to move out of the horses' way. One of them, a young lean pony, was already skittish because there had been unexpected crowds on the Causeway, and he shied back. It took some moments for the coachman to soothe him and bring the carriage up the driveway, where the doctor, Edith Pechey, her husband, the businessman, Mr Phipson, Charlotte, and Ali, waited, all with broad smiles, while Olivia had tears of relief in her eyes. Henry looked around, aware he was missing someone, before he realized Abdul wasn't around. That Abdul was still at the Byculla Club keeping guard over Manuel, who despite his contrition and fright, was as guilty as Pease and needed to be handed over to the police. Henry knew he should have done it as soon as he had had a confession, and he groaned silently. There had been too many things on his mind, and he hadn't been thinking straight.

'So many days,' Mark Twain exclaimed again, looking livelier and much refreshed after a hot bath. 'And I had just gone out for a tour of the city,' he slurped his tea with some relish, put the cup down on the low table by him and began again. 'Or maybe I am not remembering in the right order. That man, Pease, he was here in the hotel in the afternoon, just before we left for the party.'

Clara looked at him with fond irritation. 'Father, you are totally confusing us. Do you mean the party at Mr Bengalee's house?'

'There have been other parties I've missed?' he asked and everyone burst out laughing.

'Pease was there at the hotel in the afternoon, was he?' mused Henry. 'I wonder why no one spoke of that to the police then?' He felt dazed. Suddenly it seemed everyone had missed the blindingly obvious. Henry also realized they hadn't had a chance to relay Bozi's conversation earlier in the hotel to Clara and Olivia.

'If you mean the man in a loose brown coat, and those papers with him,'—Clara spoke up, from where she stood by the mantelpiece,—'he was around in the lobby. In the afternoon, I had come down with Manuel with father's suit and our gowns that had to be ironed, and suddenly, Manuel just wasn't there. He had vanished. Some minutes later, he appeared again in the ironing room, looking very embarrassed. "That man, Pease," he said, "he insists on dragging us away to his lectures and sermons." But then, Manuel too was strange, the way he vanished.'

George Kittredge tapped on the armrest of his big sofa. A long-time American businessman in India, and a friend of Phipson, Kittredge took a special interest in every American who visited. Whenever he came around to the doctors' bungalow, he always occupied that same chair that gave him a commanding view of everyone and everything. He nodded ponderously, reminding Henry that it was Kittredge alone, who among everyone gathered in that room, had not rushed out to welcome Mark Twain. Instead, he had remained seated. Suitably enthroned, Henry thought, as Kittredge spoke slowly, his every word weighted with his importance.

'He does that all the time. I refer to Arthur Pease, of course. The clerks in my office often tell me of his visits. He's always leaving those pamphlets around. The evil city can corrupt anyone, especially the newcomers and the visitors. There's so much gossip about him and those papers of his. When that happens, when he turns up, no work ever gets done.'

The long drapes of the punkah rested close to where Kittredge sat. Henry thought fleetingly of the fans he wanted to introduce into the city. In business, George Kittredge had certainly had more luck. The horse drawn trams Kittredge had introduced were a big success and now he was all excited about securing a possible license for an electric tramway system. That was just what the city needed, just as it did the electric fan. Henry secretly envied Kittredge's success, but then he had first arrived in the city sometime in the 1870s, and that was years before he, Henry, had. Kittredge was constantly moving between Boston, his hometown, and Bombay, and had made fifteen trips so far.

Henry, standing at the door of the sitting room, stole a peek into the study a door away, where on a high table, the phone sat on its neat doily. He hadn't heard the phone ring, and he was getting impatient. Why hadn't Abdul called till now? It was a small room, leading away from the hallway, and the shadow of a laburnum tree in full bloom that grew right by the netted window, made a pleasing pattern on the floor.

The hallway had a couple of elephant illustrations by Lockwood Kipling, and another of the Lahore fort by Edwin Lord Weekes, the artist who was now in Ajanta to look at the amazing cave paintings. In the sitting room where everyone was, there were the etchings and sketches of women that the celebrated painter at the JJ School of Art, M.V. Dhurandhar, had made popular. Henry strolled to the window at the far end of the hallway and looked out. There was Ali talking to the gardener, Hari, who pulled his long two-pronged rake through the shrubs, checking for snakes and nodded absently to Ali's words. Henry headed back to the sitting room, where Clara was clearing away the teacups. He took the tray from her, smiling as she led the way to the kitchen. 'Are you expecting a message?' she asked, as Henry handed over the tray to the maid who stood with her head half-veiled, her hands extended. She fairly snatched the tray from his hand, and Henry had a glimpse of startled eyes, and a gasp, as she said in halting English, 'Sahib didn't have to get the tray.'

Maya, he knew, had been teaching the local women at the Native Girls School. He shrugged, exchanged a quick smile with Clara, 'Oh, we Americans are used to doing things on our own.'

In the hallway leading to the sitting room, Clara told him about the message from the police. Superintendent Vincent would come by and record her father's statement. As they neared, the sounds of conversation became distinctly louder and more animated. 'We seem to have missed something interesting,' Henry said, as he held the door open for Clara.

It was always cool in the sitting room. The soft yellow of the walls had a calming effect, and the windows with the slanting blinds allowed the sun to gently drift in, light patches wavering amidst similar leaf patterns on the floor. There were two big armchairs, couches and low diwans, and Kittredge hunched forward, a rectangular cushion nestled on his knees, looking earnest as he said, 'This will become a heated diplomatic issue. Arthur Pease is very well-connected, with an uncle who is a member of parliament, and his father and brothers very influential in the government. You can be sure he will pull every string to get off.'

Herbert Phipson ran a hand over his bald pate, looked at his wife, Edith, before he said, 'It's all very complicated, indeed. Not just a clear case of kidnapping.'

'Kidnapping,' Mark Twain burst out, as he lay stretched on the settee. 'There was no kidnapping.' His arm dropped low beside him, and he patted the seat by him, enunciating every word. 'He was telling me about the opium trade, the smuggling, how opium has made of men, and women too, slaves of a different kind, and he said he had been trying to get the government to come down heavily on the racket. And that all the big men here,'—his voice dropped, he looked around, his eyes bright, through the lock of greying hair that fell over his forehead,—'they are all involved. The big businessmen made their fortunes from it and are becoming richer in the bargain. Pease wanted to draw attention to it. He wanted my help.'

Twain cleared his throat, and tried not to look important as he added, 'He told me he had read many of my books, and that I was a writer who knew the value of words. Unlike that man, Oscar Wilde.' He glanced with some animation toward his wife who sat opposite him, holding the morning's edition of the *Bombay Gazette* in her hands, her glasses halfway down her nose. 'Pease said something about his play. That it should never be staged. Don't you remember, my dear? We met Wilde one summer three years ago, at that hotel in Germany.'

'Four years ago, you mean,' replied Olivia slowly, 'and he was quite a sight, wasn't he, Clara?'

'Yes,' Clara stood next to Maya by the cane bookshelf, 'we were too taken up…'

'Taken aback, you mean,' interrupted her father, brushing his moustache.

'Well,' Clara hesitated, flushed, and began again, 'yes, he wore that big carnation in his lapel, and the red shoes. He made quite an impression.'

Mark Twain turned away with a slight smile, 'And he is in some sort of trouble in London. That's what Pease said. That Wilde is paying a price for his debauched ways. Now that centre that Pease runs is really something. A small cottage like place. Ah,'—he glanced towards Maya—'but you found me there. I was finally catching up on my sleep. The crows at the hotel just hadn't let me sleep. So we are back to where we were at the beginning.'

He sat back again, his hand reaching out to pull a neat cloth hand fan towards him. Henry saw Maya dart a quick look his way. She understood he was thinking about his electric fans, and that Pease was one of the first people he had approached. Twain played with the fan, brushing away Clara's offer to fan him a bit before he began again. 'I must tell you about the crows. They kept up such a cacophony, that I just couldn't sleep. The tree just outside, the tall peepul that overlooks one corner of the Esplanade seemed to house a whole colony, and after a while I just couldn't take it. I tried to sleep, I hadn't slept much before, and the last stretch of the journey from Goa to Bombay had been downright terrible, with the sudden storm. But this cawing, the mayhem, it was like a nightmare. A nightmare very like the jingle I wrote about in that story almost twenty years ago. Do you know that one?'

Henry straightened, he had been leaning against

the wall. 'The jingle, I do remember. It goes something like,'—he screwed up his eyes to remember, hoping he would not make a fool of himself and especially before Maya—'*Conductor, when you receive a fare*; *punch in the presence of the passenjare*...And then it goes on, *a blue trip slip, a buff one, and a pink one.*'

Mark Twain looked at him with delight, and everyone—Clara, Phipson, Edith, Maya, and Olivia—in the room was clapping. But not Kittredge who rarely expressed appreciation for anything not associated with him.

'That's the one,' Mark Twain said, fairly beaming, 'such an irritating thing it was. That earworm. It kept on needling me, getting in the way, just like the crows. Till I had to put it all in a story. So, where was I?' He blinked, and George Kittredge raised his hand in some apology, as he rose slowly to his feet. Everything he did, Henry knew, was with the sense of his own importance, as if he expected time to slow down to accommodate his every movement. 'Regretfully, much as I am enjoying this company, I have to go,' Kittredge said, nodding to everyone, and Charlotte rang the bell to call Ali.

A gentle tolling echoed through the house, and ended with the pattering feet of Ali, who sidled in through the side-door, came down the hallway, and salaamed his way into the room. In the manner of all long-serving attendants, he sized up the situation, and held the door open for Kittredge. But Ali was forced to open it wider as Henry, who saw the quick nod

Kittredge directed his way, accompanied him out. They followed as Ali led the way ahead, walking in an odd sideways manner, to keep them in sight, and they went back down the main hallway, past a small guestroom, its quilted red curtain waving briefly as they passed, toward the hat rack and the umbrella stand.

'You must tell him not to press charges,' Kittredge spoke low and urgently, his eyes darting towards Ali, 'Clemens, that is. It could spoil relations between us and Britain. Create difficulties, you know, what with the trade-standoff in Venezuela, and our interests in Cuba, and the Philippines. Germany will always take advantage. That Pease...'

Henry broke in impatiently, 'You did say he's well connected. And his connections let him get away with his being such a nuisance, and for so long. Goodness, Pease is the kind who would try and get his nose into everything, see the bad in everyone. I won't be surprised if he used his anti-opium crusade as a cover just to get publicity for himself, promote himself as the only do-gooder in this city.'

They heard the clopping of a horse carriage, and the afternoon heat struck Henry in the face as they walked through the main door. Kittredge had a faint smile on his face, as he shook hands. 'That's the way of all businessmen, Baker. Make your money the wrong way, and live all the right ways.'

Henry smiled, he found himself fumbling for words, 'Each to his own, I'd think. But a fellow countryman was almost kept imprisoned, for three days, and that should matter.'

Kittredge tapped with his stick on the gravelled driveway, 'It should matter, and it shouldn't. There are other stakes in all this. We just have to see the mighty big picture.'

He meant his own interests, Henry understood, and he felt Kittredge's glance rest meaningfully on him after he had boarded the carriage. The electric tramway Kittredge had set his heart on, and that was poised at a delicate stage now. He had had discussions with Viscount Sandhurst, as well as the governing council, winning over many voices, including the venerable Mr George Birdwood. Kittredge would obviously not want anything to muddy the waters. 'Baker,' it was Kittredge calling him, leaning out of the carriage that was already halfway down the drive. The boy riding on the footboard descended hurriedly to open the door, and Henry, half-turned, and stood on the steps of the house, somewhat surprised.

It wasn't quite like Kittredge to do anything out of character. He was too stiff and pompous for that. For all that he, Henry, was trade consul, Kittredge made no secret of the fact that he was the longest serving American businessman in Bombay, and had been around for two decades and more. He came down the carriage steps, lurching forward somewhat clumsily, and Henry took his time reaching him.

'Clemens, I mean Mark Twain could write a good story about it,' said Kittredge, his hand on Henry's shoulder so he could almost whisper in the other man's ear. 'Make it all a nice juicy mystery. That would give everyone a good laugh too.'

Henry nodded, his hand on his hat, and Kittredge turned back. 'We must do all we can, Henry. The country depends on us.'

This last bit of instruction left Henry somewhat amused, as he stood there, looking at the departing carriage. The late afternoon breeze was still gentle and warm on his face, and the branches of the palm trees that lined one end of the wall, loomed low, before rising again, in rhythm. A candy floss vendor passed by, ringing his bell, and Henry heard the usual clopping of horses outside on the street. The gardener, Hari, was out again with his pitchers, intending to water the dry driveway, and he inclined his head toward Henry in greeting.

Henry was glad to be back in the cool interiors of the bungalow. The blinds were pulled low over the veranda, now that evening was near, and mosquitoes and other night bugs had to be kept out. The earthen coir lamps were lit and placed strategically: one in the hallway and another just outside the sitting room, and the musty cloying smoke drifted up to him along with the heady fragrance of the jasmine creeper. 'We have another small mystery on our hands,' Maya told him with some amused resignation as he appeared through the door. 'We wanted you to come back to listen to it all.'

She gestured toward Mark Twain who was once again holding up his red diary in some mock distress. 'You see this, these notches at the centre,' Henry nodded, leaning closer to look, and noticed again the perforations, untidy and rugged, where pages had been evidently ripped off.

'It isn't just one sheet but more. Just as Miss Barton says. I wonder why someone had to do that. I was all in sympathy for his story, and his request for some writerly assistance.' Mark Twain brushed his hair away and went on, 'In fact I just wanted to get away from it all when I left the hotel for a bit. The crows at their late night concert, the man next door, who spoke a bit too loudly, maybe in his sleep.' Mark Twain chuckled in his typical way, spreading his hands, then pressing his droopy moustache back in place. 'And then the uncomfortable bed that seemed to make a noise too. And I didn't want to wake these two in the other room,'—he indicated Olivia and Clara—'Clara takes time in a new place, she's a bit nervous, and Olivia wanted to be with her. But the bed seemed to have a life of its own, making jangling, musical noises, and I thought I better go down and complain to the night manager. Then when I was on my way down, I met Pease coming up, and we both looked at each other, almost like we had seen a ghost. For we seemed to keep meeting each other.

'He still had those papers, the pamphlets, with him. He said right away that he knew why I couldn't fall asleep. The noise everywhere, and the ways of the people. He said the evil around had upset nature, and even the birds had been disturbed. He told me the people never slept, even at night, and it was little wonder that the crime rate was rising. And I had to ask then about the murder of the young woman, that all the servants were talking about. We had heard them on the stairs that evening, and even from the day-old servant, who has now disappeared for good...What's his name?' He demanded peremptorily of his wife and daughter.

'Manuel,' offered Clara, and Maya leaned back again, her head on her elbow that rested on the mantelpiece. 'And Miss Barton has got something about that matter too.'

Mark Twain's eyes gleamed at that new bit of information, but he rubbed his moustache and went on, stretching his legs, crossing them at the ankles. The dazed and drowsy man of a few hours ago had utterly disappeared, and he appeared livelier, more animated than before.

'Manuel, yes, he was edgy. And I wondered about the murder. I have read of those old gangs, the thugs, who poisoned and then strangled their victims, after stealing all their goodies. Pease said these were the most devious crimes to have ever been committed. But that things like this were happening all the time and not getting enough attention. The men who killed, robbed, and stole just to feed their opium habit. And it's a habit that's infected everyone. Everyone, he told me, is involved, and that is why the government does not wish to do anything at all. The disreputable stage actors, the dancers, the mill workers, all are slaves to this habit, because it is supposed to calm them down, soothe nerves, help them keep long hours at work.

Pease told me he could give me a tour of the city. It is at night, he said, that you will see the truths about this city. The real truths that will give you the stories you need to write about. So, we got into a carriage. He made it quite an adventure. He asked me to get my hat and coat and pull my collars over my face so no one could recognize me. All that bit about me being world-famous and that I could be kidnapped if someone recognized me in the streets.'

He stopped, he poured himself a glass of water from the ice-filled pitcher nearest him. Then noting the silence around him, he looked at all their faces and burst out laughing. 'All of you looking so stunned! Isn't this ironical?'

It was then the phone rang. A short, sharp trilling came from the study, and Maya left, saying she would answer it. 'Must be the police,' Henry murmured, leaning to hold the door open for her, 'and about time too.'

She drew him with her as they walked the few steps to the study. The sunlight was fainter now, and the shadows that strayed from outside had withdrawn to a small area around the windowsill. Maya closed the door behind them, and reaching for the phone, she told him quickly, 'I hope he isn't tiring himself too much. It's a long story, and he will have to repeat it all for the police.'

'The police will make sure it hears only what it wants or needs to.'

She picked up the phone on the fifth ring and Henry heard the operator's voice, officious and measured,

'Call from the police superintendent,' and Vincent's voice came in, just a moment later, impatient and brusque. 'Dr Ell...Miss Barton,' he said to Maya's hello. 'Er...Something important has come up. A matter of the utmost urgency. If you would kindly offer our apologies to Mr Clemens. We will be there tomorrow. I am sure he is now safe. And he will, I hope, get some necessary rest too.'

'I see,' Maya said the moment she could get a word in, 'is everything all right? Is there something...?'

'We are indeed making sure everything's in control, Miss Barton,' Vincent's voice crackled over the receiver, and Maya moved it a bit away from her ear. 'Please do offer our apologies to Mr Clemens, and we wish him a speedy recovery. We will be there tomorrow.' And with those rushed words, they heard the click of the receiver falling in place.

Henry was shaking his head, in part frustration and bemusement as Maya shrugged her shoulders. 'Quite clearly,' he said, 'this matter of Mark Twain's disappearance never mattered to them.'

'Well, they haven't covered themselves in glory in any way,' said Maya.

She walked ahead of him in the hallway grey in the dimming light and Henry felt a sadness. They had had quite an adventure, a bumbling, wildly improvised one, with some undesirable elements in their midst—he thought of Bancroft at this moment—but he had had Maya's company, and no one would ever really know nor understand how much fun that had been.

In the sitting room, Phipson had dozed off, his head resting against the sofa, his wife, Edith chatted softly with Olivia, and Clara sat quietly, lost in her thoughts, her eyes straying often to her father. Twain was looking up at the ceiling, his fingers on his forehead. 'I seem to be interrupted in my thoughts all the time,'—he said, plaintively—'and I guess you are here to tell me that the police won't be here.'

'Well, yes,' said Henry, pulling up a chair. Charlotte Ellaby said, 'I need to go back to the hospital for the evening shift. You really need to rest, Mr Clemens. I can't wait to hear the rest of your story.'

Maya followed Charlotte to the door. Twain sighed, looking at Henry. 'It's a story that will never get told, I feel. I have lost my notes, and I need to remember clearly.'

'So, he took you to the cottage? Pease, I mean.' Henry prompted, quickly. He didn't want him to lose his train of thought, or feel a new wave of fatigue once again. It seemed to Henry that Twain had gotten used to, and thrived on attention, and this explained all his liveliness when he was surrounded by all of them, hanging onto his every word.

Twain opened his mouth, his moustache looked skewed as it did every time he did so, and then closed it. He looked with some distaste at the snoring Phipson before he reached into his pocket. He took the diary out again, and pulled it open, impatient. He ran his fingers down the perforated ends where the pages had been torn out.

'Well, that bit is just what I do not remember. We were in the carriage, and he had the windows open. And after a while, I did begin to feel drowsy. Then he gave me something, a gummy kind of stuff.'

Henry stood up abruptly, his face was contorted. 'But that is just the thing.'

But Mark Twain went on as if he hadn't noticed. 'I did describe it all, when it came back to me, I mean when I could remember. We were in a boat. There was just too much colour, and light, too much noise, it was intoxicating. The gulls at sea, the colours of the sun on the glinting water, every speck glistening like a diamond where the sun fell, and the sound of the oars as the boatmen rowed. It was magical.'

He paused and looked at them. 'If you are going to ask me how I got onto that boat, when I was supposed to be in a cottage, I have no idea, no clue, not the slightest remembrance. It was there in my diary. He saw me jotting down things in it. And while it was uncomfortable, in the boat, with the constant motion, it was quite otherworldly. I felt light on my feet, and in my head,'—he said laughing. 'From where we were, mid-sea, the city looked like a floating dream place. With those swaying palm trees, the sandy beach giving way to fine-stone houses, and the tall temple lost amidst the trees that someone pointed out. I thought again of the man I had seen. A real giant of a man, he was taller than two buildings, walking on the sandy beach. I was telling Pease that this man could see quite a lot from that height, and telling him too that I had felt that way every time I had ridden those high bicycles. I could see that man again, far away in the distance, and…'

Mark Twain paused, helped himself to some iced water, wiped his lips again, and went on.

'It was really strange, seeing him then, and I remembered I had seen him the previous night too. Pease looked through his binoculars, and he had a pretty good model that he didn't allow anyone to use—and I was quite miffed about that—but he looked more upset, saying something about that man trailing him all the time. Quite a nuisance. And then I asked him if he was from the police, and that made him drop his binoculars. They swung from his neck like a pair of dead birds.'

Mark Twain laughed, his moustache appeared droopier than before. 'I had it all down here, in my diary, the pages now gone. This, and that when we returned in the boat, the man appeared closer than before. He loomed over us. I mean the tall man on stilts, and he had an American way of talking. I really thought then I had had too much of the sun. Though Pease kept passing on that gum-like thing, telling me I must have a taste of it. And on the island, where there were some real ancient statues, he said this was the most debauched place of all. Where people from the city come in stealthily, to give in to their vices. It was cool inside and looking at the ruins of the old temples there, was quite revealing. I had it all here in my diary, and I have lost it.'

The room had gone quite dark, and a woman came

in to light the gas lamps. Henry recognized her as Indu, the woman in the kitchen. Maya came forward to help Indu, the lamp close by her. The orangish light that flared up cast a glow on Maya's face, making long shadows of her lashes on her cheeks. Henry shifted and Twain, catching his eye at just that moment, smiled faintly. 'You are here a long way from home too, and our reasons for being here seem different.'

Henry flushed, wondering if he had been too obvious. As Indu lit the lamp placed near the bookshelf, and moved to the tall lamp at the corner, behind his chair, he heard a very familiar voice from outside, loud and excited, and fatigued in equal measure. 'Sahib, Sahib.'

'Abdul!' Maya exclaimed. She turned quickly, a book falling from the shelf to land at her feet.

'And about time too.' Henry rushed to the door, and then changed direction abruptly, for Abdul always entered the house through the kitchen via the side door that led in from outside. Abdul was panting, as he stood breathless with his hand on the door jamb, but he still managed a weak smile as he saw Henry.

'Sahib, I tried...'

'Why didn't you call?'

They spoke at the same time, and Henry stepped back, brushing against Maya as he did so. He steadied her with a hand, and Maya gestured to Abdul to come in. 'You need water, and something more in you, before you are ready to tell us more.'

'No,' the word came out breathless again. Abdul's

hand was against his chest, as he tried to steady his breathing. 'Sahib, I could not call.' He gulped, and gratefully drank the water Indu offered. 'I could not call. Manuel stole the phone.'

XVIII
On Manuel's Trail

This was the last thing Henry expected to hear, but Abdul wasn't done. 'He ran away. He ran away,' he repeated, and then the words came pouring out of him in a torrent. 'There were the men in the compound, sitting on the wall. The two men we saw the other day in the magic man's house. Manuel and I both saw them. And he was terrified. One moment, I had gone to drink water, the next, he was gone. I could not see him, but the two men did. I followed them too. But first I did try and call you up, and that was when I found the round thing gone, the one with numbers on the telephone. It was gone!'

'The rotary dial?' Henry said in astonishment, and just then the phone rang again. 'It's Vincent,' Charlotte's face appeared through the door, and Henry frowned. He remembered Vincent telling Maya that he would be around only the next morning.

'There's a dead body. It turned up earlier in the afternoon,' Henry heard Vincent's clipped sharp voice against his ear. 'And one of the suspects has just escaped from hospital. Mr Baker,' Vincent paused at Henry's startled 'Oh!' before he ended abruptly, 'We need you at the police station.'

'He must mean Manuel,' said Maya, flatly. 'Manuel's dead or been murdered.'

Henry looked at her in disbelief, and knew she had to be right. It fitted in with Abdul's description of Manuel's escape, and the two men on his trail.

'It must be the same men who knocked me out that night at Bancroft's home,' he mused. 'Abdul had a good look at them. I remember the hoarse voice one had, and the other one who had a very young voice, almost like a boy,' He stopped abruptly, stared at Maya, who was pulling down the blinds in the study, making the lamplight waver for a moment. 'It's Bancroft he meant,' he spluttered, looking toward the door, as he realized he might have raised his voice unnecessarily, 'Bancroft has escaped from hospital.'

'Then you must go and see what it's about, Henry,' she spoke in her low calm voice. 'Of course, it's about Bancroft. That's why he's called for you.'

~

The tall structure of the police station was visible from a long way off as Henry came up the Colaba Causeway. It seemed to him he had been making one too many trips lately to the police station. The streetlamps had already been lit, but at this time of evening, there were few pedestrians. On his last visit to ensure Bancroft's release, he had been tense and distracted, but now he felt light-headed, and things around him glowed with a heightened sense of life. He passed the padlocked doors of the goldsmiths, the embroidery workers, the furniture shops, and the sounds of everyday life from floors above came clearly to him. The shop owners lived just above their stores, and some floors were rented out to different associations to serve as boarding houses and meeting places. There was low laughter, the hum of conversation, and the ringing of cymbals. Someone or the other, Henry thought, was always at their prayers in this country.

He saw the police carriages outside the station long before he came up. This was the new Bombay police headquarters, and towering over the nearby Ashoka and peepul trees, the lone spire over the red tiled mansard roof made for an impressive sight. As he neared, he saw the rounded cupola of the police headquarters at one end, and the tower just behind came into view soon after, the tiles wan and grey in the setting sun. He saw the high bay windows, the milled railings, the balconies that lined every floor, and he was staring at the building, in rapt fascination when the carriage ground to a halt. A constable ran up, to ask first in Urdu, and then in halting English, 'Is this the Consul sahib?'

Henry looked out of the carriage window, and the man, a burly, impressively moustached Pathan, saluted, and spoke up in loud, stentorian tones. It was clear he wanted to impress his fellow constables who stood by the entrance and others who looked on from the second floor balconies. 'Vincent sahib is at the bungalow in Chandanwadi. He said the Consul sahib had to come there. That is where...' this time the constable took care to lower his voice, 'the dead body was found.'

Henry groaned, as he understood the implication of the constable's words. It could only mean that Manuel or rather his dead body had been found at Bancroft's house. And Bancroft of course had been reported as missing from the hospital where he had been taken for his injured leg.

'Of course, it's obvious he wasn't injured badly,' he said sourly, looking at Abdul, who sat by the window at the other end of the carriage, still drowsy as he slumped against the wall. Abdul had hesitated about sitting with him, but Henry had insisted. He wanted to hear more of Abdul's story, and Abdul was always useful to have around. He spoke more languages than did Henry—with his knowledge of Gujerati, Marathi, Urdu, and his own native Pashto—and his fair, lean good looks always created a good first impression, in this city where appearances were beginning to matter a lot.

'Are you awake?' Henry asked, as he looked back into the darkness. He had just given the coachman a new set of directions, and Abdul looked at him, freshly roused and just as startled to be where he was. 'I should be standing outside.'

'Stop being silly,' Henry said. He felt the hoarseness in his throat, and his hair felt sticky at the touch. He remembered he hadn't had a shower that evening, and his coat looked shabby in the dim glow that came from outside. But he was relieved on so many other counts. Mark Twain was back safely, and his shoulder no longer hurt, except when he shifted position too carelessly, and he winced as he admonished Abdul. 'I asked you to be inside, and you better get on with what you were saying. The two men, you followed them, right?'

'Hmm. Sahib, I did,' said Abdul with considerable alacrity. If he could stand up, he would, but the carriage roof was low, and that made things awkward. Henry kept the window open, the curtains drawn apart, for the two of them made the air distinctly stuffy around them.

'The roads were crowded, especially in the theatre complex, but I kept them in sight. There were carriages, carts, and peddlers of all sorts, all seeming to come straight at me, but still I never let them out of sight. Once they did stop, as if they suspected someone behind them, but I ducked in time. A sari hung out to dry from a balcony hid me for some moments. At one point, men from two different theatre companies were announcing their new plays, and they were so close, they almost came to blows. All of us, even the two men I was following, just stopped to watch.'

Abdul paused, then licked his lips. Henry shifted, feeling restless and hot. It was difficult to hear him at times with the noise outside. They were in the crowded, more lived in parts of the city, passing through narrow streets, with two- and three-storied buildings leaning down on them. People sat around on their porticos looking on at life outside, children played hopscotch or read by the lights of the streetlamps, and even at this hour, a priest moved from house to house leading by hand, a heavily garlanded cow. On seeing them, women appeared holding up utensils with candles and prayer offerings that they held before the animal, seeking to propitiate it.

'I heard someone asking for Eeshwar,' Abdul said. Henry lifted an eyebrow, and Abdul went on. 'The Victoria Company was accusing the Bhave touring company of stealing him, and some men almost came to blows.'

'I am sure the matter is well settled by now,' said Henry, as he remembered Eeshwar, the rather sullen looking string player who had agreed to be part of their makeshift performance.

'Someone mentioned he had been seen outside the Pease house,' Abdul went on. It was this that irritated Henry too. 'Really, Abdul, you seem to have done nothing but listen to gossip.'

Abdul touched his ears, seeking forgiveness. 'No, sahib, even those two men had stopped. Then one pulled the other by his vest, and they went on. The moment they passed Northbrook Garden, and were in Khetwadi Lane, I knew where they were all headed. The magic man's house at Chandanwadi.'

'That's where we are now headed,' Henry said, 'and I think you,'—he stopped as he saw the stricken expression on Abdul's face,—'we might have brought about a man's death.' He looked out, at the brick-walled houses of the native merchant houses in Girgaum, and to their left, a while ago, they had passed the grounds of the gently imposing Wilson College, the last rays of the sun making its high windows light up for some moments. More police carriages came into view the moment they turned into Chandanwadi lane. It looked very different from the last time Henry and Abdul had been there, barely two days ago. This area, as with most parts of Girgaum, the native quarter, was dominated by the locals, their houses marked by their red tiles, with walls that shone white in the morning.

Taller brick structures appeared to their right, the balconies of the upper floor with their green painted rails staring out over the first floor, the tiled roofs forming a pleasing shade. There were smaller bungalows to their left, with palm trees standing tall like skeletal sentinels. Wooden gates, low brick walls, and the louvered windows now shuttered, clearly visible on the second floors. The native houses were built differently from the more European style bungalows in Colaba. Each one had a front entrance that led to a small garden or a courtyard, with the kitchen and the inner rooms at the far end. The way Maya had once described for him. The European bungalows, on the other hand, were built in the way popular in London, and the other big cities, and Bombay now ranked among the best. He sighed, he quite liked the city, and yet he felt anxious. He hoped Mark Twain wasn't put off by all the discomfort he had recently experienced. Henry especially hoped he hadn't given a poor impression of himself. It was that moment he understood Pease's desperation, about being written about, getting more attention for his work. It was what he wanted too for himself, though he wouldn't go to Pease's desperate lengths. He didn't want so much for himself, Henry thought, just a life lived with more adventure, and with Maya, always near, always a puzzle.

'Sahib, after I lost them in the crowds, I did come back here. But...,' Abdul craned his neck to look ahead, and when he glanced back at Henry, there was a look of utter bewilderment on his face. 'There was nothing going on in the bungalow. Not a soul, not a sound. And now, just look, sahib!'

They heard the whistle as a bearded and turbaned constable on horseback rode up, pushing his way through groups of people who had gathered in curious circles, keen not to miss a thing. He cast a quick glance Henry and Abdul's way, and blew his whistle, sharp and clear again. Then he waved his baton in the air, in a commanding way. 'Tell Vincent sahib, the consul is here. And you all,' he swivelled around on his horse, turning a full circle as he took in the people around. 'All of you, clear away. This is no tamasha. Go on, let the police do its work. Go on.' He directed his horse toward a small group of men who stood, a few metres away, turbaned and in crisp starched dhotis and he urged them to go in as well. 'No by-standers here, please, on order of the superintendent.'

'Have we caught the magician?' Henry heard someone ask the constable.

'Quite a nuisance he was, with his strange ways,' said someone else.

'Like a shaman of sorts, you mean,' added someone else.

The men moved back, to stand before the gate of another bungalow. Evidently it belonged to one of them, and as Henry passed, he felt their eyes on him. 'The Consul sahib, that means…'

Henry did not understand the rest of what was said. Nor could he have if he had wanted to, for there came the sound of thumping as his carriage was urged to a halt, and then another officer on a horse, rode up. His sola topi hung on his back, and he held his baton with easy majesty.

'Mr Baker, sir, I am Assistant Superintendent Hopkins. If you please, this way.' He did not need to shout or raise his voice. There seemed to be an easy authority in how he moved, and the way his baton rested lightly on his shoulder. The small crowd dispersed, as he nodded to his men, and led the carriage toward the gate.

'Remember,' Henry whispered urgently to Abdul, 'don't say anything unless they ask you directly. Got it?'

Abdul nodded solemnly. 'Ji, yes, sahib.'

~

Hopkins said, as he reached Henry, 'This way, sir. Just follow me.' It was dark and at a few places constables stood with lanterns held high. Shadows flickered across

Hopkins' face, and the bushes around them lining the driveway looked a spectral orange in places. 'It's dark, Mr Baker, but this is a most unusual murder,' Hopkins said in a low voice, 'the second we have had in just about four days. And this one is also...'

His voice broke as they heard the tramp of boots headed their way. The tall and slightly bent figure of Vincent appeared out of the gloom. 'It's good you got here, Baker. The sight is not going to be pleasant.'

Henry took a quick look around and couldn't see Abdul anywhere. He didn't know whether to be worried or concerned. Perhaps one of the constables had elbowed Abdul out of the way, thinking he wasn't important enough to be questioned, nor could he offer evidence of any kind.

'This man, Manuel,' Vincent said, speaking brusquely, nodding to the constables who held up the lanterns, 'I believe you saw him.'

'Yes, I did,' Henry said, in a low voice. He felt the looming presence of the house to his right, dark and menacing, and the stray pebbles on the driveway gleamed white in the lantern light. The outhouse appeared immediately ahead, its door standing askew to one side, where it had been evidently broken down. It looked smaller in the dim light around, a darkness emanating from its interiors that felt intimidating.

'The chowkidar on his first round here at around seven was told by the locals about the screams. Such shouts were nothing out of the ordinary, you understand.' Vincent was looking at him carefully as he spoke, and Henry nodded. Bancroft had acquired a notoriety for himself in the few months he had been in Bombay. Even Henry had heard the stories, of the fakirs, the spirit men, the mediums, the snake charmers, and other magic men who gathered at his house, especially at odd hours, upsetting the locals of the area. There were rumours that Bancroft frequented the graveyards, the cemeteries, and the towers of silence, because he wished to commune with the dead, even work spells on them to bring them back to life. And then of late, there had been his appearances all over the city on his stilts.

'You understand, this...?' he missed some of what Vincent said for he had been lost in his own reverie. There had been something desperate and intense about Freddie Bancroft that had alarmed him in the beginning. That, and Maya's fascination with him and her wish to learn some magic tricks from Bancroft had put Henry off the man. He wondered if he could have done something to help Bancroft. The police presence was more than unexpected, and now that they were almost at the opening of the outhouse, Henry saw that the door had been pulled entirely off its hinges and rested against the wall. Two days ago, when he had accompanied Bancroft back, he remembered the door looking somewhat damaged; now it had been pulled apart entirely. He sensed the added danger to Bancroft now.

'This could be difficult for your...Mr Bancroft,' Vincent said. He clicked his fingers, and two constables ran up, lanterns held high. Henry saw the fading blue paint on the door, the cracked glass window, and then the smell that had greeted him at Pease's house assailed him again full in the face. He fell back almost by instinct and Vincent steadied him with a hand on his back.

'I understand it can be a hard sight. We found him here in the outhouse, beaten up and strangled. It is not a nice sight, Mr Baker, please let me warn you.'

~

It was his feet Henry recognized. He remembered them from when he had crept in that late afternoon, only a day or so ago. His skeletal, strangely arched feet that made that clacking soft knocking sound on the wooden floor. Manuel lay on the floor, only half of him visible in the low lamplight. What Henry saw were his bare feet, the mud still caked around his heels, and his short loincloth—which the locals called the langot—pulled well over his knees. Manuel, he thought with pity, had run till the end, desperate to evade his captors.

Henry couldn't see the rest of him. A man was bent low over Manuel's torso, presumably checking for other injuries. 'That's him?' asked Vincent. Henry swallowed, and nodded, indicating the affirmative, his eyes following the constable's lantern. 'Yes,' he whispered, drawn back again to stare at Manuel's scarred, marked feet. The man on the floor rose to his feet, and Henry saw the stethoscope trailing in his hands. He saw then the caked blood on Manuel's nose and lips, the tear on his loose upper garment. Henry's eyes, almost as if they had a will of their own, moved past the gashes he saw on Manuel's neck, the welts on his upper arms, and the arm bent at the elbow, as if he had been warding off an attack.

'It must be a shock,' said Vincent, in an unexpectedly kind voice. Henry managed a nod again, his lips suddenly dry.

'I am glad Mr Clemens is back safely. Thank you for your help and assistance on that,' Vincent's voice was soft and thoughtful. He had a way of looking into the distance, every time he paused, before his gaze turned abruptly back. 'I must admit we were outnumbered. Short in numbers. Though I do hope to get the full story. From you, and Mr Clemens too.' He looked away, bounced on his heels, before adding. 'Or I should say, Mark Twain, the famous writer.' He laughed ruefully and cleared his throat.

'I must ask you some questions,' he said, extending a hand, as he led Henry out. Then his tone completely changed, to something more official, more determined. Vincent stood erect, his face turned away from Henry presented a stern and unrelenting profile. Lifting his arm to the right, Vincent indicated the dark one-storied house ahead. Its white walls, visible through the low branches of the trees that lined the short driveway, glowered in the dim yellow streetlamps. The louvered windows were closed, and a pumpkin vine on the slanting tiled roof rustled.

'There's no getting away from facts, so I will get

to them right away. Mr Baker, your friend is in some mighty trouble.'

'My friend?' Henry stumbled for a moment on the uneven driveway, the lantern hovered erratically, he smelt the dry earth, and a whiff of the gummy opium smell came back to him. He seemed to be breathing it everywhere.

'It's a shock to you, I understand.' Vincent gestured back towards the outhouse. 'We have our methods,' he added, in a voice more assured and confident. 'We have our ways to establish guilt. But...'

They came upon a rusting iron bench, splattered with leaves, and a constable advanced, as Vincent clicked his fingers. A constable held his lantern up, while his companion swept away the leaves with his baton, before gingerly patting the ground below, thwacking it as he checked for snakes and other deadly nocturnal creatures. Just then the moon came out, its faint light drizzling through the nearest tree, and Henry shrugged, 'Oh, we could stand. That would be all right, don't you think?'

Superintendent Vincent had been about to say something else, but now his face closed up, and he looked sharply at Henry. 'Well, if you insist. You see, Mr Baker, your friend...'

'Mr Bancroft, you mean,' Henry interrupted, rubbing his shoe on the drying grass.

'Yes, Bancroft, of course,' Vincent took the correction in his stride. 'We need your permission to search his house.' He played with his baton, patting his left palm with it, and the baton's silvery end gleamed in the moonlight almost like a wand. 'There was very incriminating evidence found in that outhouse, I can tell you.'

'Opium, yes, the place reeked of the stuff.'

'Well, since you are aware of Mr Bancroft's actions.'

'Quite honestly, I never knew him well enough. And about his movements, I can assure you I really have no clue.'

Vincent looked at him, then jerked his head to the right. 'Let's go back there.' He indicated the outhouse, ablaze with the light of several more lanterns. The doctor was rubbing his forehead and speaking urgently to someone taking notes. Manuel lay on a makeshift rigged stretcher, a cloth draped over him.

'The doctor says,' Vincent said, matching his step to Baker's, 'that the death happened some three or four hours ago. In the afternoon when this area, at least the streets outside, is certainly not deserted. And as I said, we have our methods, there's no getting away from that. It's an unusual murder, very brutal.' He swung his baton, then moved it as was his wont, from one hand to the other and back again. 'Not the work of the criminal tribes, the Pardhees, the Waghares, who strangle their unsuspecting victims. But as the doctor says, this man was exhausted, tired, and hungry. His throat was parched, the tongue colourless, and the stomach had fallen in, and his chest too.'

Vincent's voice trailed away, as they reached the prone body of Manuel. The doctor and the officer making notes had turned and taken a few steps toward them. Henry saw the doctor clearly now. He was an Indian, short and slender, with a nervous quick way of talking.

'It is a most unfortunate case,' he said. 'I would say...'

Henry missed the quick nod Vincent directed the doctor's way, he only sensed a sudden movement, the way Vincent raised his voice the next moment. 'We will study the report in detail. But it is clearly not the work of the tribes we have long kept an eye on. This is a more sinister work. We will get to the bottom of it very soon. Very well then, Dr Joshi. Thank you.'

The doctor raised his hand almost to salute him, instead his stethoscope ends swung necklace-like around his chest, and he lowered his hand hurriedly. 'My report, Superintendent. It's all in here, the details,' he looked around, to his left and right, and Vincent came to his rescue once again, replying in a voice, drier than usual. 'Yes, Khan will get the report to me. Your carriage must be waiting. Dr Joshi, thank you again.' Vincent turned to Henry. 'Sorry about that. You must realize we cannot at this moment let too much information out. As I was saying, it's not the work of the tribes, whose movements we keep track of. We have our records, and our spies,' he said, a note of pride in his voice. 'They help keep an eye on them, their moves. This isn't their doing. It's something to do with the opium smuggling. Did you notice the way he was murdered?'

'You were telling me about it,' said Henry. There were just the two of them standing by the outhouse now. A lone constable stood over Manuel's dead body, a dim lantern by him. Henry looked toward the gate, as the doctor made his way out, and suddenly noticed Abdul, standing with a couple of other constables, looking quite at home amidst them. Abdul made an odd gesture with his hand as Henry caught his eye. He patted himself on the chest with a hand, and then made a gesture of patting the ground, his palms facing downward, almost as if he was reassuring Henry. He wished Vincent wouldn't take so long with his explanations. A long-drawn creak, and a distinct thwack, the sound of a wooden door falling apart had him turning his head quickly around, back toward the main house. Vincent pulled his trousers higher, smacked his palm with his baton again, and said more animatedly, 'They have taken down the door totally. Good! We need to see inside Mr Bancroft's house, and we need you as witness. I'll tell you more once we are inside.'

The hallway was dark as they entered, guided only by the wavering candle in the room ahead that had just been lit. The room smelt musty and damp, of lamp oil and dusty carpets. He brushed past an object that fell to the floor with a clank, followed by the sound of something rolling slowly on the wooden floor. As the faint light reached into the darkness, Henry saw it was a sceptre of some kind, with two bulbous ends. He was certain that was the least strange thing in Bancroft's house.

'As I was saying, do watch your step, Mr Baker,' Vincent said, as he pointed to a raised instep that led to the inner room. There was someone going around ahead, lighting the candles. There was one on the table, a stub on the window ledge, and then at last, a bigger lamp by a stand against a bookshelf popped into light.

Vincent whistled, and Henry in some irritation asked him. 'So, you obviously have an eye on Bancroft. Did you?' He wished Vincent would stop being so evasive and guarded about things.

'We take a step at a time,' Vincent said, looking toward him in the darkness. Henry suddenly knew he was enjoying this moment, relishing the importance it gave him, an omniscience that would be the envy of ordinary men like him, Henry.

Vincent cleared his throat and at last appeared to relent. 'The man, Manuel, as the doctor said, was exhausted, and starving. He was no longer in a state to put up a fight. Two of the men who attacked him—as our witnesses have established—struck him with a lethal kind of stick. The kind used to kill snakes. It's sharp at the end with those two forks. If it's slammed against the skin, it leaves cane-like marks, and the stick itself is of hardwood. That method is what has given them away. Which makes this murder somewhat complex.'

He stopped abruptly, then continued softly as he caught Henry's eye, 'And we know who we are looking for, at least one of them. If he weren't guilty at all, he would never have escaped from hospital, would he? And with an injured leg, he really can't go far.'

Henry was looking around the room, his mouth falling agape in amazement. He saw the long drapes at the windows, the magical accoutrements filling up the big table, the lamp showing up the wigs, the beards, the shiny fake crowns, and two pairs of golden coloured boots. Against one wall was stacked a pair of long sticks—an extra pair of stilts, Henry surmised—and a raised shelf full of hats. Next to it, were hooks nailed into the wall propping up more hats, swords—some curved, some of straighter length—daggers, and a spear or two.

'God in heaven,' Vincent gasped, 'this man is a sorcerer.'

'Sahib,' one of the constables spoke from behind them, trying to draw their attention, 'this way.' As they walked through to another room, leading away from a door by the table, Henry saw the rolled-up rugs stacked against the wall. The room they were in was smaller, with shelves on either side. Books and newspapers were arranged haphazardly, some with pages left open, others slipped in between the pages of other books. Old heavyset wooden chairs sat around at the centre, with a low patterned table in the middle. It was clear no servant had been in this house for many days, perhaps weeks.

'Are we looking for something specific, Superintendent?' Henry asked, his nose scrunching up, before unable to help himself, he sneezed.

Vincent's lips broke into a slight smile. 'Depends on what you mean by specific, Mr Baker.' He touched the books gingerly, wiped the dust on his finger on his khaki shirt, before asking the constable, 'Anything ahead?'

They passed a bathroom that smelled even mustier from outside, and Henry caught a quick glimpse of the grey-stoned small room, with a tin bath in the corner. They walked down a hallway to another room to the right. A big four-poster bed with the mosquito net draped around the posts stood in some lonely magnificence. Vincent walked ahead, and threw open a wardrobe, before stepping back quickly.

'A magician's house,' he said with mock resignation, 'you never know what might jump out at you.'

'That might have happened some time ago. This house looks just very abandoned,' responded Henry with some asperity. He looked up at the high ceilings, the iron beams running across the roof and felt claustrophobic. He took off his coat, and slung it over his shoulder, feeling the sweat stamp itself on him, in cloying damp patches. 'If it's the opium you think he had, all of it must be in the outhouse.'

'And what makes you so certain of that, Mr Baker?' Vincent's voice came quiet and sharp in the shimmering yellowing darkness.

Henry ran a hand through his hair, felt it crackle in the heat. 'Nothing. Just that he seems a man pretty indifferent to most things. I mean, a man not bothered about secreting away things. It's all in the open, all untidy, all spread out, and that's it.'

'Well, well, and you objected to my calling you his friend.'

Henry opened his mouth and closed it again. He had been about to retort that it took mere observational skills to understand a person, even one with so-called criminal intent. From a tree just outside the window, an owl hooted, and the men looked up startled and then at each other.

'You are right,' Henry said, in as light a tone he could muster. 'It'd be far harder to understand a friend.'

'Ha!' said Vincent, peering inside the wardrobe. He clicked his fingers and the constable at the door held up a candle. Vincent took it from him, shielding the wavering flame with a hand, as he looked his fill at what the wardrobe offered. Bancroft's coats took up half the space inside, and to the wardrobe's right, on several shelves, stacked neatly were his capes, some of velvet, others fur lined. The belts arranged in line jangled gently against each other in the faint breeze that came in from the door. The two men stared into Bancroft's wardrobe for long moments. Henry thought of the man on his stilts, so desperate to impress, so very keen to play his juggling act, and felt a fleeting sympathy. Bancroft too, had come away from New York to make a new life as a magician, to learn the magical tricks of the East. From a life as a dentist, and then an insurance salesman, Bancroft had desperately wanted to change himself, his life. His single-minded determination was so clearly obvious in how he lived. But that didn't explain the opium? Did he smuggle it because he had no other income? Or to give himself that high, otherworldly feel, to make him forget? Like the women in the mills rubbing the opium gum on their babies' tongues to make them sleep. An evil thing, a vice, had its many uses, Henry mused.

There was much that Manuel had told him, Henry found himself remembering. About the man on stilts who had followed him around, from the native lodge at Sewree, to Watson's Hotel. Vincent's voice broke into his thoughts, 'Looks like you are right. There's only the paraphernalia of a life here. Nothing criminal about it, all magical.' Henry could only manage a thin smile at Vincent's attempt at humour.

Once they were outside, Henry breathed in the evening air, taking it in big gulps. He wiped his face on his sleeve, and turned to Vincent. 'There's something you need to know. Something I have to tell you. And, I'd like my servant, Abdul, to join us.' Vincent nodded distractedly, but was looking to the outhouse where one of his constables was holding up something, gesturing for them to come up. Something that gleamed when it caught the light as the man motioned with his hands. Henry groaned inwardly. Of course, it had to be the telephone's rotary dial, plated in gold, and made of ivory. It had tempted Manuel enough to steal it.

'A telephone, sahib, part of it,' said the constable, bowing first, before holding out the squat body of the phone, the receiver hanging limply from one side. Henry felt a sliver of indignation run through him. Manuel had cut the wire connecting the phone to the socket in the wall neatly with a knife, so as to make off with the prized piece of instrument, made on order by a craftsman at Gamdevi. Now it would never work again.

'Sahib, that's the one he stole,' Abdul's excited voice broke in, and Henry fumbled as he saw Vincent frown, and look sharply at the two of them.

'Yes, he's right,' said Henry. 'This man Manuel was at my place, at the Byculla Club.' He felt the dryness catch him by the throat, and he felt immensely tired. He began slowly again, trying to think over things carefully as he said, 'Manuel, that was his name. And he was there, and he wanted protection. He had seen the men chase him. They had been dogging him for a day or more. And he knew me, having seen me with the writer at Watson's Hotel. We did intend to take him to you, but I had to get to Twain first. I had to find him, Twain, I mean.' He let his voice end on a high indignant note.

Vincent was looking at him, a look of surprise on his face. A man came forward with a pitcher and two clay cups, and the superintendent looked at him dryly. 'You took your time to come with the water, eh?'

'No one here at this time, sahib. The Nana at the end of the road, he allowed us the use of his well,' the constable explained. But Henry was already slaking his thirst, drinking in the water quickly, unmindful of the stories he had heard about poison, and cholera. Maya would have advised caution. It surprised him that he hadn't thought of Maya at all in the last few hours, and wondered what she would have made of Vincent's line of questioning.

'What this establishes, Baker, is that he was indeed a thief then,' said Vincent thoughtfully. 'Maybe Manuel wasn't his name at all.'

As Henry told him the story in more detail, quickly and speaking in low tones, Vincent's eyes never left his face. When Henry had finished, he felt the stillness around him, and far away, in the quiet night, they heard a ship's horn. 'It's ten, and really very late,' said Vincent. 'You must get home; I will get my men to call a carriage for you. There must be some about. Tomorrow we must meet.'

~

Henry dozed off almost the minute they stepped into the carriage. Abdul knelt down to loosen his shoelaces and opened the curtains a bit more to let in the night breeze. They heard the watchmen calling out their warnings in the night, and the trotting of horses as a few lone carriages passed.

'Sahib, I never finished what I had to tell you.'

Henry grunted, then groaned. There was just too much happening in one day. He wished things could be spaced out more evenly. A rescue one day, a murder the next.

'I lost the two men, remember, sahib, but I did see the magic man. He looked smaller because he wasn't on those sticks. He was limping, resting his hand on that Russian or Serbian musician's shoulder. Bozi.'

Henry's eyes flashed open, and he stared at Abdul half in disbelief and then in irritation. He had last seen Bozi when they had travelled in the carriage together only the previous day. 'It did take you long to remember this.'

'Sahib,' Abdul was squatting on the floor, his back against the seat opposite. 'Please, a thousand times I beg your forgiveness. I ran so much, and the heat was getting too much, some things I forgot then. Then with the police...'

'So, what happened?' Henry interrupted, his head against the window, soothed by the late-night breeze and the even clip-clop of the horses on the drive up the Esplanade.

It was Bozi who in some desperation had asked Abdul for help to get a carriage. Bancroft leaned on Bozi's shoulder, his face whiter than before. Abdul had hesitated, already he couldn't see the two men he was following, and had no idea where Manuel had gone. He had intended to retrieve the stolen telephone. 'Imagine,' Abdul stopped himself from venting forth on his indignation, 'we offered him refuge and this is what he does. There is really no gratitude in this world anymore.'

But it did seem Bancroft was in bad shape, and so Abdul had got Bozi a carriage. He had negotiated the fare with the driver, a hefty, tobacco chewing Pathan. The carriage was a small one-horse one that offered no cover. But these carriages were faster in the crowded, narrower lanes of the city.

'And then something made me follow them instead,' Abdul went on. 'I thought you would in any case be angry. What with letting Manuel slip out, and then his theft, I had been very careless, sahib. But I knew that the magician was up to something, and I followed them. The musician was trying to make him sit up in that open carriage, and Bancroft kept falling over him. I followed them to that man, Pease sahib's house.'

Henry sat upright then, giving Abdul his total rapt attention. 'I just followed the carriage in, slipping in through the gate. The house was in chaos, I could hear Pease shouting, asking his men to clear up things and fast. That got me really intrigued. It seemed to me that Pease wanted to hide something quickly, and I knew that the American sahib, the writer, had been here too, so I went around to the back.'

Henry could well imagine the scene for himself. After all he had been there only that morning, though it seemed a long time ago. 'You went up the small courtyard, did you see the opium patch?'

'Yes,' Abdul said, 'it had all been trampled over, and pulled up. The whole thing was a mess, as if a storm had gone through it.'

Henry let that bit of news sink in and felt somewhat deflated. That small patch with the tall blue walls around it had been a welcome riot of colour, the tomatoes, and the bulbous eggplants mingling with opium pods. It amazed him then that a beauteous thing like that could be so full of evil, and that, thought Henry, was quite the way of the world.

His thoughts had drifted, for he came back when he heard Abdul once again refer to 'Twine sahib'. 'I could hear the man, Pease, shouting in the corridor. Really sahib, he was in some panic. You let Twain sahib go, and we are going to have trouble, he kept saying. He was trying to tell the magician, what was his name'—Abdul tapped his head, and before Henry could assist, he piped up—'Bancraaft sahib, Pease was trying to tell him that he couldn't help him anymore. No more supplies, he said. I can't give you anything for your pain, or your magic. Things are already too complicated, that's what I heard him say. And the room I was in, I felt certain that was the room Twine sahib had been in. He left his walking stick, did you know?'

Henry shook his head, smiling and then he asked himself if it really behoved him to smile at a time like this. There had been a murder, still unsolved, and a man had been kidnapped, and kept hidden for three days and more. Pease could face some serious charges. It could make things unpleasant for everyone, even for Henry, for he had barged into a man's house with no permission at all.

'I guess we forgot to take it,' he said, by way of explanation. 'The stick, I mean.'

'But there were some pages he had left,' Abdul said, 'torn out of his diary, and in the bin. I saw these as I tried to listen in to what was happening, and figuring out how best to make my escape, now that I knew Bancraaft sahib was there too. I knew it was Twine sahib's writing for I had his luggage list with me, the time we came back from the Bunder with them. I can't read English, sahib,' Abdul said, as he rummaged in his kurta pocket, and pulled out the folded bits of paper, 'and these bits were really crumpled and torn, but I straightened them out as best as I could.'

Henry stretched his hand out, unable to contain his curiosity, or his own impressed expression. 'This is going to make your Twine sahib very very happy. You should be a detective, Abdul.'

XIX
An Eye to the Future

The Bombay Gazette, January 27, 1896

Labour Contractor Will Most Certainly Go Free.

Tuka Ram, the man who remains the prime suspect for the still unexplained murder of his wife, Casi, will most certainly no longer be a suspect in the case. The police have been unable to produce evidence linking Tuka to the murder. While Tuka Ram was never formally charged with the case, this admission implies that the police, and the government owe an apology to Tuka Ram, and all the millworkers who had gone on strike for a day, and even threatened to extend it. The millowners, for their part, are relieved at the latest turn in the case, and hope that work will resume as normal very soon.

The murder itself has taken some complicated twists. Another suspect, whose existence the police has been tight-lipped about, was found murdered in the most brutal way. That the police isn't saying much is a revelation of how clueless they really are. Watch this space.

Henry read the item a second time, slowly and more seriously. He knew what it was he had meant to ask Abdul before the fatigue the night before had made him forget many things. He had been looking unhappily at the stand toppled on the table, where Manuel had stolen the phone from. His story too had ended not so happily, and that was a terribly sobering thought.

'Abdul,' he shouted, rising from the commode, and peering around the door for his manservant to appear. He heard the clink of cutlery on the table and Abdul's hurried, 'Yes, sahib?' Abdul advanced with a towel, and Henry snapped, his voice muffled through the half-open door, 'Abdul, the slipper. The one Manuel had on him. Do you remember what happened to it?

Abdul looked blank for a moment, and then his eyes lit up, 'Oh yes, sahib. The one Manuel had with him. It's here all right. In the shoe rack.'

~

'That will be one more complicated story for the police. And the superintendent will think we are full of them, once he gets to know of the slipper too,' he mused to Abdul when they were once again on the way to the doctors' bungalow in Colaba. It was almost twelve in the afternoon, and Henry had slept in, catching up on sleep he had missed the last two days. Outside, it was gentle and sunny, with a soft breeze making a shushing sound in the palm trees, and there were the usual vendors out on Chowpatty, calling out their wares in raised singsong voices. They passed a man with two monkeys, dressed up colourfully, who danced to every beat of his tambourine. The gulls soared over the sandy stretches making quite a cacophony, and parakeets called from the palm trees, their multi-hued feathers melding into a mesmerizing riot of colour.

'The Superintendent will be sure to find it irritating. Though,' he said, softly to himself, running a firmer finger over his moustache, 'he will be glad to have part of it solved. In a way.'

It was the morning Maya taught at the Native Girls School. He hoped she hadn't gone to the police already about the recovered jewels. Tuka of course would have first claim to them. That was why, Henry thought, he had inveigled the girl into marriage in the first place. He shook his head in amazement. It had been such a complicated puzzle. Manuel had stolen the jewels, on Tuka's behalf, tempted by his offer. Then of all places, he had found himself a position as Mark Twain's servant. Henry found no reason to disbelieve Manuel's story, he had seemed so desperate, at the end of his tether, the way he had kept looking over his shoulder, as if death itself were approaching, and too near at hand.

Henry shuddered. He passed the gleaming yellow-white Afghan Church. Its doors were open, and the sun filtered through the stained glass windows, lighting up the pews. This sudden glimpse always filled him with sadness. The church had been built to commemorate the many lives lost in the first war against the Afghans, and it reminded him of how everything was transient, nothing stayed in the same place for long. He had been so fixated about Mark Twain the last few days; every moment, every worry and doubt had stretched on for hours, and filled up every vein and part of his skin.

Maya still wasn't back when Abdul and he drove up to the bungalow. As usual Hari and Ali stood on the patio giving their salaams. The budgerigars chirped, sitting on the white rods in their cages. Olivia was in the back garden with Charlotte, and Mark Twain and Clara were in the sitting room, Ali informed Henry as he led him inside.

'It's all right, Ali, I have been here enough times now,' Henry said laughing, nodding to Abdul who would make his way to the kitchen courtyard where the cook, and other house servants, like the assistant gardener, the cook's help, and others, usually gathered, especially when they had a moment off from their duties.

'Keep those papers safe, Abdul. I will call you in some time.'

He caught a glimpse of Charlotte and Olivia looking up at a pumpkin vine that crawled over the low thatched roof of the kitchen. The kitchen in this quaint old-fashioned bungalow was separated from the rest of the house by a blue-walled courtyard, with a clay stone oven at one corner and a bougainvillea creeper at the other end. Charlotte had kept late hours the last couple of days. Maya had told him in passing the previous day, about the mothers anxious about their irritable, sleepless babies. Something that the other doctor, Dr Edith Pechey had already suspected.

'It's what Edith already said. Some of the women work in the mills,' Maya had looked grim as she elaborated, 'and they give opium, or a paste of it, to their babies to keep them drowsy and quiet. But the police has been after the opium smugglers, and that's affected the illegal supplies...'

The wife of the labour contractor, Tuka, claimed some of it had been planted in her house to frame her, along with her husband. Henry remembered the short note in the *Gazette*. There was so much in the news, and he had looked at this bit idly. But in the light of Maya's revelations, everything seemed connected. Tuka had to keep his workers on—men and women—at the mill, make sure they never missed a single hour at work. He got a fraction, a cut from their salary, after all. It made sense for him to be in some cahoots with the opium smugglers, even indulge in a bit himself. The opium dulled the senses, made it possible for some to work mechanically, almost like machines themselves. It kept the babies quiet too, so the mothers could work long hours too. That seemed monstrous, Henry thought. Too many things needed to change.

~

As Henry entered the sitting room, he paused, pleasantly surprised, and delighted to see the change in Mark Twain. He looked refreshed, rested, and restless, for he stood up the minute Henry entered, clapped him on the shoulder, telling him that it was quite a rescue act he had pulled off. 'Miss Barton and you. What an act!'

He beamed and Henry flushed at the attention. He nodded to the women all back in the room now and smiled slightly at Charlotte's knowing smile. 'She'll soon be here,' she said, and Twain laughed too. 'I am glad to see all of you are rested,' Henry said, his eyes travelling over them. Clara wore a dark blue skirt with a top of a lighter colour, and she had taken some effort to do her hair, a pleated strand arranged on top that showed off her long turquoise coloured earrings.

'You look very pretty, Miss Clara,' he said bowing, thinking treacherously to himself that it was Maya's strange blue-green eyes that he would always associate with that colour.

Mark Twain cleared his throat, and nudged Henry by the elbow. 'Have you read this newspaper report? The murder of the poor man.' He shook his head, 'I barely knew him for an evening, and yet...'

'You would never be able to tell he was a thief, would you?' Olivia broke in shuddering. 'And to think he could enter your room freely at any time of the night?'

'And there was the matter of the needle and thread he kept asking for,' Clara chimed in, indignantly, 'and he slept in father's bed too!'

She looked embarrassed as she caught Henry's eye. That morning, with her mother, she too had been insistent that she had seen her father asleep, and Henry didn't want to remind her of that. To his surprise,

Mark Twain chuckled. 'That was funny! I would never have had an idea like that. The poor man, though. His paths crossed ours, and I wonder how long, how far he would have run.'

He looked around thoughtfully, and bent to pick the paper up from the table. 'So, it says here,' he said pulling the paper open, his eyes running over the pages quickly, before alighting on the news item that he turned in Henry's direction. 'The murder's still unsolved. That whoever did it hasn't been apprehended yet. The police are tight-lipped. It always amuses me when newspapermen write this way. Tight-lipped. Do they close their lips up tight in a straight, rigid line. Like this.'

It was hard to see Twain's lips, covered as they were by his brush-like moustache, but they laughed. 'The police did say it was an unusual murder,' began Henry, 'because their usual suspects don't have methods like these.'

'Like what?' Mark Twain asked, and Henry proceeded to tell them about the records and detailed documents the police maintained of the criminal tribes. 'The studies done by the government officials have detailed the movements, the appearances, the behaviours of certain nomadic, perpetually moving tribes. The government believes they keep shifting around, committing their crimes, and moving on.'

Mark Twain gasped, shaking his head in disbelief. 'But that is just so monstrously old-fashioned.'

'And quite wrong,' said Maya firmly. She had just

come in, and was quickly running a hand over her hair, pushing away the loose strands that fell over her face. 'It's a bit windy, outside, suddenly' she said, half-laughing, and half-complaining, 'nothing seems to stay in place.'

'I am not in disagreement with that,' said Henry lightly. He tried not to look at her, and didn't want to make that obvious either. He was happy to see her and longed to tell her more about what had transpired at Bancroft's bungalow and Abdul's latest revelations. 'I met Abdul outside,' she said. But she didn't say more, and Twain went on, 'As I was saying that is so old-fashioned. There was this French policeman. Perhaps he was a psychologist. He would make lists of head shapes, things like the cranial features, height, the facial characteristics, the build, and that would, he assumed, give the police an entire system of records about criminals in a city. But that is so cumbersome and so silly. It's not the same people committing the crimes.'

'It would mean innocents getting caught up too,' broke in Charlotte. She stood up and said briskly, 'Lunch must be ready, and then I leave for the hospital.' She turned to look back at everyone, with her hand on the handle, 'then the meeting of the Native Girls School. We hope the trust will do something in Casi's memory.'

There was a silence, and Henry broke in, 'The Bombay police are trying to improve. I do remember those two men who were sent by the Calcutta police.

They were experts in looking for fingerprints and analysing them. So, there was hope the murder would be solved. Maybe there is hope still.'

Clara interrupted, excited, and enthused, 'Father wrote about this in one of his most recent books, *Pudd'nhead Wilson, and the Extraordinary Twins*. The lawyer who collected prints on glass sides and proved that really one's fingerprints are unique. No two people have the same identical fingerprints.' She held up her palms, 'See, the shapes of the whorls, the ridges, the pores, everything's different.'

Mark Twain smiled with pleasure at Clara, 'She's right. And my story was indeed about a murder that was solved by way of fingerprints. It's a method that should help immensely. A decade ago, I wrote about it. How the impression of a thumb helped solve a murder and I was surprised even then that the method hadn't caught on. I am sure Francis Galton's book on fingerprinting will make it the most preferred way to solve a crime.' He shook his straggly mane of hair, tapping the end of the chair, 'Keeping records the way they do now, is primitive, and really unscientific.

'I was at the police headquarters yesterday,' Maya said, once they were seated at lunch. She spoke carefully, keeping an eye on the servants, who sometimes picked up the wrong kind of information, and news about Casi's jewellery, Henry was sure, was still a secret. 'So, I heard more about these much-vaunted detectives. They are developing their own method of classifying and listing the hundreds and thousands of fingerprints that will be collected under this new system. Then it will be easy to trace the criminal. In some ways. But it has to be supported by other methods too.'

'I bet,' Henry sitting opposite her, said quietly. They sat around an old table that seated eight, though there were now six of them. It was an old mahogany table made in Pune, and Phipson had got it especially made for Edith, in the days just after their engagement. The chairs had patterned backs, with a dancing peacock motif carved into the wood, and the cushions on which they sat were of fine silk. One servant served a chicken curry dish. Another held out the rice tray. There was bread, mulligatawny soup, a dish of roasted eggplant and peas, and some cutlets.

'Wearing a disguise is the best way to infiltrate a gang,' Maya mused, tearing off a piece of bread as she spoke.

'Dangerous too,' he bantered.

'Stop, you two,' said Charlotte teasingly, 'so evidently these two experts haven't been of much help in this case? In the Casi case.'

There was a silence, Maya waited for the two servants—Ali and a young boy called Hamid—to withdraw, before she resumed. 'There was little they could do apparently. The room in the lodge had been disturbed, too many people about, and then the owner also had a puja the other day to clean up the room, exorcise all the ghosts. The police, if you ask me, should have been firmer. Stopped such things before they had had a chance to check things thoroughly.'

'Ah, so whatever evidence that may have been in that room has been totally wiped out,' Mark Twain said thoughtful as he cut into his potatoes and eggplant. 'It will go down as an unsolved crime then.'

The phone rang, just as Clara shrieked. Her hands were on her throat, and her face was slowly turning red. Charlotte sized up the situation at once. 'Oh dear, you did find the curry a bit spicy.'

Maya patted her on the shoulder gently as she went out, toward the anteroom to take the call. Ali stood by the door, a look of concern on his face, holding a jug of water. 'Some water,' said Olivia, her face narrowing in worry. 'Plain rice, memsahib,' said Ali, a bit humbly. 'It helps.'

But Clara gulped down the water, and tears of relief streamed down her face. Mark Twain looked concerned. 'I had the same thing,' he said, moving his spoon through the mound of rice and curry on his plate, 'and it did not seem to affect me.'

'Samuel,' said Olivia reprovingly, 'try to feel sorry for the poor girl,' she rubbed her hand gently on Clara's sleeve in comfort. 'You must do as the man says. Take some rice...'

'Yes,' Ali said his eyes falling kindly on Clara, who was trying ineffectually to wipe her tears, 'try and keep the rice in your mouth for a bit. It will be okay.'

The cook, Mehboob Khan, had appeared at the door, a worried look on his face, 'I had put only little spice, memsahib. Some red pepper,' he murmured, over and over again. Charlotte gestured to him with her hand, it will be all right, she meant to say. 'Clara,' she said her voice gentle, 'try and think of more cheerful things. Really, the first time you have it is always the hardest.'

'In anything,' Twain said in a dry voice, 'even in love.' And he looked at Henry meaningfully in a way that made him redden.

XX

A Cinderella Like Ending?

Maya returned to say that Superintendent Vincent had called to apologize again. He would not be there that evening either. There were some complications, Maya said, some possibility of disturbances and protests again in the Girgaum area. The workers planned to take a march out in support of Tuka Ram.

'That isn't likely to put our Superintendent in a good mood,' mused Henry, as everyone rose from the table to return to the sitting room. Henry lingered, hoping to get a quick word in with Maya. But she wasn't looking at him, in fact, it seemed to Henry that she was trying not to catch his eye. Telling himself he was being far too sensitive, he touched her on the shoulder, forcing her to look up.

'I'll go and meet Vincent then. In fact, I must,' he said. He couldn't understand why he felt this awkwardness. Later he would tell himself that it was the fact that Maya hadn't shown much concern. That she hadn't asked how the previous evening had gone, especially his meeting with Vincent. It was quite in contrast to her worry over him some days ago when he had been injured in the fracas at Bancroft's house.

She frowned, 'But you met him yesterday, didn't you?'

'Ah yes. Some things just didn't come up for discussion. Like the slipper Manuel found, one of a pair. Abdul says it's still at home.

He stopped abruptly. It was the first time in six months that he had used the word, 'home' to describe the rooms he occupied at the Byculla Club. Two rooms for himself, and an office, and a smaller one for Abdul. Maybe a place grew on one, with all its familiar spaces, and the memories each space soon acquired. The table in his office, the electric fans that, once the city's planned grid system began to work, would change working ways drastically, the lychee tree just outside, and the lounge chair, the bay window behind it from where the late afternoon sun filtered in.

Maya eyes widened at his revelation. She made to say something and then hesitated. She shook her head to get an errant strand out of the way, then she said, 'I'll go and see Freddie.' She kept her eyes on Henry, as he stepped back, his face flushing at her mention of Bancroft. 'Abdul told me he did see him in Pease' house.' She looked around, and reached out, her hands moving toward him. But Henry stepped back, knocking against a tall flower vase crammed with dahlias. He caught it just as it fell, and heard her words come over him. 'He will get into a mess bigger than before. The opium links him with Pease somehow. But Freddie would never…'

He stepped away from her and moved to the door, 'Freddie isn't quite a babe in the woods. He did follow Manuel. He did see him at the lodge, and followed him. He could have...'

'I understand, Henry,' she said, looking at her hands, and then back at him, defiant, 'And as for Freddie, maybe he's just way in over his head.'

'You'd think this way of Freddie, of course,' he said, knowing he had a sneer in his voice, and that he sounded hateful, 'He's teaching you many a trick or two. I am sure you enjoy his company.'

And he opened the door, and walked out, not bothering to hold the door open for her.

~

The Clemenses were leaving for the hotel too, and Henry offered to accompany them, before going onto the police headquarters at Crawford Market. All of them were leaving around the same time, and outside, on the driveway, there was a flurry of activity. Hari rushed to the gate to bring in the carriages. Charlotte and Maya were returning to the Native Girls' School in one, and Henry was careful not to look her way. Her face was flushed in turn, but she was smiling as she kissed the Clemenses goodbye and told them that she looked forward to their next meeting. Charlotte and Edith had planned a proper trip, complete with a picnic to the Elephanta caves.

Mark Twain took out his pipe the minute they were seated in the carriage, and smiled at Henry. This was the time he liked Bombay best, Henry thought, smiling absently back at Twain. The city too was growing on him, its late afternoon slowness, and the way the sun drifted in past the low branches, the surf glinting like silver dots in the sea, and the boats moving in a mesmerizing stillness.

'I will need to send a telegram to my manager,' Twain said, puffing out a stream of smoke that wafted out of the window and swirled somewhere around the horse's ears. 'He's been asking if things have gone on as per schedule.' He looked amused, and gave his low-throated laughter, 'I wanted to tell him, if I could, that the last four days had gone in a daze.' Everyone chuckled, Olivia shook her head amusedly as she glanced toward her husband.

'But one can't make too big a deal about it, right? There's the bigger picture, isn't there?' asked Mark Twain, frowning, his deep brown eyes fixed on Henry.

Henry allowed himself a slight smile. He told himself he mustn't think too much about Maya. Maybe she felt a magician with uncertain prospects and dubious practices, was far less dull, less predictable than a trade consul with promising job prospects ahead.

'There are big things and small things,' he said calmly, 'you know about the Venezuela border matter, I am sure. The Venezuelan government and the British in Guyana are clashing over the border areas, and President Cleveland has every right to get involved. If the news of a famous, well yes, you are world-famous'—as Mark Twain smiled faintly, and his moustache wobbled again—'writer gets more attention, with newspapers screaming headlines like "British muddle up American writer's visit," or something like that, it can aggravate things.'

'Yes, writers are quite in the news these days,' Twain said meaningfully, and the discreet shake of his head meant that Henry was not to bring up the Oscar Wilde matter. The *Bombay Gazette* had put out a small salacious story about Wilde's imprisonment. He was lodged at Reading Gaol having already served a year of his imprisonment in very difficult circumstances. No one was giving Wilde any sympathy whatsoever. Wilde had, Henry had read, been jeered at, and spat on, when he appeared on the railway platform on his transfer to Reading, thirty miles west of London. His trial had scandalized many, and Twain perhaps, was being discreet in not wanting to bring up the matter before the ladies.

'Well, this matter ended well, and I am sure the rest will go as per scheduled,' Henry said, feeling he sounded a tad officious. 'The British government here will be careful; I will make sure of that too.'

'That was quite something,' Twain said, 'the days I knew nothing about seem to have been the most exciting. Two murders, and both unsolved. I wish I could be around to have you both solve it.'

'Both?' Clara and he had asked the question simultaneously, her eyes darting towards Henry, before she blushed delicately. Her father smiled at her, before turning back to Henry, 'Miss Barton and you, quite a pair of detectives.'

'Well,' Henry laughed, feeling oddly sad at that comment, 'my man, Abdul, who is just behind, was quite something too,' He looked out of the window, thinking it was perhaps the last time Maya and he would do something together. 'Olivia and Clara were really worried. We would have wanted their stay to be memorable in other ways.'

'All's well that ends well,' said Clara smiling, 'and I am sure we haven't seen the last of you, Mr Baker.'

She gave him a look full of meaning, and Henry smiled back, wishing he could find a way to make Maya jealous too. She could so easily pull the knife into him by the mere mention of a certain Freddie Bancroft. Clara was a pretty woman, and devoted to her parents. He shuddered invisibly at the thought of him making up a foursome with Clara, and always travelling in the wake of Mark Twain. That would be the end of all hopes for more adventures, all on his own. He would not mind having someone like Maya, she would only spice things up. But Maya, his lips tightened at the thought, evidently had other preferences.

~

Vincent looked at him in barely concealed irritation as Henry came up. There had been a reporter from the *Bombay Gazette* and then someone from the *Manchester Guardian* just before, he informed Henry tersely. 'This is a big city, and I have other things to do than speak to reporters about a no longer missing American writer.'

Later, Henry would think it was his anger over Maya that had made him so very outspoken, before the crusty police superintendent, 'Well, for Mark Twain's rescue, and the fact that he came to no harm, you don't really have yourself or the Bombay police to thank.'

Vincent had the grace to offer him a stiff smile and a nod of acknowledgement. 'I do thank you for your...your unconventional methods, Mr Baker. I am glad he's doing all right. We will have Mr Pease in for questioning soon.'

'Isn't it too late already not to question him?' Henry persisted. 'His hypocrisy is so plainly evident. A man who speaks against opium, grows it himself, and has packs of it...'

Vincent heard him out patiently, before he stepped back and invited Henry to the chair facing him, 'Mr Pease has the permission to do so. Yes.' he nodded as Henry gasped. 'The recovering addicts many a time ask for opium, and he gets them off it gradually. Not at once, for that could have detrimental effects. He did ask for permits to grow the poppy, but as for the packs you mention...'

'There could be a connection, don't you see? The packs in Tuka's house, meant for some of the workers.'

Vincent raised his eyebrows, almost in disbelief. 'Are you saying there are addicts everywhere?'

'No, no,' Henry said leaning forward and then realizing it looked too desperate, he sat back on the cushioned cane chair, and said insistently, 'Dr Ellaby at the hospital has been telling us of the irritable babies, the anxious mothers. Many from the mill—The Bombay Spinning Mill, the New Empire, the ED Sassoon mills—are workers got by Tuka Ram. That is why he's so powerful, even some prominent people in the city speak in his support. I would not be surprised if Tuka has his fingers in this opium ring.'

Vincent didn't take his eyes off him, listening intently, before he finally broke in. 'We haven't given up on him at all. As I mentioned, Manuel wasn't the man who murdered the young woman. We...'

'You did mention this yesterday, Superintendent, I needed to tell you about something else. Manuel did come by just the day before he was unfortunately murdered. He did tell us what happened. I did tell you he was in the room, and had slithered under the bed, after taking the jewels.'

Vincent nodded, though he had already started looking impatient, 'Look I need...'

'It won't take long,' Henry was insistent. 'The man who actually murdered her, I mean Casi, left behind his slippers.' Vincent's eyes widened, before a slow understanding smile broke out on his face. 'We have one of those. One of a pair. It will be quite a Cinderella Act going around to see whom it fits.' Vincent's eyes narrowed as he followed Henry's explanation carefully, then slapped his forehead in amazement, 'The other one, of course Manuel had it. Just as you told me!'

'Exactly, my point,' Henry smiled in a conspiratorial way, 'It will match Tuka's in every way. You can get Tuka to step into it, and it'll fit him with ease. I don't think he expected to leave them behind, but a criminal will always incriminate himself.'

'Do you have the other slipper?'

'It was in my rooms at the club, and my man Abdul is carrying it about with him. Vital piece of incriminating evidence so we dared not have it out of sight,' Henry said, rubbing his chin tiredly. 'And those two men who attacked me, were the same men who tailed Manuel. For my manservant Abdul did have a look at them. Well, one of them was called Balram, and the other had a thin, whinnying kind of voice.'

Vincent rose to his feet, nodding. 'We must get that slipper then. And we expect those two men to be arrested soon enough. They can't get out of the city with the checks we have placed, and the Koli fishermen have been strictly warned not to take any stranger out to sea.'

~

It was evening when he left the station, and he felt suddenly bereft. He would have taken a ride by the sea, if he had planned an evening with Maya, or even gone to the theatre, but they had had that terrible exchange some hours earlier. He had been rude, Henry admitted, but he wasn't ready to make up. She has to make a choice, he said stubbornly to himself. 'Let's go back to the doctors' bungalow,' he said impulsively to Abdul, 'Maybe we get another nice meal there. I am tired of the clubhouse dinners.'

Abdul wasn't very successful in hiding his smile.

He guessed Henry's intentions at once, and Henry didn't bother to hide his own rakish smile either, as the carriage Abdul summoned came to a halt beside them. 'We will give your papers to Mark Twain. I just forgot somehow. At least he can write a story on this if he wants to.'

What if Maya had no wish to make a choice, he thought, alone in the carriage, for Abdul preferred sitting up front with the coachman. 'I would be hypocritical if I didn't see things her way,' Henry spoke aloud to himself. 'She wants adventure in the way I do too.' Two people, he thought sadly, if bound by romance, could never have adventures together. Romance, love, was its own separate adventure. This one adventure, with her, had ended far too quickly, and too soon.

Epilogue

'Pease makes Peace then,' Mark Twain said the next afternoon when they met at the Victoria Terminus railway station. This was an impressive Gothic building, designed by the master architect Frederick Stevens. Its turrets, carved gateways, pointed arches ranged on either side of a central high arch, intricate railings, high glazed windows had already made it a world-famous structure. The train to Baroda, a distance of a day or so, was already at the platform, and Mark Twain and his family stood outside saying their goodbyes.

Henry looked away, as Maya made the explanation. 'Yes, he didn't want too many skeletons come tumbling out of the cupboard. What with that opium racket he was part of, with Tuka, and even Bancroft…' Her face turned red, as she looked Henry's way. 'A preacher but doing just the opposite. But for Peace, it was all settled tactfully.'

'The hypocrite,' Olivia sniffed into her perfumed handkerchief, and Clara looked away too. Henry told her about the things she might see in Baroda, for its maharaja, a very enlightened ruler, had built a fine city, complete with a university that drew students from all over India. It had well-maintained gardens, and a world-class zoo as well. Clara nodded, still looking unhappy and Henry berated himself, knowing he was part cause of this.

'Good relations matter. Isn't that a key tenet of diplomacy?' mused Maya, in the end, 'You must see more of Bombay when you are back from Baroda. And we must do that Elephanta picnic.'

'And I have my papers back,' Mark Twain said, chuckling, 'I can make a story out of this any day. It will make for a real juicy adventure story.'

This time Henry caught Maya's eye and they exchanged a quick impulsive smile.

They were standing close together as the train pulled away, and he had her arm around her shoulder, as the train became a round black sphere caught in dizzying black smoky clouds. She didn't move away. Instead, she rested her head against him, and Henry drew her closer to him. If he kissed her, then and there, as he wanted to, would that mean a breach of propriety? This was a very starchy city, after all. He was thinking these thoughts when he felt Maya's hands on his cheeks, and it was then, he slowly bent down to kiss her, a kiss he wanted to go on forever. He would remember this moment for the rest of his life.

Acknowledgements

I began work on this novel in 2019. It took definite shape when I studied with Bret Lott at Vermont College of Fine Arts during a postgraduate semester that unfolded in the midst of a Covid summer in 2020. Mary Logue, Minnesota-based editor, and writer of several crime novels including the Claire Watkins series, ran her fine editorial eye over this manuscript.

Almost two decades ago now, Shama Futehally read my first manuscript, and left me always in her debt. I am grateful for friends like Vatsala Kaul-Banerjee, Arpita Das, Moazzam Sheikh, Dipankar Das, Renu Panika, Gurusharan Singh, and Shruti Pandey. I miss Deepa Rathore and Nandita Agarwal, both of whom passed away in recent months and I miss them both. I met fellow writers, Tim Bridwell, Carolyn Ogburn, Donald Quist, Cristina DeSouza, and Camilla Sanderson, at VCFA and cherish their friendship. Naresh Fernandes, Aman Khanna, Nandini Ramnath, and Arunava Sinha at *Scroll.in* have always been encouraging and supportive. I'd like to thank Tarun Saint, and Thomas Abraham at Hachette India, for encouraging me to write more detective fiction.

Friends at the *Economic and Political Weekly* where I worked for eight years have always been special: Gauraang Pradhan, Padma Prakash, Deepali Shekhar, Nutan Patel, Leela Solomon, Kamal Fanibanda and James Rumao. Subba Rao, Luis Fernandes, Jayanthi Mahalingam and Meera Nair, were the very first editors I had when I first thought I could become a writer. Ram Reddy, first my editor at EPW and later at *The India Forum*, encouraged me to explore new areas of historical research. Maithreyi Krishnaraj has always cheered me on through my writing life, and Shanta Gokhale has been inspiring, as a writer, and in her emails to me. Ravi Singh and Renuka Chatterjee of Speaking Tiger have been absolutely the best: they liked this manuscript and have been supportive through the process. Rima Zaheer, as my editor, has been wonderful to work with. I'd like to thank Aruna Ghosh, who first read this manuscript for my publisher.

My mother, Uma Chakrabarty, introduced me first to works of mystery and detective fiction, from Satyajit Ray's Feluda to Agatha Christie, Erle Stanley Gardner, and Ngaio Marsh. Here in New Jersey, which has been home to me in recent years, Ajay and Devyani liked this story when I narrated it to them: briefly and succinctly, but without any spoilers (I hope!). And of course, Mark Twain, whose novels featuring Tom Sawyer and Huckleberry Finn, I read while growing up in Odisha. For a long time, though, I always knew him as the writer of *The Prince and the Pauper,* and the chaotically irreverent short story, 'The Celebrated Jumping Frog of Calaveras County.'

ALSO IN SPEAKING TIGER

COMING BACK TO THE CITY

MUMBAI STORIES

Anuradha Kumar

In Parel's Jupiter Mills chawl—one of the few remaining in Mumbai—live many long-time residents. Among them, Pooja, restless and trapped in an unhappy marriage, who finds joy in her flourishing dabba service and attempts at learning English, even as her husband Mahesh flirts with the underworld and dreams of zipping through the streets in his boss's yellow Mercedes-Benz. Pooja's friend, Vasudha, a scheming single mother who hopes to give her daughter a better life in the treacherous city. And their upstairs neighbour, Dr Joshi, a famed artist, who has hidden away two paintings—one of a murder he witnessed, and the other a striking portrait of Pooja.

In the parallel Mumbai of high-rises that loom over the city's slums and chawls live the affluent few: Suhel, a confirmed bachelor, who finds himself falling in love—first with a portrait and then its subject, Pooja. An upcoming politician of dubious repute, Mahesh's boss Ghatge, whose devious intentions could destroy the peace of Jupiter Mills. A young and disturbed journalist Raina Gupta who opens up old wounds when she interviews veteran activist Neera Joshi about the mill-workers' strike of the 1980s and her scandalous affair with its assassinated leader. And Dr Sneha Desai, a successful but lonely radiologist, fighting to restart her sex-education classes for adolescents in a municipal school.

In the Mumbai of mills and malls where everything—especially land—is at a premium, the chawl becomes the target of greedy real-estate barons and sleazy politicians, thus bringing together this interconnected cast of characters.

As vast and diverse as Mumbai itself, *Coming Back to the City* draws us effortlessly, completely into the lives of the people who animate the maximum city, even as they are consumed by it—people caught in a web of unexpected love, desperate ambition and endless, addictive optimism.